Exploring Inequality in Europe

Exploring Inequality in Europe

Diverging Income and Employment Opportunities in the Crisis

Edited by

Martin Heidenreich

University of Oldenburg, Germany

Cheltenham, UK • Northampton, MA, USA

Published by
Edward Elgar Publishing Limited
The Lypiatts
15 Lansdown Road
Cheltenham
Glos GL50 2JA
UK

Edward Elgar Publishing, Inc.
William Pratt House
9 Dewey Court
Northampton
Massachusetts 01060
USA

A catalogue record for this book
is available from the British Library

Library of Congress Control Number: 2016931740

This book is available electronically in **Elgar**online
Social and Political Science subject collection
DOI 10.4337/9781783476664

ISBN 978 1 78347 665 7 (cased)
ISBN 978 1 78347 666 4 (eBook)

Typeset by Servis Filmsetting Ltd, Stockport, Cheshire
Printed and bound in Great Britain by TJ International Ltd, Padstow

Contents

Contributors

Franziska Buttler is Associate of the International Office of the Business School Berlin.

Martin Heidenreich is Jean Monnet Chair for European Studies in Social Sciences and Director of the Jean Monnet Centre for Europeanisation and Transnational Regulations at the University of Oldenburg, Germany.

Cathrin Ingensiep is a researcher and PhD student in the Department of Social Sciences of the University of Hamburg, Germany.

Sabine Israel is a researcher and PhD student in the Department of Social Sciences of the University of Oldenburg, Germany.

Jenny Preunkert is a researcher in the Department of Social Sciences of the University of Oldenburg, Germany.

Christian Reimann is at the Brandenburg University of Technology, Germany.

1. Introduction: the *double dualization* of inequality in Europe

Martin Heidenreich

1.1 HORIZONTAL EUROPEANIZATION AND THE EUROZONE CRISIS: TWO DETERMINANTS OF THE EUROPEANIZATION OF SOCIAL INEQUALITY

The process of European integration is being increasingly faced with the need to ensure the social integration of Europe's citizens. Until the 1980s, the crises afflicting the European integration project mainly concerned the relationship between sovereign nation-states and supranational institutions and policies. During the more recent crises surrounding the Maastricht Treaty (1993), the European Constitutional Treaty rejected by the French and Dutch populations in 2005, the current financial, economic and sovereign debt crisis which began in 2008 (Giddens 2014) and the migration and refugee crisis since 2015, the relationship between European citizens and the protagonists of the European integration project both at the national and the European level has become central (Fligstein 2008). The long-standing permissive consensus among Europeans, which for decades enabled the deepening and enlargement of the European Union (EU) in an expertocratic, elite-driven way, is gradually eroding (Hooghe and Marks 2009). The EU is evolving from an intergovernmental arena into a social space characterized by closer interdependencies between European citizens. This is not only a result of geographic proximity and a partly common, conflict-ridden history, but it is mainly the result of the common political, legal, economic, monetary and social framework which has liberalized European markets, facilitated cross-border mobility and created a common currency for, currently, 19 of the 28 EU Member States. Therefore, it is not surprising that Europeans are increasingly aware of the impact of European political institutions, processes and decisions on their living conditions.

This growing awareness of the supra- and transnational influences on living conditions has been reinforced by the sovereign debt crisis in the eurozone. Beginning as a global financial crisis in 2008, this crisis turned into a sovereign debt crisis in 2010 and led to the erosion of trust in EU institutions and other EU Member States (Armingeon and Ceka 2013; Braun and Tausendpfund 2014). It also gave rise to Eurosceptic and populist parties in many European countries, bitter conflicts concerning the regulation of the euro area and the financing of bailout programmes, and the possibility of some countries leaving the eurozone or even the EU.

The starting point of this volume is the assumption that the erosion of trust in the EU, the euro and other EU Member States is the outcome of these two processes, namely horizontal Europeanization and the sovereign debt crisis. Firstly, social inequalities are increasingly perceived in a European context. Europeans compare their living situation not only with their compatriots, but also with other Europeans. This reflects the increasing economic interdependencies, cross-border relations and cross-border networks in the EU (cf. Mau and Mewes 2012). Europeans with more cross-border relations have better opportunities for coping with unemployment, financial difficulties and other biographical challenges (Chapter 8). These processes of horizontal Europeanization, but also the impact of EU policies on national policies (cf. Featherstone and Radaelli 2003), are reflected in increasingly transnational perceptions of social inequalities. This has been termed the Europeanization of social inequalities.

Secondly, the erosion of trust in the EU is also the result of the financial, economic and sovereign debt crisis in Europe that has affected European economies since 2008 and that has not yet ended, as shown by the debates on a third bailout programme for Greece in 2015 and the still deficient institutionalization of the euro. This crisis has led to an unprecedented level of institutionalized solidarity among the EU Member States (as indicated by the financial volume of the bailout funds ESM (European Stability Mechanism), EFSM (European Financial Stability Mechanism) and EFSF (European Financial Stability Facility); cf. Chapter 9), but also to very different impacts on the living conditions of Europeans and a serious deterioration in the social situation, particularly in Southern Europe. This can be illustrated by two selected indicators which refer to the individual and the household level – unemployment (Figures 1.1 and 1.2) and deprivation (Figures 1.3 and 1.4). Figures 1.1 and 1.3 are based on national means which have been aggregated by common European country groups in order to illustrate different trajectories in Europe. These figures especially highlight the split between Scandinavian and Continental European countries on one side and the Eastern and Southern European countries on the other side. In addition, they also illustrate the deterioration of employment and living conditions in Southern Europe in relation to Eastern Europe. This shows the reorganization of centre–periphery

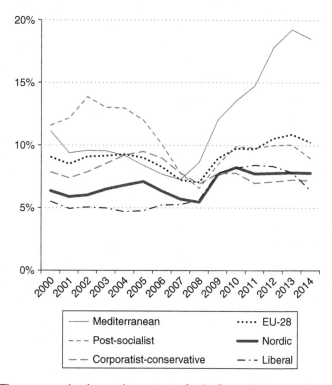

Note: The average national unemployment rates for the five employment regimes (cf. Gallie and Paugam 2000) are weighted by the respective labour force. The countries have been grouped as follows: Liberal: UK, IE; corporatist: NL, LU, FR, DE, BE, AT; Mediterranean: PT, MT, IT, ES, EL, CY; post-socialist: RO, SK, SI, PL, LV, LT, HU, EE, CZ, BG; Scandinavian: DK, SE, FI. The differences between the regimes are highly significant.

Source: Own calculations based on Eurostat, table [une_rt_a].

Figure 1.1 Regime-specific unemployment rates in the EU-28 (2000–2014)

relations in Europe and the restructuring of the European periphery during the eurozone crisis.

Besides these territorial separation lines, the European population is also socially divided. Figures 1.2 and 1.4 illustrate that Europeans are affected differently by unemployment and deprivation according to their age, gender, migration background and educational levels. Apart from the territorial cleavages which dominate public discourse, the EU is also a social space. Younger persons with a lower education and a migration

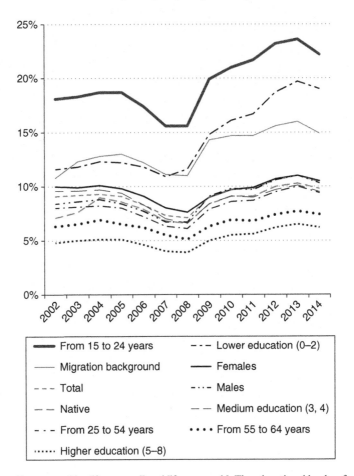

▬▬ From 15 to 24 years	– – – Lower education (0–2)
——— Migration background	▬▬ Females
– – – Total	– ·· – Males
— — Native	— — Medium education (3, 4)
– · – From 25 to 54 years	•••• From 55 to 64 years
······ Higher education (5–8)	

Source: Eurostat, tables [lfsa_urgaed] and [lfsa_urgacob]. The educational levels refer to the ISCED classification.

Figure 1.2   *Unemployment rates by socio-demographic background (EU-28; 2002–2014)*

background suffer on average much more from unemployment and deprivation than highly educated, older natives – and these negative effects have become more pronounced since the crisis.

The objection could be raised that the Mediterranean or corporatist-conservative countries or older and younger persons are not homogeneous and that the previously mentioned territorial and social characteristics interact: the situation of a young Spaniard is much worse than a German

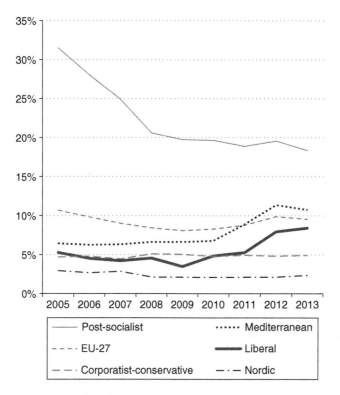

Note: The severe material deprivation rate measures the percentage of the population that cannot afford at least four of the following items: (1) to pay their rent, mortgage or utility bills; (2) to keep their home adequately warm; (3) to face unexpected expenses; (4) to eat meat or proteins regularly; (5) to go on holiday; (6) a television set; (7) a washing machine; (8) a car; (9) a telephone. See Figure 1.1.

Source: Own calculations on the basis of Eurostat, table [ilc_mddd21].

Figure 1.3   *Severe material deprivation in different EU regions (EU-27; 2005–2013)*

of the same age. This is the reason why we test our arguments in the following chapters on the basis of micro-data using multivariate methods. In order to grasp the multidimensionality of inequality, we use various indicators which refer either to the individual (in the case of unemployment, but also in the case of long-term unemployment, temporary employment or wage levels) or to household-related living conditions (in the case of deprivation, but also in the case of poverty).

A major result of our analyses, which is also illustrated by the previously

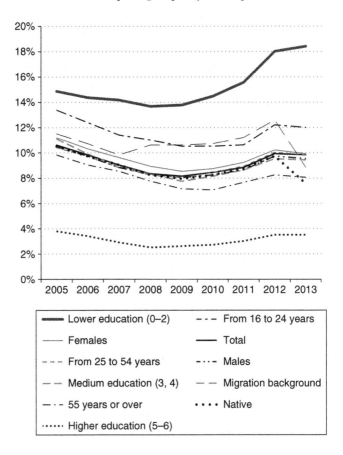

Source: See Figure 1.3. Eurostat, tables [ilc_mddd11], [ilc_mddd21]. [ilc_mddd14] and [ilc_mddd16].

*Figure 1.4   Severe material deprivation by socio-economic background
            (EU-27; 2005–2013)*

discussed four figures, is the *double dualization thesis*: the living situations of Europeans are divided along territorial and social or socio-demographic lines (Mau et al. 2012). On the one hand, after a decade of prosperity and convergence, the eurozone crisis has contributed to an increasing dualization of life chances, especially between Northern and Southern Europeans. On the other hand, life chances are diverging between younger and older, migrant and native, male and female, and high- and low-skilled employees. The following chapters show that this double dualization can be observed not only for the two indicators taken here as an illustrative example, but also for other dimensions of social inequality: income inequality and subjective socio-economic insecurity (Chapter 2), persistent poverty (Chapter 3), long-term unemployment (Chapter 4), low pay (Chapter 5), temporary contracts (Chapter 6), unmet medical needs (Chapter 7) and life satisfaction (Chapter 8).

From a sociological perspective, the institutionalization of these territorial and social cleavages differs fundamentally between a nation-state or other forms of a political union and a loose intergovernmental association of sovereign states. While a nation-state tries to replace territorial cleavages with social cleavages (in order to avoid irreconcilable conflicts between different ideologies or regional identities which favour separatist movements; Heidenreich 2003), an intergovernmental association is characterized by bargaining relations between different nations which aggregate and articulate the interests of their citizens. Between these two opposite forms of interest aggregation, three different forms of conceiving the Europeanization of social inequalities can be distinguished. This will be discussed in the next section (1.2). In order to introduce the following analyses, major results will be discussed in a comparative perspective in section 1.3. In the last section, these chapters are briefly summarized (1.4).

1.2 BEYOND THE METHODOLOGICAL NATIONALISM OF INEQUALITY RESEARCH: THREE VARIANTS OF THE EUROPEANIZATION THESIS

Social inequalities have been analysed so far almost exclusively in the national context, or from an internationally comparative perspective (Alderson and Nielsen 2002; Wilkinson and Pickett 2009; OECD 2015). There are compelling reasons for such a national frame of reference. Since the end of the nineteenth century, at least in Europe, the national welfare state has become the central guarantor of social security (Castles et al. 2010). Even in a globalized world, the perception and articulation of social risks and inequalities as well as attempts by the public to reduce them take place largely at the national level. Nation-states are the largest known levels on which norms of equality and solidarity are effectively institutionalized. Social security benefits and taxes, unions and wage bargaining systems, education and training, public systems of interregional redistribution – all these institutions are mainly institutionalized at the national level. This was especially the case in the post-war period of egalitarian capitalism, which was characterized by relatively closed national economies, national wage-bargaining and educational systems, and by national welfare states (Kenworthy 2004). These observations have formed the basis of the 'methodological nationalism' of inequality research, i.e. the assumption that nation-states are the natural unit of analysis for patterns of social inequality due to the congruence of territorial, political, economic and social borders and cognitive frames of perception (Smith 1983: 26; Beck 2007). In a world dominated by nation-states, culturally homogeneous democratic welfare states have been the primary focus of requests for civil, democratic and social rights (Rokkan 1999).

However, despite the predominantly national framework of analysis, supra- and transnational developments also shape the distribution of income and the living opportunities of people. The rise in national inequalities, but also the decline of between-nation inequalities, has been explained by the globalization of goods, services, labour and capital markets (Alderson and Nielsen 2002; OECD 2011; Milanovic 2013), and by skill-biased technological change, i.e. by the increasingly important role of specific qualifications and skills in the context of global technological competition.

In addition to global trends, the EU has also become an essential unit for the generation and regulation of inequalities (Beckfield 2006; Fligstein 2008; Heidenreich 2003). At least until recently, the economic, monetary and legislative integration and regulatory harmonization in Europe has led to a convergence of the standards of living in the EU. Since the Great Recession (2008–2009) and the subsequent sovereign debt crisis in Europe (2010–2015), however, the negative effects of an incomplete monetary union have also become obvious. The necessity of adapting employment and wage levels instead of devaluating the own national currency euro and the European-wide limits for sovereign debts have led to restrictive public policies, more generally termed as austerity policies (Blyth 2013)

This demonstrates the need for inequality research to overcome the 'methodological nationalism' of inequality research by taking into account the multiple geographical references of social inequality in a multiscalar perspective, analysing inequalities as the outcome of socio-spatial processes which take place in distinct spatial units (Brenner 2001: 604), for example the regions, the nation-states and the EU.

In such a multiscalar context, this book claims that we are witnessing a *Europeanization of social inequalities*. This concept 'refers to transnational processes caused by the European integration, which shape the distribution of scarce and desired goods and positions thus shaping the life chances, the social identities, the interests and values of individuals and social groups' (Heidenreich and Wunder 2008: 33). This concept highlights both the objective dimension of social inequalities, which is the European impact on the distribution of resources and positions, and its subjective dimension, namely the transnationalization of the reference groups and standards of equality. It claims that social differences between autonomous EU Member States are no longer merely evaluated as social disparities in unrelated social spheres, but as social inequalities in a common social space characterized by transnational frames of reference and by conflicts between transnational social groups regarding privileged access to more or less advantageous social positions and resources. The social and economic heterogeneity of Europe, which for centuries was contained in closed nation-states (Rokkan 1999), is returning to the fore. This concept can be understood in at least three different ways (see Chapter 2 for the case of income inequalities). Firstly, as an indicator of the growing importance of Europe for the analysis and comparison of national inequalities; secondly, as a reference to the growing importance of European and more specifically EU-related factors which influence patterns of social inequality; and, thirdly, as a reference to transnational frames of references. This analytical separation is loosely inspired by the classical distinction made by Geiger (1932) between the description of the unequal distributions of social resources and relations (*Lagerungsbild*), its explanation by different, often class-related, strategies and dynamics (*Schichtungsbild*), and the subjective perceptions, mentalities and lifestyles of the individuals (*Mentalitätsbild*).

In the first perspective, which is still firmly rooted in the methodological nationalism of inequality research, Europe is conceived as an international social space, in which the patterns and developments of within-state inequality can be compared and the evolution of total and between-state inequality can be analysed – for example, the divergence or convergence of individual standards of living or the increasing or decreasing share of between-state inequality. In this perspective, the nation-state is still the main point of reference for the diagnosis of equality and inequality. Inequality indices therefore reflect the distribution of socially valuable goods and opportunities among the population of a specific country. Here, Europeanization refers to the increasing importance of Europe as a point of reference for the comparison of national patterns of inequality: '(T)he more Europeanization there is, the more the principle of comparability replaces the principle of the incomparability of social inequality between nation state spaces' (Beck 2007: 695). In contrast to the third concept, in which the people in the involved countries also compare their living situations with persons in other countries, these comparisons are limited to the scientific sphere. The standards of equality of the respective individuals still refer to national reference groups. Between EU Member States, territorial cleavages are dominant.

In the second perspective, the Europeanization of social inequalities refers to the economic, political and monetary integration of Europe and its impact on life chances. This is close to the usage of the term in political science in which Europeanization refers to the

> (p)rocesses of (a) construction (b) diffusion and (c) institutionalisation of formal and informal rules, procedures, policy paradigms, styles, 'ways of doing things' and shared beliefs and norms which are first defined and consolidated in the making of EU decisions and then incorporated in the logic of domestic discourse, identities, political structures and public policies. (Radaelli 2003: 30)

This definition conceives of the EU as a supranational political and administrative space, and focuses on its impact on political changes in the national arena. Examples of the impact of European policies on the social and income situation of the population are the influence of the common market on economic growth and income (Fligstein and Stone Sweet 2002), the impact of the political and legal integration of Europe on living conditions (cf. Beckfield 2009) and the impact of a common currency and the recently strengthened eurozone-wide coordination of national economic policies on standards of living (Blyth 2013). In this case, territorial cleavages are still dominant, but EU-wide policies may provide social rights to selected social groups (e.g. to farmers, workers, women, students, transnationally mobile EU citizens).

In the third understanding, the Europeanization of social inequalities refers to the increasing relevance of transnational norms, standards of equality and frames of reference (Delhey and Kohler 2006; Fahey 2007; Kangas and Ritakallio 2007). Whelan and Maître (2009: 118) distinguish between a weak and a strong version of this argument: 'The former proposes that a common standard relating to an acceptable level of participation in one's own society emerges as a consequence of knowledge of conditions in other societies (. . .) The stronger version requires (. . .), that people perceive themselves as part of a larger European stratification system.' Besides territorially conceived interests, cleavages between different social groups cutting across national lines become more important – for example between winners and losers of Europeanization processes (Fligstein 2008). Other indicators of the emergence of transnational standards of evaluation are the generally lower life satisfaction in poorer EU countries (Chapter 2) and the surprisingly high level of declared solidarity between EU citizens (Gerhards and Lengfeld 2015).

In a perspective inspired by Rokkan (1999), these forms of Europeanization can be seen as indicators that, in addition to territorial cleavages between different European nations, socio-economic cleavages between advantaged and disadvantaged social groups become more important. An international or supranational Europe becomes a European societal sphere. An international Europe is dominated by conflicts between central and peripheral regions and countries; it can be integrated by inter-governmental negotiations and agreements, as liberal intergovernmental-ism has taught us (Moravcsik 1998). In a supranational Europe analysed by neofunctional approaches, economic and political interdependencies require common rules which are developed and monitored by suprana-tional institutions such as the European Commission or the European Court of Justice. In both cases, interests are conceived first of all in a national perspective. A transnational conception transcends such a ter-ritorial definition of identities, norms of equality, interests, and conflicts, focusing instead on the living situations, practices, interests and perceptions of transnational social groups defined for example by age, gender, educa-tion, migration experiences, occupation, lifestyle or mobility. Conflicts and bargaining processes also emerge along social lines and not only territorial lines. This would undermine the exclusive responsibility of the nation-state regarding the definition and articulation of social interests. Its emergence would imply that European integration and growing cross-border transac-tions and interdependencies between Europeans would lead to a partial 'unfreezing' of nationally defined interests (Ferrera 2003). The EU would become a contested terrain for issues which were previously the exclusive domain of the nation-state and which are now also the sphere of com-peting civil society actors, trade unions, business associations and other interest groups. Conflicts in Europe would not only be conflicts between central and peripheral countries and regions, but also between 'winners' and 'losers' of Europeanization processes (Kriesi et al. 2006). Even if such a European societal sphere seems a very distant vision, the aforementioned results on the Europeanization of solidarity in the EU and indicators of the third understanding of the Europeanization of social inequalities might indicate that the eurozone crisis might contain the possibility of transcending the mostly territorial cleavages of the EU.

In sum, the Europeanization thesis comprises the concept of compar-ing national inequality patterns in a European context (*international perspective*), the concept of explaining the patterns and dynamics of social inequalities in terms of the *supranational regulation* of the European economies and societies, and the concept of the emergence of *transnational standards of equality and frames of reference*. These three concepts refer to different causal mechanisms. In the first case, Europeanization is the result of spatial and historical proximity and some basic similarities (e.g. as highly industrialized or knowledge-based countries with an advanced welfare state and a democratic order) which allow for comparison. In the second case, the drivers of Europeanization processes are EU policies such as the abolishment of internal border controls or the introduction

of a common European currency. In the third case, the causal factors
are increasing cross-border contacts, networks, debates, transactions and
transnational social conflicts between different socio-economic groups.

1.3   SOCIAL INEQUALITIES IN THE EUROZONE CRISIS: FIVE TRENDS

A major reason for the Europeanization of social inequalities, especially
during the period of time that we analyse in this volume, is the introduction of the euro in, currently, 19 EU Member States. This currency union
is characterized by a discrepancy between the Europeanized monetary
policy and the still national fiscal policies. At the EU or eurozone level
no political authority exists with sufficient financial capacity to deal with
the three challenges of a currency union (Shambaugh 2012; De Grauwe
2014): (1) the illiquidity of Member States due to excessive public debts;
(2) the illiquidity of banks due to excessive private debts; (3) cyclical
economic downturns. The first challenge would require either a regime
for dealing with insolvent states, Europe-wide bailout funds or a central
bank which functions as the lender of last resort; the second challenge
requires a banking union which also includes a common responsibility for
the resolution of heavily indebted banks; and the third challenge requires
an anti-cyclical fiscal policy at the eurozone level (for example, automatic
stabilizers as a European unemployment insurance).

   Given the absence of such a Europe-wide fiscal capacity, Friedman
(1997) predicted early on that the introduction of the euro 'would exacer-
bate political tensions by converting divergent shocks that could have been
readily accommodated by exchange rate changes into divisive political
issues'. The essential question is which adjustment mechanisms can buffer
the effects of economic shocks after the abolition of flexible exchange rates.
While flexible exchange rates allow a quick adaptation of nominal wages
and prices by means of a devaluation, such an adaptation in a currency
union requires either high cross-border mobility, high international transfer payments, increasing public debts, a flexible labour market that allows
productivity increases by closing down unproductive businesses, or flexible
nominal wages in order to compensate for the loss of flexible exchange
rates. In the eurozone crisis the most important buffers to external economic shocks have been wages and the employment level. In particular,
Southern European countries and also Ireland had to regain their competitiveness in relation to the export-led Northern European countries (Hall
2014) through a real depreciation. The result has been a rearrangement
of social inequalities in the EU and especially in the eurozone that can be

summarized in terms of five trends: (1) polarization of European labour markets; (2) restructuring of the European centre–periphery relations due to the relative decline of Southern Europe and the continuing convergence of Eastern and Western Europe; (3) increasing national employment, income and health inequalities; (4) subjective Europeanization of inequalities; and (5) an impact of the EU on social inequalities. These five trends are summarized on the basis of the following chapters:

1. *Overarching importance of the labour market as a buffer in the eurozone crisis.* Among the variety of mechanisms by which a country can react to asymmetric economic shocks after the abolition of flexible exchange rates, the labour market was the most important 'shock absorber'. This explains the social crisis with very high and diverging unemployment levels (cf. Figures 1.1 and 1.2). While the income disparities in the enlarged EU remain broadly stable, the variation of regional and national unemployment rates has sharply increased since 2007 (Figure 1.5). The increasing variation of regional and national unemployment rates reflects the absence of alternative buffers for asymmetric economic shocks (Chapter 8). As a consequence, the level of poverty and persistent poverty risks are also growing, while the exit rates out of poverty are very low (Chapter 3).

2. *Restructuring of European centre–periphery relations.* The economic and income convergence between Northern and Southern Europe in the former 15 EU Member States has come to an at least temporary halt, while the economic and income convergence continues between the currently 28 Member States of the EU – mainly due to a convergence between Western and Eastern Europe (Chapter 2). In sum, economic and income disparities in the EU remain stable because the increasing gap between the North and South is partially compensated by the East–West convergence (Figure 1.5). This overall stability, however, conceals the strong economic growth of many Eastern European countries (Poland, Lithuania, Latvia, Romania and Bulgaria) and the stagnation and decline of most Southern European countries.

3. *Increasing social inequalities within the European nation-states.* As previously mentioned, the gap between the social risks of higher- and low-skilled employees, healthy and chronically-ill employees, migrants and natives as well as younger and older persons has increased since the beginning of the crisis (Emmenegger et al. 2012: 373; Schwander and Häusermann 2013). Especially for younger persons, the fact of being temporarily employed becomes a serious social and unemployment risk – an indicator of the dualization of labour markets between insiders

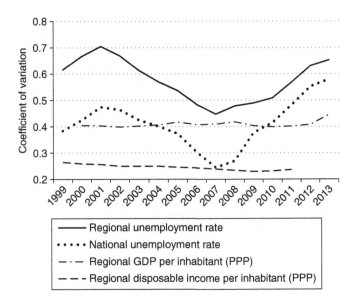

Source: Regional unemployment rates, gross domestic product (GDP) at current market prices and disposable income (PPS per inhabitant) by NUTS 2 regions [lfst_r_lfu3rt] and [nama_r_e2gdp] nama_r_ehh2inc. The coefficient of variation ratio has been calculated as the weighted standard deviation of the respective indicator to the weighted mean.

Figure 1.5   *Regional variation of economic, unemployment and income*
            inequalities in the EU-27 (1999–2013)

with permanent contracts and outsiders with temporary contracts (Chapters 4 and 6). Further indicators of the social dualization of nation-states are poverty rates and persistent poverty rates (Chapter 3). High poverty and deprivation rates often imply substandard living conditions and psycho-social stress stemming from the inability to afford basic items. These circumstances bring about an increased need for medical care for the deprived in particular, but also for the unemployed and chronically ill, who find their access to healthcare increasingly restricted due to costs and administrative hurdles to benefiting from free access (Chapter 7). However, a positive development is the continued increase of women in the labour markets (Chapter 5).

4. *Increasing Europeanization of perceptions and opportunities.* The crisis has eroded the trust of the European population in EU institutions (Chapter 8). This is also the result of the perceived Europeanization of social expectations and groups of reference (Chapter 2). Especially during the crisis, the economic situation is not only valued in relation to

other compatriots, but increasingly also in relation to other Europeans, which explains the declining life and income satisfaction in poorer countries (Chapters 2 and 8).

5. *Impact of the EU on social inequalities.* The multi-level analyses in the following chapters show that in addition to individual and household-related factors, national context factors are important determinants of social inequalities. Examples are the influence of social security on the risk of poverty and social exclusion (Chapter 3). In addition, EU policies and their outcomes – especially common market regulations, monetary integration and European-wide regulation of public expenditures ('austerity'), but also activation policies (Chapter 4) – also have an impact on individual and household-related patterns of inequalities (for example on the provision of health services; cf. Chapter 7).

In sum, the dualization of labour markets, the reorganization of European centre–periphery relations, the perceived Europeanization of inequalities and the impact of EU decisions are major dimensions of the current social crisis in the EU. Due to the common market and monetary union, the EU has also become a political and administrative space that has a decisive impact on patterns of social inequalities – and this is increasingly also perceived by its citizens. Overall, the social and territorial differences of living conditions (income, poverty, deprivation, health status and general life satisfaction) have increased in Europe since the beginning of the financial, sovereign debt and economic crisis in 2008. The 'double dualization' between advantaged and disadvantaged social groups and between Northern and Southern European countries has deepened during the crisis. After a decade of substantial capital flows to Southern Europe which have reduced economic divergences in Europe, social inequalities within and between the EU Member States are increasing in some dimensions and are threatening the social bases of European integration.

1.4   STRUCTURE OF THE BOOK

This book broadens the hitherto dominant national framework of inequality research by taking into account European factors that shape income inequality, access to employment opportunities and other social inequalities. By analysing the double dualization between the winners and losers of the crisis, the segmentation of labour markets and the perceived quality of life in Europe, this book contributes to a better understanding of the patterns and dynamics of inequality in an integrated Europe. Our analyses are in general based on micro-data provided by Eurostat – in particular the

European Union Statistics on Income and Living Conditions (EU-SILC)[1] and the Labour Force Survey – which are often combined with data on the national context and European policies in multi-level analyses. These data cover both some years before and the years of the eurozone crisis.

In Chapter 2, Martin Heidenreich specifies the previously explained international, supranational and transnational understandings of the Europeanization of inequalities for the case of income inequality. Firstly, it is shown that the move towards increasing national income inequalities has been reversed, especially in the former 15 EU Member States. Secondly, national and regional patterns of income inequality are also shaped by the growing economic integration at the European level. Thirdly, the subjective perception of economic stress is not only shaped by national frames of reference but also by transnational ones.

In Chapter 3, Cathrin Ingensiep discusses the evolution of persistent poverty and its national determinants during the economic and financial crisis. She asks which institutional factors prevent long-term poverty. In the analysis based on EU-SILC longitudinal data, it is shown that persistent poverty mostly affects the already disadvantaged social groups. Social expenditure – but not low national unemployment levels – is essential for preventing long episodes of poverty. Temporary and permanently poor people are affected differently by these national factors. While a higher unemployment rate does not alter the risk of becoming long-term poor, growing social expenditure reduces this risk. Hence, during the crisis, job security cannot be seen as a safeguard against long-term poverty, while social expenditure protects people from persistent poverty.

In Chapter 4, Martin Heidenreich discusses the changing social distribution of unemployment and long-term unemployment risks during the eurozone crisis. These risks are interpreted as the result of three different, overlapping forms of labour market segmentation: firstly, the institutionally stabilized polarization between labour market insiders and outsiders; secondly, the occupational dualization of high- and low-skilled employees and occupations; and, thirdly, the marginalization of disadvantaged social groups. It can be shown that (long-term) unemployment risks especially increase for low-skilled people and occupations, single parents, migrants and ill people. Women, older and permanently employed people are relatively less affected by short-term unemployment but are more affected by long-term unemployment. Hence, the current crisis strengthens the occupational and social dualization of labour markets, endangering the inclusiveness and long-term growth potential of the European economy and societies.

In Chapter 5, Martin Heidenreich discusses whether the financial, economic and sovereign debt crisis has also had major effects on the employment and earnings conditions of women. On the basis of macro- and micro-data, this chapter discusses whether this crisis and the austerity policies in the countries most affected by the crisis have had a negative effect on the employment and wage conditions of women (*austerity*), whether the *inclusion* of women in the labour market has continued, and whether the *dualization* of the labour markets has also affected the employment and earnings situation of women, and in which dimensions. The austerity hypothesis can be generally refuted. Secondly, during the crisis, the shift towards more inclusive employment patterns has continued. The gender gaps in employment and unemployment rates have continued to shrink, especially in Southern European countries, which have been the bulwark of the male breadwinner model in Europe. Particularly during the crisis, high unemployment rates have contributed to the erosion of traditional gender relations. Thirdly, the employment profiles of women clearly differ from their male counterparts. Employed women are generally more highly qualified, mostly employed in the service sector, and are overrepresented in atypical and low-paid jobs. This indicates a particular pattern of labour market inclusion which is based on a dualization between low- and high-skilled women – some women are the winners of the eurozone crisis, while others are the losers – and also of the continuing inclusion of women in the labour market.

In Chapter 6, Christian Reimann analyses the development of atypical employment relationships and their individual and national determinants from 2002 to 2013 on the basis of the European Labour Force Survey. Labour market reforms have increased temporary employment rates in Europe since the 1970s. This development led to a dualization between permanently employed insiders and temporarily employed outsiders. However, national institutions as well as economic and labour market structures remain very different. The thesis of this chapter is that the insider–outsider divide increasingly depends on individual characteristics such as gender, age and educational attainment, while national particularities are losing their importance in determining the risk of being temporarily employed. It is shown that national institutions and structures have lost their explanatory power, particularly during the years before the crisis. This de-territorialization of social inequalities can be interpreted as an indicator of Europeanization processes affecting the labour market segmentation. With the onset of the crisis in 2008/2009, however, the situation changed. National institutional factors such as employment protection, unemployment rate and economic growth once again influence the risk of temporary employment – an indicator of the renationalization of employment policies.

In Chapter 7, Sabine Israel adopts a transnational perspective to assess the health consequences of the eurozone crisis and its austerity policies for the population in the European peripheral countries. Physical, psycho-social and medical health determinants which commonly explain poor health among people of low income are included in the analysis in order to describe the diffusion of adverse social conditions. On the basis of EU-SILC, two sets of disadvantaged countries are compared from 2006/2007 to 2011/2012: West European countries which are subject to Economic Adjustment Programmes (EAPs), and East European countries which are subject to Balance of Payment Programmes (BoPs). It is shown that deprivation, arrears and access to healthcare are worsening in the majority of the peripheral countries. The BoP countries Latvia and Romania display increased barriers to healthcare, while mortgage problems are turning into a problem in Ireland and Greece. Moreover, deprivation affected more than three-fifths of the population in Greece, Hungary and Latvia in 2011/2012. While the sharpest increase in adverse social determinants can be observed in the lower-income quintiles, self-perceived poor health is mostly diffused among the people in the lowest – but also in the second- and third-income – quintile, bringing the social gradient in health to its demise. This surprising result can be explained by the relative improvement in the social position of the poorest, but also by means-tested exemptions from payments of services such as healthcare, which shift the cost burden towards higher-income quintiles.

In Chapter 8, Franziska Buttler starts from the observation that post-war Europe is characterized by new transnational interrelations. European Integration opened up new opportunity structures that may help individuals to achieve a certain standard of living and to deal with unpleasant life events. This raises the question of whether processes of horizontal Europeanization have opened up new possibilities and enriched opportunities. It can be shown that individuals who make transnational experiences are more satisfied with their lives than other people. A similar relationship can be observed on the country level as well. Nation-states which are open towards other European countries in the social domains of tourism, working abroad, immigration and European higher-education exchange increase the chances of higher individual life satisfaction. Hence, social transnational interrelations are beneficial for the utilization of resources which help to deal with problematic occurrences in life, especially in times of crisis.

In Chapter 9, Jenny Preunkert discusses the question of whether the previously discussed evolution of social inequalities – especially the high (youth) unemployment rates and the vast poverty, social exclusion and health problems – is also shaped by the political reaction to the sovereign debt crisis. She discusses the question of whether the conditions imposed by the eurozone bailout funds have contributed to the social problems faced by Southern European Member States and Ireland. In addition to an economic dimension, do the eurozone bailout funds also have a social dimension? Are the previously mentioned social problems relevant political issues in the management of the European crisis? The analysis shows that the social problems have been recognized within the European crisis policy, yet to this day social security systems have been mainly treated as a cost factor that has to be reduced. Additional social assistance has only been demanded for specific disadvantaged social groups.

ACKNOWLEDGEMENTS

This book is the result of a research project on the Europeanization of social inequalities, which was supported by a grant from the German Research Foundation (DFG) (grant no. HE 2174/12-1). The research took place at the University of Oldenburg in the context of the DFG-funded research unit 'Horizontal Europeanization' (FOR 1539). The authors would like to thank their fellow authors for their suggestions and comments, Eckard Kämper (DFG) and the scientific advisory board (Bernhard Ebbinghaus, Max Haller, Jo Reichertz, Peter Wagner, Anja Weiß and Theresa Wobbe) for their active and benevolent support of our research group, Isolde Heyen and Kerstin Zemke for their invaluable administrative support, and Natalie Chandler for her linguistic revision of our articles.

NOTE

1. EU-SILC (Statistics on Income and Living Conditions) is an EU-wide survey on income, poverty and living conditions in Europe which started in 2004, initially in 13 countries and by 2013 in 32 countries (EU-28 plus Iceland, Switzerland, Norway and Serbia). Data for Bulgaria and Romania have been available since 2007, data for Malta since 2008, and data for Croatia since 2010. EU-SILC is not a common survey, but tries to unify and harmonize the concepts employed – for example the concept of disposable income – and the survey methods. It is based on uniform definitions and methodological minimum standards. It consists of a household questionnaire and an individual questionnaire for household members aged 16 years and over. It covers in detail the income and material living conditions of households in Europe. Both with regard to sampling and data collection, the SILC data are still subject to considerable problems. Despite the methodological problems in terms of representativeness, accuracy, comparability and coherence, the EU-SILC data are currently the only available data source for comparative international and supranational analyses of income and living conditions in the EU.

REFERENCES

Alderson, A.S. and F. Nielsen (2002), 'Globalization and the Great U-Turn. Income Inequality Trends in 16 OECD Countries', *American Journal of Sociology* **107** (5): 1244–1299.

Armingeon, K. and B. Ceka (2013), 'The Loss of Trust in the European Union During the Great Recession Since 2007: The Role of Heuristics from the National Political System', *European Union Politics*, doi: 10.1177/1465116513495595 (online).

Beck, U. (2007), 'Beyond Class and Nation: Reframing Social Inequalities in a Globalizing World', *The British Journal of Sociology* **58** (4): 679–705.

Beckfield, J. (2006), 'European Integration and Income Inequality', *American Sociological Review* **71** (6): 964–985.

Beckfield, J. (2009), 'Remapping Inequality in Europe', *International Journal of Comparative Sociology* **50** (5–6): 486–504.

Blyth, M. (2013), *Austerity: The History of a Dangerous Idea*, Oxford: Oxford University Press.

Braun, D. and M. Tausendpfund (2014), 'The Impact of the Euro Crisis on Citizens' Support for the European Union', *Journal of European Integration* **36** (3): 231–245.

Brenner, N. (2001), 'The Limits to Scale? Methodological Reflections on Scalar Structuration Progress', *Human Geography* **25** (4): 591–614.

Castles, F.G., S. Leibfried, J. Lewis, H. Obinger and C. Pierson (2010), *The Oxford Handbook of the Welfare State*, Oxford: Oxford University Press.

De Grauwe, P. (2014), *Economics of Monetary Union*. 10th revised edition, Oxford: Oxford University Press.

Delhey, J. and U. Kohler (2006), 'From Nationally Bounded to Pan-European Inequalities? On the Importance of Foreign Countries as Reference Groups', *European Sociological Review* **22**: 125–140.

Emmenegger, P., S. Häusermann, B. Palier and M. Seeleib-Kaiser (eds) (2012), *The Age of Dualization: The Changing Face of Inequality in Deindustrializing Societies*, Oxford: Oxford University Press.

Fahey, T. (2007), 'The Case for an EU-wide Measure of Poverty', *European Sociological Review* **23** (1): 35–47.

Featherstone, K. and C.M. Radaelli (eds) (2003), *The Politics of Europeanization*, Oxford: Oxford University Press.

Ferrera, M. (2003), 'European Integration and National Social Citizenship', *Comparative Political Studies* **36** (6): 611–652.

Fligstein, N. (2008), *Euroclash*, Oxford: Oxford University Press.

Fligstein, N. and A. Stone Sweet (2002), 'Constructing Polities and Markets: An Institutionalist Account of European Integration 1', *American Journal of Sociology* **107** (5): 1206–1243.

Friedman, M. (1997), Why Europe Can't Afford the Euro – The Danger of a Common Currency, *The Times*, 19 November. Accessed 8 October 2015 at www.project-syndicate.org/commentary/the-euro--monetary-unity-to-political-disunity.

Gallie, D. and S. Paugam (eds) (2000), *Welfare Regimes and the Experience of Unemployment in Europe*, Oxford: Oxford University Press.

Geiger, T. (1932), *Die soziale Schichtung des deutschen Volkes. Soziographischer Versuch auf statistischer Grundlage*, Stuttgart: Enke.

Gerhards, J. and H. Lengfeld (2015), *European Citizenship and Social Integration in the European Union*, London and New York: Routledge.

Giddens, A. (2014), *Turbulent and Mighty Continent: What Future for Europe*, Cambridge: Polity.

Hall, P.A. (2014), 'Varieties of Capitalism and the Euro Crisis', *West European Politics* **37** (6): 1223–1243.

Heidenreich, M. (2003), 'Regional Inequalities in the Enlarged Europe', *Journal of European Social Policy* **13** (4): 313–333.

Heidenreich, M. and C. Wunder (2008), 'Patterns of Regional Inequality in the Enlarged Europe', *European Sociological Review* **24** (1): 19–36.

Hooghe, L. and G. Marks (2009), 'A Postfunctionalist Theory of European Integration', *British Journal of Political Science* **39** (1): 1–23.

Kangas, O.E. and V. Ritakallio (2007), 'Relative to What? Cross National Pictures of European Poverty Measured by Regional, National and European Standards', *European Societies* **9**: 119–145.

Kenworthy, L. (2004), *Egalitarian Capitalism*, New York: Russell Sage Foundation.

Kriesi, H., E. Grande, R. Lachat, M. Dolezal, S. Bornschier and T. Frey (2006), 'Globalization and the Transformation of the National Political Space: Six European Countries Compared', *European Journal of Political Research* **45** (6): 921–956.

Mau, S. and J. Mewes (2012), 'Horizontal Europeanisation in Contextual Perspective: What Drives Cross-border Activities Within the European Union?', *European Societies* **14** (1): 7–34.

Mau, S., J. Mewes and N.M. Schöneck (2012), 'What Determines Subjective Socio-economic Insecurity? Context and Class in Comparative Perspective', *Socio-Economic Review* **10** (4): 655–682.

Milanovic, B. (2013), 'Global Income Inequality in Numbers: In History and Now', *Global Policy* **4** (2): 198–208.

Moravcsik, A. (1998), *The Choice for Europe: Social Purpose and State Power from Messina to Maastricht*, Ithaca, NY: Cornell University Press.

OECD (2011), *Divided We Stand: Why Inequality Keeps Rising*, Paris: OECD.

OECD (2015), *In It Together: Why Less Inequality Benefits All*, Paris: OECD.

Radaelli, C. (2003), 'The Europeanization of Public Policy', in K. Featherstone and C. Radaelli (eds), *The Politics of Europeanization*, Oxford: Oxford University Press, pp. 27–56.

Rokkan, S. (1999), *State Formation, Nation-building, and Mass Politics in Europe*, Oxford: Oxford University Press.

Schwander, H. and S. Häusermann (2013), 'Who Is In and Who Is Out? A Risk-based Conceptualization of Insiders and Outsiders', *Journal of European Social Policy* **23** (3): 248–269.

Shambaugh, J.C. (2012), 'The Euro's Three Crises', *Brookings Papers on Economic Activity* **44** (1): 157–211.

Smith, A.D. (1983), 'Nationalism and Classical Social Theory', *British Journal of Sociology* **34** (1): 19–38.

Whelan, C.T. and B. Maître (2009), 'Europeanization of Inequality and European Reference Groups', *Journal of European Social Policy* **19** (2): 117–130.

Wilkinson, R.G. and K. Pickett (2009), *The Spirit Level: Why More Equal Societies Almost Always Do Better*, London: Allen Lane.

2. The Europeanization of income inequality before and during the eurozone crisis: inter-, supra- and transnational perspectives

Martin Heidenreich

2.1 INTRODUCTION: THE EUROZONE CRISIS AS A CHALLENGE FOR INEQUALITY RESEARCH

Disposable income is the essential economic basis for most households. The evolution and distribution of income is thus in the focus of the public and scientific debate (DiPrete 2007). It has been claimed that since the Great Recession of 2007–2009 and in the subsequent eurozone crisis income inequalities in the European Union (EU) have strongly increased (Blyth 2013: 15), European societies are becoming increasingly dualized (Emmenegger et al. 2012), the gap between insiders and outsiders has deepened (Lindvall and Rueda 2014), and the middle classes in European countries are eroding (Mau 2014). Empirically, however, inequalities of disposable income in the EU-27, in the EU-15 and in the eurozone have basically been stable since 2008. In some countries strongly affected by the crisis (e.g. Portugal, UK, Latvia) they are even declining.[1] This does not imply that the Great Recession and the subsequent financial, sovereign debt and economic crisis in Europe had no effect on inequality. On the contrary, the dissatisfaction with the current situation is immense and threatens to undermine the EU and its cohesion.[2]

However, highly aggregated, selective and relative inequality indicators focusing on national patterns of inequality, for example the cited Gini index of national income inequality, might not adequately reflect the ways in which people perceive inequality. Firstly, sometimes higher or lower parts of the income distribution ('the richest 1%', the 'poor'. . .) might be more important for the perception of inequality as the median of the distribution on which the Gini index focuses.

Secondly, other dimensions beyond income might be more important than disposable income (for example unemployment, earnings or wealth, gender or class, educational or employment inequalities or social mobility), as social inequalities are a multidimensional phenomenon (cf. however DiPrete 2007 for the overarching importance of income and earnings inequality). The crisis has first of all contributed to an increase in labour market inequalities in the EU (see Chapters 1 and 4).

Thirdly, besides the national frame of reference on which the usual inequality coefficients are based, a European or transnational frame of reference might also be important. The 73 per cent of Greeks or the 66 per cent of Bulgarians who evaluated the current financial situation of their households as bad in 2012 might not have done this because national inequality has increased in their countries or because their income has decreased (which only has been the case in Greece), but because they perceived their financial situations as bad compared with other Europeans (Figure 2.1). Such an observation requires a different concept of income inequality which conceives of inequality not only as an unequal distribution within one country, but also within Europe (cf. Heidenreich and Wunder 2008). The current dissatisfaction with the social and political situation in the EU may indicate the emergence of a transnational understanding of inequality: not only inequality within or between nation-states, but also the differences between individual living situations in different European countries are increasingly considered as indicators of inequality (and not only as disparity, i.e. as characteristics of unrelated social positions; cf. Blau 1977: 5).

In the introductory chapter this development was described as the Europeanization of social inequality. The aim of this chapter is to discuss the three previously distinguished understandings of this concept with regard to income inequality and to provide empirical evidence of the corresponding trends in the EU before and during the eurozone crisis: (1) When Europe is conceived of as an international social space, the research question is whether the trends towards higher within-state and lower between-state inequalities which were observed before the crisis (OECD 2011) have also continued during the crisis or whether the re-emergence of centre–periphery divisions and increasing between-state inequalities can be expected (Emmenegger et al. 2012). In section 2.2 it will be shown that the previously observed convergence of inequality between EU Member States has come to an at least temporary halt during the eurozone crisis. (2) When the EU is conceived of as a supranational political and administrative space, the question is raised as to whether the economic and political integration of the EU, and more particularly the common market, the currency union and austerity policies, have a negative effect on income

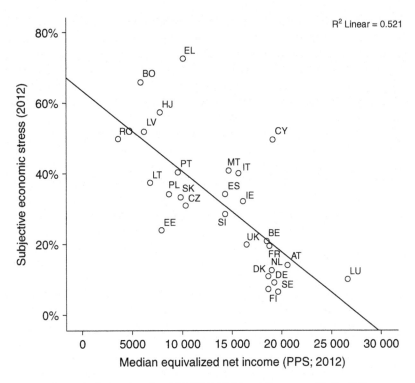

Source:	Own calculations based on EU-SILC (2012) and Eurostat, table ilc_di03.

*Figure 2.1	Subjective economic stress and disposable income (in PPS, EU-27; 2012)*

inequality. (3) When Europe is conceived of as a transnational social space, the research question is whether the social integration of Europe has contributed to the emergence of a European frame of reference for the perception of social inequalities. It will be shown that the perception of economic stress is not only shaped by individual living conditions and national contexts, but also by the national and transnational income position of the respondents (section 2.4). The empirical bases for these analyses are aggregate data provided by Eurostat on the national and regional contexts and the EU-SILC micro-data 2005–2013 which allow the evolution of income inequalities to be analysed before and during the crisis (see Chapter 1). In conclusion, the chapter stresses the need for a better understanding of the European-wide and transnational inequality dynamics, particularly in the current crisis (section 2.5).

2.2 INCOME INEQUALITIES BETWEEN AND WITHIN EU MEMBER STATES

In this section income dynamics within and between EU Member States before and during the financial, sovereign debt and economic crisis in the EU will be analysed in the framework of the first Europeanization concept. On the basis of Beckfield (2009) and Blyth (2013), *it can be expected that the trend towards increasing national inequalities is also continuing during the crisis, while the trend towards declining between-nation inequalities has been reversed due to austerity policies and the re-emergence of centre–periphery differences (H1).*

Until the beginning of the global financial crisis in 2008, national inequalities in most European countries had been increasing since the 1990s (Atkinson et al. 2010; OECD 2011). The reasons for this can be summarized under the banners of technology and globalization. Inequality grew due to skill-intense technological developments and increasing flows of capital, goods, services and people which raised the cross-border competition between various locations (Alderson and Nielsen 2002; OECD 2011). However, national institutions and policies such as employment and welfare regimes and private living forms also play a significant role. This explains why the level of income inequality clearly varies between the still-egalitarian income structures in the Scandinavian countries and the higher inequalities of many Central and Eastern European and most Southern European countries.

Despite the criticism of European austerity policies and their inequality-enhancing potential, national inequalities in the former 15 Member States of the EU and in the EU-27 slightly decreased from 2008 to 2013 (Figure 2.2). From 2008 to 2013, the Gini coefficient of income inequalities increased in eight EU countries by more than one percentage point (in Cyprus, Croatia, Hungary, Luxembourg, Denmark, Estonia, Spain and Italy), while it decreased in seven countries (Belgium, Latvia, the Netherlands, Poland, Portugal, Romania and the UK). Not even in the countries most affected by the crisis can a clear trend be observed. In the five countries that have been subject to Economic Adjustment Programmes (EAPs) (Cyprus, Greece, Ireland, Spain and Portugal; cf. Gros et al. 2014), inequalities have clearly increased only in Cyprus and in Spain, while they have decreased in Portugal. In Greece and Ireland inequality remained practically stable. This relative stability of national inequality pattern contrasts clearly with the increasing inequalities before the crisis. In the first decade after the introduction of the euro (1999–2008), the Gini coefficient of income inequalities increased in 13 EU countries by more than one percentage point, while it decreased clearly

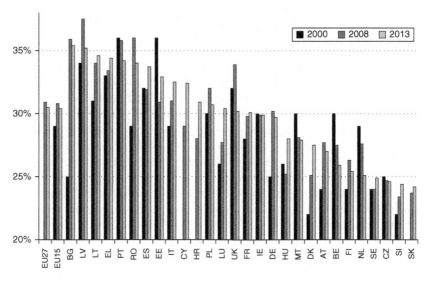

Source: Eurostat, table ilc_di12, accessed on 24 December 2014.

Figure 2.2   Income inequality in European countries. Gini-coefficients of equivalized disposable income (2000, 2008 and 2013)

only in five countries (Spain, Belgium, Malta, Ireland and Estonia). In sum, in contrast to H1, the trend towards increasing income inequalities has stopped during the crisis.

The evolution of between-state inequality will now be discussed. Before the crisis, income inequalities between the EU Member States decreased (Heidenreich and Härpfer 2010). This was mainly due to the economic and legal integration of the Southern and later Central and Eastern European countries into the common European market, but it was also a result of the monetary integration of the eurozone, which initially reduced the interest rate differentials between the former 'high' and 'low' inflation countries and thus stimulated huge capital flows into the quickly growing countries in the Southern, Northern and Eastern periphery. The question is whether this pattern has also continued in the current situation or whether this trend has been reversed – especially due to the deterioration of the situation in Southern and Eastern Europe (cf. Emmenegger et al. 2012 for the expectation of an increasing dualization and polarization of the EU).

Figure 2.3 gives an overview of the level and income inequality in Europe and in selected national states.[3] This figure is based on the income distribution of the European population. Each European is included independently from his or her nationality. On the basis of this figure, the pan-European

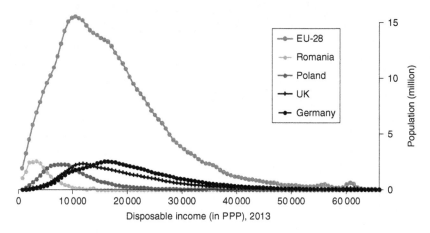

Source: EU-SILC UDB 2013. The results of the 2013 survey refer to the income situation in 2012.

Figure 2.3 Income distribution in the European Union (EU-28) and in Germany, the UK, Poland and Romania (2013)

income inequality has been calculated as Gini=0.339 (2013), which is higher than the Gini-coefficient given by Eurostat (0.305; table ilc_di12). The reason for this difference is that Eurostat calculates the European-wide coefficient as the weighted mean of the national values, thus ignoring between-state inequalities as a major source of inequalities in the EU. The former method is justified if the EU is considered a Single Market, but not as a societal field characterized by common standards of equality and solidarity. The latter method assumes common, European-wide standards of equality. Table 2.1 compares these two ways of calculating income inequality and poverty. In contrast to the income inequality in the USA, income inequality even throughout the whole EU is considerably lower.

These two alternatives also shape the debate on poverty (Fahey 2007). If a national poverty threshold of 60 per cent of the *national* median income is assumed, 16.5 per cent of Europeans are poor. If a European poverty threshold of 60 per cent is assumed, 23.6 per cent of the EU population is poor. The composition of these groups differs strongly. In the first case, people in countries with an unequal income structure and a residual minimum income system are especially considered to be poor (e.g. more than 20 per cent of Bulgarians, Greeks, Croatians and Romanians). In the second case, Europeans in poorer countries are mostly affected (e.g. 94.9 per cent of Romanians, 77.2 per cent of Bulgarians, 48.2 per cent of Latvians and 64.6 per cent of Lithuanians). This confirms the

Table 2.1 *Income inequality and poverty in the EU (2013; survey year 2012) and in the USA*

PPP	EU 15	EU 25	EU 28	USA
Income inequality, based on weighted national values (Gini)	0.305	0.287	0.304	
Income inequality (Gini)	0.300	0.318	0.339	0.382 (2013)
Income inequality (decile ratio)	4.034	4.590	5.553	5.811 (2013; LIS)
Poverty (60%; national thresholds)	16.3%	16.2%	16.5%	
Poverty (continental threshold)	13.5%	19.1%	23.6%	24.1% (2013; LIS)

Source: Own calculations on the basis of EU-SILC UDB 2013; OECD (2011: 24). http://www.lisdatacenter.org (Key Figures as of 10 December 2014).

observation that poverty in Europe is concentrated in poor countries, while in the USA 'the main cause of inequality is that regardless of state, there are rich and poor people' (Milanovic 2011: 176).

However, before and even during the crisis, the general pattern described by Milanovic is changing. In the enlarged EU-25 and EU-27, the between-country inequality (calculated on the basis of the mean logarithmic deviation) is strongly decreasing – in the EU-25, for example, from 30.5 per cent (2005) of total income inequality to only 19.7 per cent (2013); in the EU-27 from 38.8 per cent (2007) to 30.7 per cent (2013) (see Table 2.2). In the former EU-15, however, a different pattern can be observed: convergence before and divergence during the crisis. While the between-nation inequality in 1997 still amounted to 10.7 per cent of total inequality (Heidenreich and Härpfer 2010), it declined by 2010 to 4 per cent – an indicator of the rapid homogenization of the core European countries due to the common market, the introduction of the common currency and the regulatory homogenization of Europe. In the former EU-15, inequality was no longer predominantly a matter of countries; the segmentary differentiation of the social space was increasingly replaced by a functional one. However, since the beginning of the euro crisis, this convergence process has been reversed and the previous centre–periphery difference is returning. The between-nation inequality has increased from 4 per cent (2010) to 9.1 per cent (2013) of total inequality. In short, in the former European core region the convergence process has been reversed; in the enlarged EU it has come to a halt.

Table 2.2   Inequalities of disposable income within and between nations in the EU (survey years 2005–2013, PPS, MLD)

	EU 15				EU 25				EU 27			
	Gini	MLD total (=100%)	Within nation inequality (in % of total inequality)	Between nation inequality (in % of total inequality)	Gini	MLD total (=100%)	Within nation inequality (in % of total inequality)	Between nation inequality (in % of total inequality)	Gini	MLD total (=100%)	Within nation inequality (in % of total inequality)	Between nation inequality (in % of total inequality)
2005[1]	0.292	0.150	93.5%	6.5%	0.334	0.157	69.5%	30.5%				
2006[1]	0.288	0.148	94.3%	5.7%	0.326	0.153	72.1%	27.9%				
2007[2]	0.296	0.155	93.1%	6.9%	0.331	0.160	72.2%	27.8%	0.354	0.244	61.2%	38.8%
2008	0.298	0.157	93.5%	6.5%	0.328	0.163	75.4%	24.6%	0.349	0.234	64.0%	36.0%
2009	0.294	0.152	95.8%	4.2%	0.321	0.157	78.5%	21.5%	0.341	0.219	67.1%	32.9%
2010	0.294	0.154	96.0%	4.0%	0.319	0.160	79.7%	20.3%	0.339	0.217	68.4%	31.6%
2011	0.297	0.160	95.0%	5.0%	0.319	0.167	81.2%	18.8%	0.339	0.218	69.8%	30.2%
2012	0.298	0.164	93.0%	7.0%	0.318	0.174	81.2%	18.8%	0.338	0.220	69.4%	30.6%
2013	0.300	0.165	90.9%	9.1%	0.319	0.184	80.3%	19.7%	0.338	0.219	69.3%	30.7%

Notes:
(1) Without Bulgaria, Malta and Romania.
(2) Without Malta.

Source: EU-SILC, own calculations. Percentages refer to the decomposition of the income inequality in within-nation and between-nation inequality.

In conclusion, while national income inequalities before the crisis grew, national patterns of income inequality remained broadly stable during the crisis – with huge national variations, however. The first part of H1 has to be refuted. Total income inequality in the EU is still lower than in the USA. Before the crisis, income inequality between EU Member States was strongly declining. The economic position of a person was increasingly less determined by the nation-state in which he or she was living. This meritocratic convergence process has been interrupted and partially reversed during the crisis – especially due to the European financial, economic and debt crisis in which the median disposable income (PPS) decreased in Greece by 25 per cent, in Ireland by 12 per cent and in the UK by 9 per cent from 2008–2013, while it increased in Slovakia by 42 per cent, in Poland by 36 per cent and in Romania by 29 per cent (Eurostat, table ilc_di04). The second part of H1 thus has been confirmed: the crisis has reversed the European-wide convergence process.

2.3   THE DETERMINANTS OF REGIONAL AND NATIONAL PATTERNS OF INCOME INEQUALITY

As an example of a supranational understanding of the Europeanization thesis, I will turn now to the question of whether the patterns of inequality are shaped not only by particular regional and national context factors but also by European decisions and patterns. The dependent variables are national and (where possible) regional levels of inequality.[4] These patterns can be explained by the regional economic and labour market structures, national institutions, global interconnections and also by European policies. This will now be explained.

Economic and employment structures play a decisive role in national and regional patterns of income inequality. A higher employment share of the *industrial sector* means in general lower levels of inequality, because industrial workers are usually more unionized and covered by collective wage agreements – according to Kuznets (1955) a central reason for egalitarian wage and income structures. Furthermore, the *labour market structure* also affects the distribution of disposable income. Kenworthy (2004) has shown that a higher employment rate (especially of women) is the basis for a more egalitarian distribution. Even though a higher labour force participation rate might be associated with an expansion of low-wage activities, the disposable income of the household will increase when more people per household have a job. More inclusive labour markets, i.e. a higher employment rate of women in particular, will thus be associated with higher income and lower inequality if households with low incomes benefit over-proportionally from additional employment opportunities (Kenworthy and Pontusson 2005). It can therefore be expected that more inclusive labour markets (e.g. indicated by higher female employment rates) and a strong industrial sector will favour lower income inequality. Secondly, *national institutions* such as a strong welfare state – indicated by high social security expenditures – will favour egalitarian income structures (Kenworthy 2004). Thirdly, a significant part of the effects of economic integration is the result of *European integration*, since the EU is the most internationalized economy in the world and a decisive factor in the current economic crisis. Beckfield (2009: 490) shows that the economic integration of the EU is associated with an increase in income inequality. Fiscal consolidation policies – especially since the beginning of the global and European financial and economic crisis – might also contribute to higher inequalities (Blyth 2013). *The European integration in goods, services, capital and labour markets and austerity policies might thus contribute to higher income inequality (H2).*

The explanatory variables used in the following analysis are explained in detail in the appendix Table 2A.1. Whenever possible, data for the NUTS2 level are used because more disaggregated data in most cases do not exist. The resulting data set has a hierarchical structure, i.e. the level of income inequality in a region is to be explained firstly by the regional economic, employment and labour market structures, and secondly by the national institutional context, the openness of national product, capital and labour markets, and the relevance of the European and global context for the respective country. Thirdly, these contextual effects on regional and national patterns of inequality differ from one year to the other. This structure can be analysed by multi-level models, which include data from j regions ('level 2') of i countries ('level 1') in k years ('level 3') (Rabe-Hesketh and Skrondal 2012: 385).

Initially, the regional and national income distributions are analysed without explanatory variables. A two-level model (Table 2.3, column 1) takes into account only the national variations of inequality patterns: $y_{ijk} = \beta_1 + \zeta_i^{(1)} + \varepsilon_{ijk}$[5] In the next step, the differences in income equality between different regions of a country will be taken into account (Table 2.3, column 2).

Besides the effects of the regions and countries – which are 'nested' effects because each region is part of a country – the effects of the respective survey years have to be taken into account. In our case, time will be included as a crossed random effect, which implies that all the territories are affected similarly by the economic situation or other events or characteristics associated with the survey year (cf. Rabe-Hesketh and Skrondal 2012: 433 for a similar

Table 2.3 Determinants of national and regional income inequality (Gini) before and during the Great Recession (2005–2013) in 24 EU Member States

	Two-level empty model (2005–2013) (1)	Three-level empty model (2005–2013) (2)	Three-way error-components model (2005–2013) (3)	2005–2013 (4)	2005–2008 (5)	2009–2013 (6)
Industrial employment				−0.13*	−0.14**	−0.21**
				(−2.38)	(−2.82)	(−4.69)
Female employment rate				−0.09**	−0.10**	−0.12**
				(−2.62)	(−3.17)	(−3.34)
Social expenditures				−0.11+	−0.38**	−0.17
				(−1.66)	(−4.72)	(−1.62)
Fiscal austerity				0.01	0.06	−0.01
				(0.31)	(0.76)	(−0.40)
EU Single Market Integration				−0.07*	−0.10+	−0.10**
				(−2.45)	(−1.87)	(−2.84)
Constant	27.90**	27.90**	27.88**	27.49**	26.72**	27.35**
	(38.67)	(38.65)	(39.00)	(44.13)	(46.70)	(51.61)
No.	1140	1140	1140	1100	550	550
Log-likelihood	−2779	−2772	−2358	−2241	−1112	−1154
Wald_chi²				19.32	39.08	74.67
ψ[(1)] (between-nation variance)	13.54	13.55	10.55	6.35	5.18	3.80

$\psi^{(2)}$ (between-region variance)	0.28	5.08	3.12	3.35	3.24
$\psi^{(3)}$ (inter-temporal variance)		0.56	0.51	0.49	0.13
ψ (residual variance)	6.74	2.15	2.18	1.61	2.18
Between-state ICC	0.66	0.58	0.52	0.49	0.41
Between-region ICC	0.01	0.28	0.26	0.32	0.35
Between-year ICC		0.03	0.04	0.05	0.01
Pseudo-R^2			0.661	0.653	0.681
AIC	5563	4726	4501	2244	2329
BIC	5578	4751	4551	2287	2372

Notes: + p < 0.10, * p < 0.05, ** p < 0.01; in parentheses: t-values.

Source: Multi-level analysis based on regional and national inequality indicators calculated on the basis of EU-SILC UDB 2005–2013 and SOEP. Contextual variables provided by Eurostat.

three-way error-components model). This model is reproduced in column 3 of Table 2.3. Three different intra-class correlations (ICC) can be calculated on the basis of this model. The 'between-nation' intra-class correlation ($\psi(1)/(\psi(1) + \psi(2) + \psi(3) + \theta)$) indicates how similar the income inequalities are within one country. The 'interregional' ICC, which is calculated as the variance between different regions of the same state, refers to the additional explanatory contribution of the regional level. The 'between-year' ICC refers to the correlation for the same year across regions.

As an 'empty model' without explanatory variables, model (3) also serves as a point of reference for the following models. As suggested by the previously proposed hypotheses, it will be tested in models (4)–(6) if and to what extent income inequality is shaped by regional economic and labour market structures, national institutions, and European and global market integration. Methodically, this requires that the explanatory variables x_2, x_3, x_4 and the corresponding coefficients β_2, β_3, β_4 must be taken into account in addition to the national ($\zeta_i^{(1)}$), regional ($\zeta_{jk}^{(2)}$) and temporal effects ($\zeta_k^{(3)}$): $y_{ijk} = \beta_1 + \beta_2 x_2 + \beta_3 x_3 + \beta_4 x_4 + \ldots + \zeta_i^{(1)} + \zeta_{jk}^{(2)} + \zeta_k^{(3)} + \varepsilon_{ijk}$. The quality of the estimate is indicated by the log-likelihood value. The Bayes and Akaike information criteria AIC and BIC indicate the fit of the models. The proportion of explained variance in the overall model can be calculated in analogy to the squared correlation coefficients (r^2) of a multiple regression as the correlation between the estimated and actual level of income inequality.

H2 will now be tested for the whole period taken into consideration (column 4) and the years before the crisis (2005–2008, column 5) and during the crisis (2009–2012, column 6). The results are surprisingly similar for all the three time frames: a higher share of industrial employment is strongly correlated with lower inequality. As expected on the basis of Kenworthy (2004), a higher share of female employment is also correlated with lower inequality in nearly all dimensions, since a higher employment rate of women is associated with a higher household income, especially of poorer households. As expected, both regional indicators are associated with more egalitarian income structures. At the national level, the welfare state indicated by the level of social expenditures has the expected effect on egalitarian patterns of income. The economic integration in Europe which is tested by the corresponding sub-index proposed by König and Ohr (2013) has a significant negative effect on income inequality before and during the crisis. This can be taken as an indicator for the egalitarian dynamics of the EU, which fosters the convergence of its Member States via their economic integration. However, no significant effect of fiscal austerity, which in the eurozone is also the result of European coordination and supervision of fiscal policies, can be observed. Hypothesis H2, which focuses on the effects of the economic integration in Europe, can be thus only partially be confirmed.

The effects of the crisis on income inequalities are still limited as the comparison of models (5) and (6) shows. The effects of the industrial sector and of European economic integration on egalitarian income patterns become stronger and the effect of social expenditures becomes weaker. But other variables (for example the unemployment rate) do not have an additional significant effect on inequality.

In sum, the patterns of national and regional income inequality are predominantly shaped by national economic and labour market structures and national institutions (especially national welfare policies). Countries with a higher share of industrial employment, a high female employment rate and high social expenditures are characterized by more egalitarian income patterns. Economic integration in Europe has a negative impact on income inequality, which might be an indicator of the egalitarian dynamics of European integration not yet counterbalanced by fiscal austerity.

2.4 SUBJECTIVE ECONOMIC STRESS: THE EUROPEANIZATION OF PERCEIVED INCOME INEQUALITY

In the next step, the determinants of subjective economic stress will be discussed on the basis of the third Europeanization concept, which conceives of Europe as a transnational space. The assumption of the Europeanization of living conditions will be tested on the basis of the question of if and to what extent subjective economic stress – the inability to make ends meet – is shaped not only by individual, household-related, regional or national factors, but also by the income level in a European and transnational context (Fahey 2007; Heidenreich and Wunder 2008). At least at the macro-level, this indicator is highly correlated with subjective poverty (Figure 2.1). Taking the example of Greece, the discrepancy between national indicators and subjective perceptions can be illustrated. While the national poverty rate increased only by 1.6 percentage points during the crisis, the available income declined from the beginning of the crisis (2008) until 2012 by 16 per cent, while the reported difficulties in making ends meet increased from 54.5 per cent to 72.8 per cent. This – and not the slight increase in the national poverty or inequality rates – might be a more plausible explanation for the increase of the perceived economic stress. The Europeanization thesis therefore claims that subjective feelings of deprivation and poverty are also explained by a *European respective transnational frame of reference* (cf. Delhey and Kohler 2006; Fahey 2007; Kangas and Ritakallio 2007; Heidenreich and Wunder 2008; Goedemé and Rottiers 2011). Whelan and Maître (2009: 118) explain the underlying

Europeanization concept as a strong one, since it implies 'that people perceive themselves as part of a larger European stratification system (a thesis which they however reject both in their weak and their strong versions). Furthermore, the perception of being advantaged or disadvantaged within this system would have to play an important role in individuals' evaluations of their own life circumstances.' Thus, Europe is conceived of as a social space for the development and perception of social inequalities.

Empirically, economic stress will first of all be influenced by *personal and household-related living conditions*: women, younger and older people, low-skilled persons with routinized jobs, singles, single parents, migrants and the unemployed are the groups which are most strongly affected by poverty. These groups also exhibit the highest risk of feeling poor. In addition, the *economic, labour market and institutional context* of the European countries will also influence the perceived economic stress. More specifically, strong egalitarian institutions, for example advanced systems of social security, a strong industrial sector and high (female) employment levels reduce subjective risks of economic stress. In addition to the variables included in section 2.3, the regional respective national level of income inequality is also included because a more egalitarian society might reduce status competition and thus the perceived economic stress. Similar to section 2.3, the influence of austerity policies and European economic integration will also be tested. In addition, the effect of economic adjustment programmes is tested. On the basis of happiness research, it can be expected that the most important factor in reducing subjective economic stress will be a high income.[6] Drawing on the Europeanization thesis and Figure 2.1, I expect *that the level of disposable income is evaluated as high or low not only in relation to the average national income, but also in relation to European and transnational standards (H3)*. This hypothesis will be discussed on the basis of the previously explained EU-SILC data.

The question of whether a person has difficulties in making ends meet has been recoded as a binary variable in order to better distinguish people with serious difficulties from other people. Therefore, multi-level binary logistic regressions and more specifically the logistic two-level random intercept models which can be calculated with the xtmelogit algorithm of STATA 13 will be used (Hox 2010: chapter 6). The variables used in these models and the expected effects are described in the appendix Table 2A.1. The coefficients in Table 2.4 are average marginal effects (AME) which express the average effect of the respective category of the independent variable on the dependent variable in comparison to the reference category. In contrast to odds ratios, AMEs can be compared across groups, samples and models (Mood 2010).

In Table 2.4, the occupational, qualificational and ascriptive

Table 2.4 Subjective economic stress of the European population (2005–2012)

	2005	2006	2007	2008	2009	2010	2011	2012
Women	0.002+	0.002		0.002	0.005**		0.003*	0.004**
	(1.67)	(1.52)		(1.39)	(4.04)		(2.07)	(3.09)
Age group (ref.: 25–54 years)								
15 to 24 years	−0.002	0.002		−0.006*	−0.011**		−0.015**	−0.021**
	(−0.65)	(0.78)		(−2.56)	(−4.92)		(−6.28)	(−8.82)
55 years +	−0.059**	−0.059**		−0.060**	−0.070**		−0.067**	−0.067**
	(−30.04)	(−31.52)		(−34.87)	(−40.20)		(−37.64)	(−38.12)
Household type (ref.: adults with children)								
One person household	0.036**	0.040**	0.013**	0.037**	0.029**	0.003	0.033**	0.031**
	(13.43)	(15.43)	(5.84)	(15.99)	(12.25)	(1.36)	(13.97)	(13.16)
Adults, no child	−0.001	0.001	−0.020**	0.003+	−0.005**	−0.029**	−0.005**	−0.009**
	(−0.55)	(0.66)	(−13.52)	(1.77)	(−3.20)	(−19.93)	(−2.78)	(−5.40)
Single-parent household	0.119**	0.125**	0.124**	0.121**	0.117**	0.126**	0.124**	0.122**
	(28.02)	(30.38)	(31.55)	(31.14)	(29.81)	(31.85)	(31.16)	(31.52)
Foreigner or born abroad	0.061**	0.052**	0.045**	0.055**	0.061**	0.056**	0.054**	0.048**
	(20.01)	(17.80)	(16.19)	(20.62)	(23.15)	(21.56)	(20.54)	(18.69)
Health	0.134**	0.123**	0.102**	0.126**	0.127**	0.109**	0.136**	0.131**
	(57.70)	(55.30)	(50.50)	(58.79)	(58.35)	(51.34)	(61.14)	(59.46)
Educational level (ref.: high)								
Low	0.065**	0.064**	0.045**	0.070**	0.069**	0.047**	0.059**	0.063**
	(22.29)	(22.76)	(17.08)	(27.67)	(27.52)	(19.47)	(22.91)	(24.93)
Medium	0.033**	0.037**	0.032**	0.039**	0.038**	0.032**	0.035**	0.035**
	(12.49)	(14.63)	(13.23)	(17.35)	(17.12)	(14.27)	(15.15)	(15.82)

Table 2.4 (continued)

	2005	2006	2007	2008	2009	2010	2011	2012
ISCO skill levels (ref.: operating, repair)								
Simple tasks	0.008**	0.007**	0.013**	0.007**	0.008**	0.007**	0.011**	0.011**
	(4.57)	(3.81)	(7.99)	(4.33)	(4.45)	(4.28)	(6.18)	(6.32)
Complex tasks	-0.025**	-0.025**	-0.021**	-0.025**	-0.027**	-0.030**	-0.027**	-0.028**
	(-8.96)	(-9.34)	(-8.44)	(-10.72)	(-11.31)	(-12.62)	(-11.59)	(-12.19)
Problem-solving, creativity	-0.057**	-0.055**	-0.051**	-0.051**	-0.054**	-0.059**	-0.054**	-0.050**
	(-20.74)	(-20.43)	(-20.27)	(-21.14)	(-22.26)	(-24.72)	(-20.40)	(-19.29)
Unemployed (household)	0.133**	0.119**	0.128**	0.123**	0.149**	0.154**	0.134**	0.141**
	(62.36)	(55.99)	(60.52)	(57.09)	(74.31)	(79.75)	(67.88)	(72.17)
Disposable income (deciles)	-0.015**	-0.008**	-0.006**	-0.007**	-0.011**	-0.015**	-0.011**	-0.011**
	(-15.23)	(-8.06)	(-6.54)	(-6.93)	(-11.28)	(-15.40)	(-11.09)	(-11.61)
Disposable income, in % of national median (deciles)	-0.024**	-0.031**	-0.030**	-0.031**	-0.027**	-0.025**	-0.029**	-0.028**
	(-33.57)	(-43.57)	(-43.59)	(-42.06)	(-35.35)	(-33.62)	(-38.00)	(-36.06)
Industrial employment	-0.002**	-0.002**	-0.002**	-0.002**	-0.003**	-0.004**	-0.004**	-0.004**
	(-11.80)	(-11.97)	(-12.84)	(-13.92)	(-16.88)	(-22.05)	(-24.16)	(-21.90)
Female employment	0.002**	0.000	-0.001**	-0.000+	-0.000	-0.000	-0.003**	-0.000
	(5.10)	(0.44)	(-3.48)	(-1.79)	(-1.26)	(-1.53)	(-14.15)	(-1.13)
Unemployment	0.006**	0.004**	-0.001	0.002**	0.003**	0.003**	-0.002**	0.004**
	(8.04)	(4.56)	(-1.13)	(3.78)	(7.17)	(7.15)	(-3.47)	(6.82)
Social protection	-0.007	-0.006	-0.007+	-0.011*	-0.015**	-0.014**	-0.012**	-0.011*
	(-1.54)	(-1.12)	(-1.66)	(-2.24)	(-3.03)	(-2.86)	(-2.73)	(-2.56)

Inequality (Gini)	0.004	0.014+	0.015*	0.004	0.002	0.003	0.008	0.005
	(0.59)	(1.95)	(2.18)	(0.51)	(0.29)	(0.46)	(0.95)	(0.66)
Fiscal austerity	0.034+	0.016	−0.039**	0.002	−0.001	0.002	−0.002	−0.014
	(1.67)	(0.59)	(−2.76)	(0.16)	(−0.06)	(0.31)	(−0.35)	(−1.22)
EU Single Market Integration	−0.004	0.000	0.000	−0.001	−0.002	−0.001	−0.001	−0.001
	(−1.50)	(0.11)	(0.16)	(−0.46)	(−0.68)	(−0.38)	(−0.38)	(−0.30)
No.	301 448	309 886	328 691	363 302	359 048	356 583	354 498	359 860
chi²	35 626	38 269	36 913	42 776	44 919	45 735	46 760	47 483
Between-country variance	0.476	0.48	0.457	0.613	0.472	0.513	0.421	0.48
Variance (total)	3.766	3.77	3.746	3.903	3.762	3.803	3.711	3.77
Intra-class correlation	0.127	0.127	0.122	0.157	0.125	0.135	0.113	0.127
McFadden pseudo-R^2	0.136	0.146	0.139	0.138	0.144	0.148	0.155	0.152
AIC	281 000	283 000	285 000	335 000	336 000	333 000	326 000	337 000
BIC	281 000	284 000	286 000	335 000	337 000	333 000	326 000	338 000
Log-likelihood	−140 000	−142 000	−143 000	−167 000	−168 000	−166 000	−163 000	−169 000

Note: Table 2.4 shows the results of different binary logistic two-level random intercept models with the dependent dichotomous variable 'serious difficulties in making ends meet' (yes or no). The figures refer to the interviewed persons from 24 EU countries. In 2007 and 2010, age and sex could not be included in the model due to multi-collinearity. The coefficients are average marginal effects (cf. Mood 2010). Figures in parentheses: t-values. The AIC (Akaike information criterion) and the BIC (Bayes information criterion) are measures of the relative quality of the statistical models. Legend: + p < .1; * p < .05; ** p < .01.

Source: Own calculations on the basis of the last revisions of EU-SILC UDB 2005–2012.

characteristics of the respondents are included in the models for the years 2005–2012 in order to determine which individual and household-related factors influence the risk of subjective economic stress. These models also include the indicators for the national and transnational income position of the respondents, which is at the core of this section. In addition to these individual factors, the previously discussed contextual variables have been included.

While the perceived economic stress of *female* respondents was not significantly higher before the crisis, this changed during the crisis because since 2009 women have a higher perceived risk. The perceived risks of *prime-aged persons* have been always higher than the risks of older people. From 2008 this difference also became significant in comparison to younger people, which shows that the people at the core of the labour market are strongly affected. *One-person households and singles* had a significantly higher risk before and during the crisis; since 2007, adults without children have a significantly lower risk than adults with children. The perceived economic stress for *migrants* both before and during the crisis was much higher than the risk for natives. Furthermore, *bad health* was a major economic risk both before and during the crisis.

Indicators of a dualization in the population are sharp differences between the perceived risks of various *skill and occupational groups* (Emmenegger et al. 2012). In comparison to highly skilled people, the economic stress of *medium- and low-skilled people* was consistently and significantly higher. In a similar vein, the economic stress of the population varies with their *occupational profile*. For people with complex tasks (e.g. technicians and associate professionals or retail managers (skill group 3)), or tasks that require problem-solving, decision-making or creativity (e.g. professionals or sales and marketing managers (skill group 4)), perceived economic stresses are significantly lower than those of employees with simple (skill group 1) or operational, repairing and information-processing tasks (e.g. clerical support workers, services and sales workers, skilled agricultural workers, craft workers, plant and machine operators and assemblers (skill group 2)). In comparison with more skilled persons, during the crisis employees with simple skills reported increasing difficulties in making ends meet. Unsurprisingly, *being unemployed* or having an unemployed person in the household leads to a sharp increase in the perceived economic stress (up to 14 percentage points).

Indicators for the economic, employment and welfare system of the respective countries have also been included in addition to the individual and household-related factors. As expected, a higher share of the industrial sector, higher female employment rates, lower unemployment rates and higher expenditures for social protection significantly reduce economic stress in most of the years. Income inequality, fiscal austerity and the EU Single Market integration had no consistent effect on subjective economic stress.

In the next step, the indicators for the relative income position of the respondents compared to the national and European median were included in order to test H3. As expected, both income indicators are negatively correlated with economic stress. The position in the transnational income hierarchy has a weaker effect on subjective poverty. An international income position improved by one decile reduces economic stress by 1.5 (2005) respective 1.1 (2012) percentage points. In contrast, 2.4 respective 2.8 percentage points are linked to an improvement in the national income position. However, this also implies that the international income position has a strong effect, even though the national income position has been already included in the model. This result supports the thesis of the transnationalization respective Europeanization of subjective economic stress. In the years from 2005 to 2012, subjective economic stress is lower by approximately 4 percentage points for each higher income decile. Approximately one-quarter of this decrease can be attributed to the transnational income position and three-quarters to the national income position. The proportion explained by the transnational income position in contrast to the national position did not increase during the crisis.

In sum, a comparison of economic stress before and during the current crisis shows that the patterns at the individual and household level basically reflect the objective living conditions of the population. Singles, single parents, migrants, low-skilled persons with elementary jobs and the unemployed had higher economic stress than other people. This pattern was unexpectedly stable before and during the crisis. Apart from this high stability, a number of changes can also be observed. Since 2009, women have reported more difficulties than men in making ends meet, while younger people perceive lower risks than before. Both observations are counter-intuitive because employed women are the relative winners of the crisis, while younger people face high unemployment risks during the crisis. Unsurprisingly, higher incomes reduce economic stress. However, it is not at all self-evident that the position in the European and transnational income hierarchy – and not only the position in the national hierarchy – shapes feelings of economic insecurity. A huge amount of national differences in subjective deprivation can be explained by three variables: industrial employment, unemployment and social protection. In total, the subjective perception of a person's own financial limitations is surprisingly stable.

2.5   SUMMARY AND OUTLOOK

The methodological nationalism of inequality research assumes that the social relations and institutional structures that shape the distribution of living and income opportunities can be analysed mostly within the boundaries of a nation-state. This assumption is challenged by the Europeanization of markets, governance structures and social relations. A key challenge for the sociology of social inequality is thus the investigation of transnational, especially European, spatial references. In this chapter, three different Europeanization conceptions were described and illustrated taking the example of income inequalities. Firstly, Europe was conceived of as an international social space in which national patterns of income inequality and the evolution of between-nation inequality can be compared. Secondly, Europe was conceived of as a politically regulated economic field which shapes the social situations of households and individuals, and, thirdly, as an emerging social field shaping the perceptions of income inequalities.

First of all, the development of within- and between-nation inequality was analysed. The previously-ascertained increase in within-nation inequality and the decline in income inequality between EU Member States came to a halt during the Great Recession and the eurozone crisis. This mostly reflects the deteriorating conditions in Mediterranean countries. While most of the post-socialist countries successfully weathered the storm (especially Slovakia, Poland, Romania and Bulgaria), Southern European countries had to deal with the withdrawal of the huge inflows of capital which they received after the creation of the common European currency in 1999. This shows that the Europeanization of income inequality cannot be equalized with a European-wide convergence of living conditions. On the contrary, the Europeanization of economic and social conditions, especially in the five Western European bailout countries during the eurozone crisis, implies a clear differentiation and deterioration in living conditions. This shows that inequality is not only shaped by national institutions, but to a large extent also by European processes of convergence und divergence.

Secondly, in addition to regional economic and labour market structures and national institutions, European economic integration also shapes regional and national patterns of income inequality. This shows that European integration promotes more egalitarian income structures.

Thirdly, the factors at the individual, household, national and transnational level which shape the subjective economic stress in Europe were analysed. Unsurprisingly, being a native, healthy and high-qualified man in a prime-age group and with a skilled occupation strongly reduces economic stress in comparison to migrants, women and low-skilled singles. A strong industry, low unemployment and a developed welfare state likewise reduce subjective economic stress. In addition to these individual and national factors, a rank in the national and European income hierarchy also reduces economic stress. The fact that the individual position in the transnational income hierarchy has a strong and significant effect in comparison to the effect of the position in the national income hierarchy can be interpreted as strong support for the hypothesized Europeanization of frames of reference.

Income inequality therefore cannot be analysed solely in the national context. Especially in the current economic, financial and sovereign debt crisis, it has become evident that income inequality is increasingly also being generated and regulated at the European level. In the current recession this is documented in the at least temporary halt of the economic convergence process which has characterized the EU for decades. The standards with which a person evaluates his or her own living conditions also seem to be increasingly defined in a European and transnational context. A key challenge for the sociology of social inequality is therefore the investigation of multiple and also European frames of reference.

NOTES

1. The Gini-coefficient of equivalized disposable income (source: Eurostat, table ilc_di12) decreased from 2008 to 2013 in the EU (27 countries) from 30.9 per cent to 30.5 per cent, in the EU (15 countries) from 30.8 per cent to 30.4 per cent, and increased in the euro zone (18) from 30.4 per cent to 30.6 per cent. Eurostat calculates these Gini indices as the weighted average of the national values. In Cyprus, the Gini index increased from 29.0 per cent to 32.4 per cent and in Spain from 31.9 per cent to 33.7 per cent, while it decreased in Portugal from 35.8 per cent to 34.2 per cent. In Greece, inequality increased by one percentage point, while it remained stable in Ireland.
2. In June 2014, for example, 68 per cent of the Europeans were not satisfied with the way inequalities and poverty is addressed in their respective home countries (Special EB (Eurobarometer) 418). Thirty-two per cent of the Europeans identified social inequalities as being among the EU's two biggest challenges (Special EB 413). Thirty-two per cent of the Europeans felt, in spring 2014, that there was a risk of falling into poverty. This share 'has increased significantly in many Member States since January–February 2009: Spain (43 per cent, +26 percentage points), Greece (56 per cent, +22), Croatia (47 per cent, +21), Cyprus (44 per cent, +21), Slovakia (44 per cent, +17), Slovenia (37 per cent, +15) and Portugal (38 per cent, +14)' (EB 81, spring 2014, p. 26)
3. All the following calculations are based on the latest available versions of the EU-SILC data (e.g. EU-SILC UDB UDB_c13_ver 2013-2 from 1 August 2015). The different measures of inequality mentioned above have been calculated for the survey year 2012 – where the income data for 2011 were collected – for the EU-28 Member States. In all cases we use the disposable income (HX090; reference year: mostly previous calendar year), the 'new OECD' equivalence scale (HX050), the weighting factor (RB050) and the conversion rates and purchasing power parities proposed by EU-SILC and described in the corresponding manual. We ignore missing values and zero incomes and replace

incomes that are higher than 99 per cent of the national population by an upper limit which corresponds to the 99th percentile. Similarly, a lower limit is applied for incomes below the first percentile. This top- and bottom-coding which reduces the effect of possibly spurious outliers (Burkhauser et al. 2008) explains the differences to the figures published by Eurostat. My figures therefore systematically underestimate the top part of the income distribution, but they avoid the distortions linked to accidental outliers. Data for Romania and Bulgaria are available since 2007, data for Malta since 2008 and data for Croatia since 2010.

4. In general, patterns of income inequality differ clearly within a state. Even in relatively egalitarian countries such as Germany, the inequality in Hamburg (Gini for 2012: 0.30) is much higher than in Trier (Gini 2012: 0.20). The inequality in Northern Ireland (Gini = 0.27) is lower than in London (Gini = 0.34).

5. In this model y_{ijk} refers to regional inequality in the kth year in the jth region in the ith country. β_1 (Gini = 27.9 per cent) indicates the mean inequality of all regions and countries, $\zeta_i^{(1)}$ the difference between the overall mean β_1 of the total sample and the value of the country i. ε_{ijk} is the error for the region j and the country i in the jth year. $\zeta_i^{(1)}$ und ε_{ijk} are assumed independent of each other and identically distributed (i.i.d.) with mean 0 and the variances $\psi^{(1)}$ and θ. This variance (13.54) amounts to 66 per cent of the total variance (20.56). Two-thirds of the variance therefore originates within the European countries, i.e. they are to be attributed either to the peculiarities of the region or the year.

6. This expectation reflects the observation that life satisfaction increases with income (according to Kahneman and Deaton 2010, up to an annual household income of US$75 000 which in 2010 equated to 60 000 Euro).

REFERENCES

Alderson, A.S. and F. Nielsen (2002), 'Globalization and the Great U-Turn. Income Inequality Trends in 16 OECD Countries', *American Journal of Sociology*, **107** (5), 1244–1299.

Atkinson, A.B., E. Marlier, F. Montaigne and A. Reinstadler (2010), 'Income Poverty and Income Inequality', in A.B. Atkinson and E. Marlier (eds), *Income and Living Conditions in Europe*, Luxembourg: Office for Official Publications of the European Communities, pp. 101–131.

Beckfield, J. (2009), 'Remapping Inequality in Europe', *International Journal of Comparative Sociology*, **50** (5–6), 486–504.

Blau, P.M. (1977), *Inequality and Heterogeneity: A Primitive Theory of Social Structure*, New York: Free Press.

Blyth, M. (2013), *Austerity: The History of a Dangerous Idea*, Oxford: Oxford University Press.

Burkhauser, R.V., T. Oshio and L. Rovba (2008), 'How the Distribution of After-Tax Income Changed Over the 1990s Business Cycle: A Comparison of the United States, Great Britain, Germany and Japan', *Journal of Income Distribution*, **17** (1), 87–109.

Delhey, J. and U. Kohler (2006), 'From Nationally Bounded to Pan-European Inequalities? On the Importance of Foreign Countries as Reference Groups', *European Sociological Review*, **22** (2), 125–140.

DiPrete, T.A. (2007), 'What has Sociology to Contribute to the Study of Inequality Trends? A Historical and Comparative Perspective', *American Behavioral Scientist*, **50** (5), 603–618.

Emmenegger, P., S. Häusermann, B. Palier and M. Seeleib-Kaiser (eds) (2012),

The Age of Dualization: The Changing Face of Inequality in Deindustrializing Societies, New York: Oxford University Press.

Fahey, T. (2007), 'The Case for an EU-wide Measure of Poverty', *European Sociological Review*, **23** (1), 35–47.

Goedemé, T. and S. Rottiers (2011), 'Poverty in the Enlarged European Union. A Discussion about Definitions and Reference Groups', *Sociology Compass*, **5** (1), 77–91.

Gros, D., C. Alcidi, A. Belke, L. Coutinho and A. Giovannini (2014), *State-of-play in Implementing Macroeconomic Adjustment Programmes in the Euro Area: Short Version*, Ruhr Economic Papers No. 482. Accessed 19 March 2015 at http://dx.doi.org/10.4419/86788548.

Heidenreich, M. and M. Härpfer (2010), 'Einkommensungleichheiten in der Europäischen Union', in M. Eigmüller and S. Mau (eds), *Gesellschaftstheorie und Europapolitik*, Wiesbaden: VS, pp. 245–273.

Heidenreich, M. and C. Wunder (2008), 'Patterns of Regional Inequality in the Enlarged Europe', *European Sociological Review*, **24** (1), 19–36.

Hox, J. (2010), *Multilevel Analysis: Techniques and Applications*, New York and Hove: Routledge.

Kahneman, D. and A. Deaton (2010), 'High Income Improves Evaluation of Life But Not Emotional Well-being', *Proceedings of the National Academy of Sciences*, **107** (38), 16489–16493.

Kangas, O.E. and V. Ritakallio (2007), 'Relative to What? Cross National Pictures of European Poverty Measured by Regional, National and European Standards', *European Societies*, **9** (2), 119–145.

Kenworthy, L. (2004), *Egalitarian Capitalism*, New York: Russell Sage Foundation.

Kenworthy, L. and J. Pontusson (2005), 'Rising Inequality and the Politics of Redistribution in Affluent Countries', *Perspectives on Politics*, **3** (3), 449–471.

König, J. and R. Ohr (2013), 'Different Efforts in European Economic Integration: Implications of the EU Index', *Journal of Common Market Studies*, **51** (6), 1074–1090.

Kuznets, S. (1955), 'Economic Growth and Income Inequality', *The American Economic Review*, **45** (1), 1–28.

Lindvall, J. and D. Rueda (2014), 'The Insider–Outsider Dilemma', *British Journal of Political Science*, **44** (2), 460–475.

Mau, S. (2014), 'Transformation und Krise der europäischen Mittelschichten', in M. Heidenreich (ed.), *Krise der europäischen Vergesellschaftung?*, Wiesbaden: VS, pp. 253–279.

Milanovic, B. (2011), *The Haves and the Have-Nots: A Brief and Idiosyncratic History of Global Inequality*, New York: Basic Books.

Mood, C. (2010), 'Logistic Regression: Why We Cannot Do What We Think We Can Do, and What We Can Do About It', *European Sociological Review*, **26** (1), 67–82.

OECD (2011), *Divided We Stand: Why Inequality Keeps Rising*, Paris: OECD.

Rabe-Hesketh, S. and A. Skrondal (2012), *Multilevel and Longitudinal Modeling Using Stata, (Third Edition)*, Volume I: Continuous Responses. College Station, TX: Stata Press.

Whelan, C.T. and B. Maître (2009), 'Europeanization of Inequality and European Reference Groups', *Journal of European Social Policy*, **19** (2), 117–130.

APPENDIX

Table 2A.1 Explanatory variables used, their operationalization and their expected and observed effects

Variable	Operationalization	Data source	Expected	Observed
Dependent				
Gini (in %)	Inequality of disposable household income per equivalent adult (in %)	EU-SILC (hx090), SOEP		
Subjective poverty	'Thinking of your household's total income, is your household able to make ends meet, namely, to pay for its usual necessary expenses?' (1: **With difficulties** or great difficulties; reference group: no serious difficulties)	EU-SILC (hs120)		
Independent micro-level				
Gender	1: 'Male' (ref. category); 2: 'Female'	EU-SILC (rb090)	0	+ (since 2009)
Age class	1: 15–24 years; 2: 25–54 years; ref. category; 3: 55 years and older	EU-SILC (rx020)	+ for youth	– lower for youth
Household type	1: 'One-person household'; 2: 'Adults, no children'; 3: 'Single parent household'; 4: 'Adults with children'; (ref. category)	EU-SILC (hx060)	+ for singles	+ for singles
Migration status	Foreign nationality or born abroad (0: Domestic origin (ref. category); 1: Foreign origin)	EU-SILC (pb210 (a)	+	+
Health	Self-perceived health (1: 'bad or very bad'; 0: 'Very good, good or fair')	EU-SILC (ph010)	+	+
Educational level	Highest ISCED level attained (3: Tertiary education – levels 5–6; ref. category; 2: Upper secondary and post-secondary non-tertiary education (3–4); 1: Pre-primary, primary and lower secondary education (0–2))	EU-SILC (pe040)	+	+
Occupational skill level (ISCO08)	1: Simple and routine physical or manual tasks; 2: Operating machinery and electronic equipment; driving	EU-SILC (pl050; pl051)	+ for simple tasks	+

Variable	Expected	Observed	Description	Data source
			vehicles; maintenance and repair … manipulation, ordering and storage of information (ref. category); 3: Complex technical and practical tasks; 4: Problem-solving, decision-making, creativity	
Unemployed	+	+	At least one unemployed person in the household of the respondent	EU-SILC (pl031; pl031)
Disposable income	−	−	Disposable equivalized net income in PPP (recoded in deciles)	EU-SILC (hx090)
Disposable income in % of national income	−	−	Disposable equivalized net income in PPP divided by national median income (recoded in deciles)	EU-SILC (hx090)
Independent macro-level				
Industrial employment	−/−	−/−	Employment share (per cent of total employment) in industry (NACE C–F)	Eurostat, [lfst_r_lfe2en2]
Female employment	−/−	−/(−)	Female employment rates in % of all women aged 15–64 years	Eurostat, [lfst_r_lfe2en2]
Unemployment rate	+	+	National unemployment rate (in per cent of the population aged 15–64 years)	Eurostat, [lfst_r_lfe2emprt]
Social protection	−/−	−/−	Social protection expenditure includes social benefits, administration costs and other expenditure linked to social protection schemes (% of GDP)	Eurostat, [spr_exp_sum]
Income inequality	+	0	Gini index of national or regional income inequality	EU-SILC (hx090), SOEP
Fiscal austerity	+/+	0/0	Change of primary balance in comparison to previous year; in % of GDP, 2014)	Eurostat [gov_10a_main]
EU Single Market Integration	−/−	−/0	EU single market (for goods, services, capital and labour)	König and Ohr (2013)

Note: The expected and observed effects mentioned at first for the independent macro-level variables refer to the effects on patterns of income inequality; the other signs refer to expected and observed effects of the respective variables on the risk of meeting serious difficulties in making ends meet. '+' refers to an effect significantly higher than zero, '−' refers to an effect significantly lower than zero; '0' to an effect that does not differ significantly from zero.

Source: EU-SILC 2005–2013; SOEP; Eurostat.

3. Determinants of persistent poverty. Do institutional factors matter?

Cathrin Ingensiep

3.1 INTRODUCTION

The scientific and political debate about poverty has intensified at the European level since the announcement of the 2020 goals. They comprise the fight against poverty and social exclusion as one of five central targets of the European Union (EU) until 2020. In order to specify this intention, several indicators have been chosen, one of them being income poverty. In addition, its definition was enlarged by having a look at people who are long-term poor. Short-term episodes of poverty can mostly be bridged by running down savings, restricting lifestyle or borrowing money (Headey et al. 1994). Long-term poverty, on the other hand, causes serious distress (Fouarge and Muffels 2000). Permanent poverty has serious and long-term consequences for well-being, health and social relations. These effects are qualitatively different from short-term poverty episodes (cf. Whelan et al. 2003), giving rise to a broad, sometimes ideological debate on 'cultures of poverty' and poverty traps (Bowles et al. 2006). In any case, persistent poverty has serious and long-lasting effects on the life satisfaction of individuals, families and descendants (Corcoran 1995; Duncan 1996) – effects which have been well known since the publication of the classical study of Jahoda et al. (2002) on the psycho-social consequences of long-term unemployment in an Austrian community during the Great Depression.

Based on cross-sectional data, poverty is mostly described in a static perspective. As a consequence, the number of people is measured independently of the duration, frequency and incidence of poverty (Stevens 1999). But such a perspective is not satisfactory for describing the cumulative effects of poverty (Groh-Samberg 2005). The analysis of longitudinal data is required to identify the following (Carter and Barrett 2006): the contrast between people in constant poverty and those affected only for a short period of time, and the evolution of the respective proportions during the current sovereign debt and economic crisis in Europe. During this crisis, poverty has increased within European countries. The severity of this development varies between different Member States. Policy responses to the crisis have included fiscal consolidation and the reduction of debt to GDP ratio. Duiella and Turrini (2014) showed that social expenditure has helped to curb the rise in poverty and has been sheltered from fiscal consolidation policies.

This chapter treats different types of poverty biographies in Europe over the duration of four years in a comparative perspective and explains them by individual, household-related and national factors. On the individual level, the question is which socio-demographic characteristics influence the likelihood of being temporarily or persistently poor. Moreover, it will be shown which national context factors – especially welfare state regulations – determine the risk of becoming and remaining poor. In addition to existing analyses of permanent poverty (Maître et al. 2011), the chapter will also discuss whether the current crisis is influencing the impact of the national context on persistent poverty.

The chapter is structured as follows. First, the current state of the art of longitudinal poverty research and own research hypotheses are outlined. The data and the operationalization of permanent poverty will then be described, followed by the first empirical results of the national distribution and evolution of persistent poverty. In the next step, the role of individual, household-related and national factors on different types of poverty are discussed. The chapter concludes with a short summary.

3.2 THE ADVANTAGE OF MEASURING PERSISTENT POVERTY

The classical approach towards poverty is to define a household-related minimum income threshold and classify individuals either as 'income poor' or 'non-poor'. The currently adopted minimum income threshold, also used by the EU, defines individuals as being poor if their equalized disposable income, i.e. the total income of a household, after taxes and social expenditures and including social benefits and weighted by the number and age of household members, is below 60 per cent of the national median income. This approach is often criticized because measuring the financial means of a household is not sufficient for describing an individual's standard of living. An alternative approach is therefore to adopt a multi-dimensional view of poverty, for example on the basis of a concept of material deprivation (Fusco et al. 2011; Whelan and Maître 2012). However, in this chapter we will stick to a limited and somewhat reductionist concept of poverty in order to discuss the temporal dimension in more detail. Aggregated poverty rates at a given point of time can only give a snapshot of a more or less stable situation of poverty, deprivation and social exclusion. Dynamic poverty research describes not only phases of poverty. Different phases during the life course are taken into consideration and linked to other events. Poverty can occur both as a short, isolated episode and as a repeated and continuous phenomenon. This is crucial for understanding the nature of poverty in the social context. Studies show that long-term poverty has a significantly stronger negative impact on life quality than short episodes (Corcoran 1995). Poverty is often accompanied by unemployment, which also leads to a gradual exclusion from social life. It remains unclear how the group in poverty, apart from socio-structural characteristics, can be described in terms of the length of time they remain in poverty. It is therefore necessary to examine the proportion of persistent poverty as a share of all poor. In this way the question of whether poor people are a stable group of persistently poor, durably excluded people can be answered. Beck (1986) challenges this assumption and diagnoses a 'democratization' of poverty, which dissolves the boundary between affected and unaffected individuals. He assumes that a growing portion of the population is – at least temporarily – exposed to unemployment and poverty (Beck 1986: 149). Poverty therefore might not be the destiny of a stable, durably excluded group and the basis for a marginalized, inter-generationally transmitted 'culture of poverty', but rather a temporary phenomenon affecting multiple social classes in various phases of their lives. This individualization of poverty, also shown by Leibfried et al. (Leibfried et al. 1995; Buhr and Leibfried 2009; Groh-Samberg 2005), thus has to be analysed in a life course perspective, as it may be the result of specific events, such as divorce and job losses, which can effect also individuals from all kinds of socio-economic backgrounds (Carter and Barrett 2006; Groh-Samberg 2005). Therefore, it is necessary to analyse poverty in a synchronic and diachronic perspective by distinguishing between the poverty risk of specific vulnerable groups and the biographical occurrence of poverty at different life stages (Beck 1986: 149).

3.3   PERSISTENT POVERTY

Most poverty studies, for example Whelan et al. (2003) and Dennis and Guio (2003), focus on poverty at a particular time, since longitudinal data are rarely available. In addition, sometimes a specific treatment does not even seem necessary because 'there is a near-linear relationship between rates of persistent poverty and current poverty across EU countries', at least at the macro-level (Jenkins and van Kerm 2011: 20). This argument involves an ecological fallacy. It is therefore necessary to analyse poverty dynamics at the individual and household level. Furthermore, individual, household-related and national factors may have a different impact on temporary and persistent poverty. It has already been shown that unemployed, single parents as well as younger and older people are the groups most affected by the risk of persistent poverty (Jenkins 2000; Jenkins and Rigg 2001). This is largely consistent with the findings from cross-sectional studies. Younger and older people are especially prone to being poor (Aassve et al. 2007; Cantillon et al. 2003; Deaton and Paxson 1997; Grootaert and Braithwaite 1998). Job loss and unemployment is the most important factor for slipping into poverty (Gallie et al. 2003). Atypical jobs and low education also matter (Tilak 2002). On the basis of Muffels et al. (2000), Maître et al. (2011: 2) assert 'that the same contributing factors influence persistent poverty but are operating in a cumulative manner and with greater magnitude'.

In general, it is assumed that the household is the central instance that pools individual incomes, resources and risks. Children and other dependent family members especially increase the probability of being permanently poor, while a higher number of employed people reduces unemployment risks.

National mechanisms must also be checked with regard to whether they provide social support to leave short-term poverty episodes quickly. Activation policies and social benefits and services might prevent long-term unemployment. Therefore, it can be assumed that the level of social benefits has an impact on the extent of persistent poverty. This is also true for labour market regulations. Paid work is still the main source of income. Consequently, an inclusive labour market with high employment and low unemployment rates is the best protection against poverty experiences, although the group of working-poor is steadily rising (see for example Gardiner and Millar 2006; Gießelmann and Lohmann 2008; Marx and Verbist 1998). Economic factors such as gross domestic product (GDP) growth might also influence on the duration and length of poverty episodes. These factors will be taken into account in the next section.

3.3.1 Institutional Determinants of Persistent Poverty

Current poverty analyses mostly use cross-sectional data (Kenworthy 1999; Kim 2000; Korpi and Palme 1998). New datasets, however, also allow the dynamic aspects of poverty to be investigated in a longitudinal perspective, even though most papers using longitudinal data only analyse the situation in just a few selected countries inside (Fouarge and Muffels 2000) and outside the EU. We are aware only of Caminada et al. (2012) and Whelan et al. (2003) that focus on the entire EU. Investigations into the institutional and macroeconomic determinants of poverty are also rather rare (Dafermos and Papatheodorou 2013).

The intention of this chapter is to contribute towards filling this gap in the use of longitudinal data for poverty analysis. However, as there are many studies on the impact of socio-demographic factors on poverty, this study focuses on institutional factors. They are important for explaining the cross-country variation of poverty dynamics (Dafermos and Papatheodorou 2013; Damioli 2010).

At this point, previous research on the impact of inequality, social expenditures and unemployment will now be summarized. For most households labour is the most importance source of income, while unemployment is an important reason for poverty. Therefore, labour market institutions significantly affect income inequality and poverty (Brady 2003; Checchi and García-Peñalosa 2008; Defina and Thanawala 2001; Gustafsson and Johansson 1999). Whereas a short phase of unemployment can be bridged by saved money, the impact of a long-term unemployment is perceived to be detrimental (Dafermos and Papatheodorou 2013). Even employed people are in danger of poverty during an economic downturn due to lower wages (Moller et al. 2003). A greater unionization is associated with reduced income inequality (Alderson and Nielsen 2002). Consequently, high unemployment and long-term unemployment rates have a negative effect on persistent poverty. Social protection is also an important determinant of poverty for the European countries. Behrendt (2002: 338) concludes 'that countries with high social spending tend to reduce poverty more effectively than countries with a lower social expenditure ratio'. Moller et al., however, show that generous welfare benefits contribute to an increase of poverty 'because they act as disincentives for recipients to seek work' (Moller et al. 2003: 27). In contrast, Caminada and Goudswaard (2012: 21) cannot confirm 'that higher social expenditure goes along with lower poverty levels'.

3.3.2   Crisis – The Role of the Welfare State

During the economic crisis, the GDP fell in real terms in all European countries in 2009 (Karanikolos et al. 2013). As a consequence of the crisis, many workers were laid off and unemployment increased substantially. Moreover, people able to keep their jobs were confronted with wage cuts (Verick 2009). *We therefore expect that the influence of the unemployment rate on persistent poverty decreases during the crisis (H1a). In contrast to people who are temporarily poor, it is furthermore expected that this factor increases the likelihood of staying in poverty (H1b).* Most countries reacted to the crisis with budget cuts. Consequently, the economic downturn of the EU led to changes in welfare policies. Social protection and unemployment benefits were in particular affected. Richardson concludes that 'due to the onset of the financial crisis, the life of the average family (and the young family) has got harder' (Richardson 2010: 498). The most important intervention was the change in the amount of benefits. Considering 'temporary postponements or reduction to payments, some benefits were simply. . .closed' (Richardson 2011: 25). *As a consequence of the austerity policies we expect a growing influence of social expenditure on poverty (H2a). Furthermore, it is expected that long-term poor people in particular are suffering from cuts in social expenditure because they are unable to quickly exit from poverty (H2b).*

3.4 METHODS AND DATA

In this section, data and methods are discussed and the operationalization of persistent poverty and other variables will be explained.

3.4.1 Data

The investigation of dynamic patterns of poverty requires longitudinal data. For the 28 EU Member States, the EU-SILC database is the only source for comparative income data in a longitudinal perspective. The longitudinal part of the EU-SILC is designed as a rotating panel. In general, interviewed households and people are followed over four years. This therefore represents the maximum time span that individuals remain in the panel. In addition, every year the panel loses a quarter of its respondents and a new quarter is added. As a consequence, in every wave the data contain only a quarter of people with data for the full four years. This results in a small sample size. Additionally, an important concern about panel data is the effect of panel attrition. In the case of vulnerable groups, this rate might be higher and the attrition is not necessarily equally distributed throughout the countries (Maître et al. 2011). In order to compare different time spans, data from 2006–2009 to 2009–2012 is used. The first waves of the longitudinal datasets are not used due to the limited number of countries. In fact, 19 countries are included in the analysis, whereas in the descriptive part all countries available were used. For the analytical part, Austria (AT), Belgium (BE), Cyprus (CY), Czech Republic (CZ), Denmark (DK), Estonia (EE), Spain (ES), Finland (FI), France (FR), Iceland (IS), Italy (IT), Lithuania (LT), Latvia (LV), the Netherlands (NL), Norway (NO), Poland (PL), Portugal (PT), Slovenia (SI) and the United Kingdom (UK) are included. Germany, as the biggest European country, does not feature in this dataset and there is no complete data for the new Member States Romania and Bulgaria.

3.4.2 Methods

In most cases a cross-national comparison regarding poverty dynamics is adopted. In this article, a logistic regression on persistent poverty is adopted in order to analyse the influence on the binary dependent variable of persistent poverty. The two-step approach using logistic regression will be used in a multinomial logic with persistent poverty as the reference. In the first step, a distinction will be made by comparing the non-poor to the persistent poor, excluding the temporarily poor. In a second step, a comparison between the transient poor and the persistent poor will be made. We will include explanatory factors on both the individual and the national level (for details see Table 3.1). Many scholars (Maas and Hox 2004, 2005; Snijders 2005; Stegmueller 2013) point out that multi-level estimators are inefficient if there are less than 30 countries. To have a longer time span, the number of countries has to be reduced due to missing data. As a consequence, multi-level analysis cannot be applied. In order to control for nested structures despite these limitations, cluster-robust standard errors are used. This method is widely applied in country comparative research (Hoechle 2007; Thompson 2011), but it also has its critics (King and Roberts 2014). The comparison between different years with differences in the number of observations is made possible by calculating average marginal effects (Mood 2010).

3.4.3 Definition of Poverty and Persistent Poverty

In this section the concept of persistent poverty will be defined and explained. Persistently poor people are first of all poor. A person is considered poor if he or she lives in a household with less than 60 per cent of the national equalized disposable median income. Persistent poverty can be defined in different ways (Duncan and Rodgers 1991). One possible approach is the fraction of n-years in poverty. Adopted by the EU, this definition counts the years spent in poverty over an arbitrary chosen time span (in most cases limited due to data restrictions). Following the EU, we will define persistent poverty as those people who were in poverty in the survey year and in at least two out of the three preceding years.

Regarding long-term poverty types over four years, in addition to the persistent poor and people who have never been poor during the whole period, other possible courses of poverty can be assigned to the different types of temporary poverty. This includes households that have spent only

Table 3.1   The variables used, their operationalization and their expected effects

Variable	Operationalization	Data source	Expected effect
Dependent			
Persistent Poverty	1: 'being in poverty in the current year and in at least two out of the three preceding years' 0a: 'never poor' 0b: 'not persistent poor'	EU-SILC Definition: Eurostat 2010	
Independent micro-level			
Sex	1: 'male' (ref.) 2: 'female'	EU-SILC (rb090)	
Age class	1: 18–24 years 2: 25–54 years (ref.) 3: 55 years and older	EU-SILC (rx020)	
Household type	1: 'one person household' 2: 'two adults, no children' 3: 'adults with children' (ref.) 4: 'single parent household' 5: 'not classified'	EU-SILC (self-defined)	
Educational level	Highest ISCED level attained 1: Pre-primary, primary and lower secondary education (0–2) 2: Upper secondary and post-secondary non-tertiary education (3–4) 3: Tertiary education – levels 5–6; ref. category	EU-SILC (pe040)	
Individual activity status	1: 'at work' (ref. category) 2: 'unemployed' 3: 'retired' 4: 'other inactive'	EU-SILC (rb210)	
Independent macro-level			
Income inequality	Gini index of national income inequality	Eurostat	+
Social protection	Social protection expenditure (% of GDP)	Eurostat (ESSPROS)	−
Unemployment benefits	Net replacement rates for a married single-earner couple with two children, average wage in the initial phase of unemployment	OECD	+

one year in poverty over the period as well as recurring poverty profiles containing a number of short, unconnected episodes. At this point, the major problem of temporary observations becomes apparent. The people who were poor during the first year of the observation period can therefore either have been poor for a short episode or they are already permanently poor. Due to the limitation of four years, it is not possible to figure out the exact length of poverty episodes. This problem, which is known as censoring (Brzinsky-Fay and Kohler 2010; Dijkstra and Taris 1995), restricts findings from analyses and produces blurred results. Many innovations in methods deal with the handling and analysis of this problem (Foster et al. 1984), while there is a distinction between right and left censored cases. Left censoring means that you cannot include the individual's previous years into the analysis. The impossibility of observing the period is called right censoring.

To determine the levels of various factors relating to different poverty types, certain assumptions have to be made and certain limitations have to be introduced. Some explanatory factors are in general constant, while others vary. After an individual reaches a certain age, it can be assumed that the level of education won't change significantly. Possible and even likely, however, is a change in the household configuration due to a person moving in or out. Contextual factors have been selected from the third year of measurement, while the effects of political decisions on actions helping people to leave poverty are evaluated on the basis of the most recent data.

Individual factors are included to control for gender, age and household status. Moreover, as described above, the educational level has a great influence on poverty. The economic status as income from work as the main income source is also included. The macro-level is represented through the most common measure of income inequality, the Gini-index. Moreover, the unemployment rate and social protection expenditure (as an indicator for social benefits received) are included.

3.5 RESULTS

In this section an overview of national patterns with respect to different types of poverty and transition rates will now be given. In all countries, around 70 per cent of the interviewees were never poor from 2008 to 2011. Permanently poor people make up the largest share of people in Bulgaria and Romania, where the share is above 15 per cent. In contrast, the share in Sweden, Czech Republic and Iceland is under five per cent. Temporary poverty is more widespread in all countries. The highest values are those of the UK (23 per cent) and Lithuania (24.7 per cent). The proportion

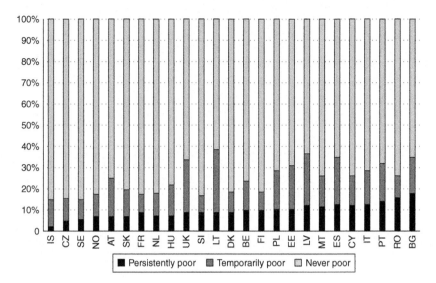

Note: Different poverty types in % regarding the time span 2008–2011, non-poor people included.

Source: EU-SILC longitudinal 2008–2011. Own calculations.

Figure 3.1   Distribution of poverty types (2008–2011) in European countries

of people who spent at least one year of the four years in poverty can be derived from the addition of permanent and temporary poverty. While in Sweden this proportion is 15 per cent of all people, the almost 40 per cent share in Bulgaria and Latvia is more than twice as high. The likelihood of being affected by poverty for at least one year is therefore very strong in these countries.

The share of persistently poor people is not directly connected to the actual poverty rate. Figure 3.2 shows the poverty rate in 2011 together with the distribution of all poor people in persistent and non-persistent poverty. With the exception of the UK and Lithuania, the proportion of permanently poor people accounts for more than half of all people affected by poverty in 2010. Especially in Romania, Belgium and Cyprus this value stands at about 75 per cent. This clearly shows that to a large extent poverty is a permanent phenomenon. The distribution of persistent poverty is independent from the overall national poverty level. This can be illustrated by an example: although Spain and Sweden have very different poverty rates for the year 2011 (19 per cent in Spain, 8 per cent in Sweden),

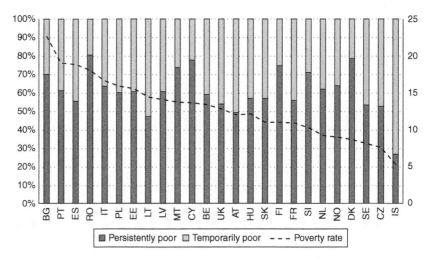

Note: Share of people persistent and temporary poor with regard to all poor people (2008–2011). Added: country's poverty rate in 2011.

Source: EU-SILC longitudinal 2008–2011, Poverty Rate: Eurostat. Own calculations.

Figure 3.2   Share of people in persistent poverty

the two countries do not differ in terms of the occurrence of persistent poverty (in both countries it is around 54 per cent of all poor people). It can be said that high poverty rates are not directly connected to high levels of long-term poor people.

   In the final step, the development of persistent poverty over time will be shown. Using all five waves, the countries of the EU can be grouped in two clusters. The first group shown in Figure 3.3, comprising the UK, Norway, Finland and France, exhibits growing persistent poverty rates. The countries hit hard by the crisis form a second group. Portugal, Spain and Estonia as well as Iceland show an especially high rate in the years 2011 and 2012 in contrast to the preceding years. Only Poland, a country which had a positive economic trend throughout the crisis, shows a decline in persistent poverty rates when the first and last year of the evaluation are compared.

   After the descriptive analysis of patterns of persistent poverty, the influences of the micro and macro factors were tested. In the first step, a logistic regression was performed to estimate the probability for someone with typical persistent poverty values in contrast to non-poor people. Therefore, individual and national factors are included in the logistic model. In the second step, the same analysis was performed with a division between

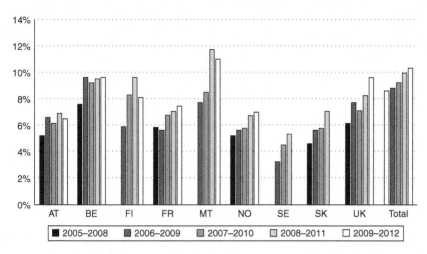

Note: Share of people persistent poor for all waves. Countries with growing percentage of persistent poverty are displayed.

Source: EU-SILC longitudinal (2005–2008, 2006–2009, 2007–2010, 2008–2011, 2009–2012). Own calculations.

Figure 3.3   *Change in the share of persistent poor people (% of all) – countries with rising rates*

long-term and short-term poor people. This step will shed a light on factors determining leaving or remaining in poverty.

On the individual level, age is highly relevant for the risk of becoming permanently poor. In contrast to the expectation that younger and older groups are especially hit by poverty risks, the analysis shows that the age group 25–54 years faces the highest risks. Consequently, younger people may experience shorter poverty traps and so may older people. With regard to the individual main activity, the findings are in line with the literature. Unemployed and inactive people especially are prone to longer poverty episodes. This is not true for retired people, which fits with the age effects mentioned before. If the development over time is examined, it becomes clear that the main activity status especially loses impact; being employed no longer prevents very much against poverty. In 2009, the unemployed group faced a 22 per cent higher risk of being long-term poor. In 2012, this impact is 2.5 percentage points lower, showing a probability under 20 per cent. This development is the same regarding the results that compare persistently poor people to transient poor people. Employment status therefore does not prevent against persistent poverty, which is due

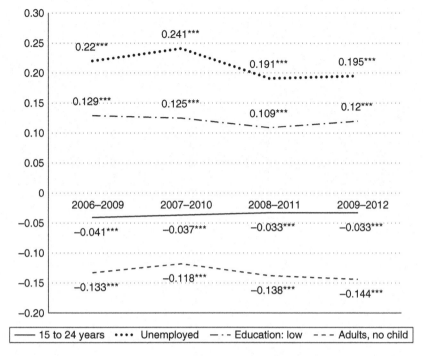

Figure 3.4   Development of the individual risks of being permanently poor between 2006–2009 and 2009–2012 in Europe

to high poverty rates. In the case of education, the group with the highest degree of education faces the lowest risks. This effect is constant over time and also detectable when comparing short- and long-term poor people. Education thus not only results in income-generating opportunities but also in strategies for keeping the household above the poverty level. The household structure also plays an important role in predicting the probability of being in persistent poverty. The fact of having children is negatively connected to poverty. Households with children had a slightly higher risk of becoming poor in 2012 – around 14 per cent higher than households without children. If the difference between persistent and temporary poor is examined, the change of the effect is the other way around. In 2012, a family was less prone to falling into poverty for a longer time than in 2008, although the risk is still higher compared to childless people. This not only shows that the risk of being persistently poor is spread differently between groups; it also becomes clear that effects on the individual level differ for short- and long-term poverty. As a consequence, severe poverty hit vulnerable groups the hardest during the crisis. However, in addition to the disadvantaging effects for vulnerable groups, persistent poverty became more widespread in society during the crisis.

Next, the aim was to also analyse the influence of the institutional level. In the first step, comparing persistently poor people to people never affected by poverty showed factors which influence the poverty experience. As these are not only unique for persistent poverty, in the second step, the temporary poor and persistent poor were compared to show the specific factors that characterize persistent poverty.

The factor of income inequality is highly significant for all years, increasing from 2009 to 2012 by about 1 percentage point. Although the literature was rather unclear about the relationship between poverty and inequality, the investigation of persistent poverty shows a low but significant connection. Countries with a higher Gini-index are characterized by higher persistent poverty rates. This effect is even intensified during the crisis by higher diverged wages. Social expenditure influenced the probability of persistent poverty over the entire time span analysed. The influence decreased slightly on a highly significant level. Consequently, a higher rate of social expenditure relative to the GDP has a positive impact on persistent poverty, but this influence did not increase during the crisis. Countries are unable to prevent poverty through social protection, as the amount of money might not be high enough and the group of needy people is greater. The hypothesis H1a therefore has to be rejected. The unemployment rate is only significant in the first year. The models for the years 2010 to 2012 do not show an influence of the unemployment rate for persistent poverty. This supports hypothesis H2a. During the crisis, having a job as a safeguard against poverty loses importance. Due to lower wages, a higher rate of unemployment does not negatively affect persistent poverty.

As observed earlier, the unemployment rate does not make a difference when comparing the different poverty types of transient and persistent poor people. Therefore hypothesis H1b can be confirmed. Only in 2009 did a higher unemployment rate lead to a higher probability of being long-term poor in people who were already poor. In contrast, higher social expenditure does prevent against persistent poverty, so there hypothesis H2b has to be rejected. As social spending went up by one standard deviation, the chance of being persistently poor is around 4 per cent lower in the years 2009 to 2012 than in the time spans before. This is slightly less

Table 3.2   *Effects on the risk of being persistently poor compared to non-poor people*

	2006–2009	2007–2010	2008–2011	2009–2012
	Risk of being persistently poor			
Social expenditure	−0.024***	−0.015*	−0.011*	−0.019***
	(−3.67)	(−2.51)	(−2.12)	(−4.33)
Income inequality	0.028**	0.029***	0.027***	0.038***
	(−3.19)	(−3.96)	(−3.66)	(−4.76)
Unemployment rate	0.023***	0.008	0.005	0.003
	(−4.47)	(−1.4)	(−0.81)	(−0.63)
No.	41 137	42 255	43 050	42 820
R^2	0.210	0.206	0.208	0.202
AIC	22 402	22 515	22 452	22 611
BIC	22 540	22 653	22 591	22 750
Log-likelihood	−11 185.49	−11 241.54	−11 210.18	−11 289.70

Notes: Logistic regression on the risk of being persistently poor in the four-year time span compared to never poor people; taking into account the country level; the coefficients are the average marginal effects, confidence intervals in brackets. Individual factors are included in all models (see Table A3.1), full results are displayed in the appendix at the end of the chapter.
Significance levels: *** ($p < 0.001$), ** ($p < 0.01$), * ($p < 0.05$), + ($p < 0.1$).

than in the year 2009 (5.0 per cent), but still a highly important factor. Income inequality measured through the Gini-index does not play a role distinguishing between those two groups. Therefore, in an unequal society, the risk of becoming long-term poor is no higher than in countries with a more equal society.

3.6 CONCLUSION

Persistent poverty is a growing problem (Figure 3.3). The share of persistently poor people grew during the crisis in most European countries. This chapter has raised the question of whether the influence of institutional and personal factors on persistent poverty changed during the crisis. Furthermore, it has shed light on the factors affecting persistent poverty, which differ compared to temporary poverty. Individual factors play an important role in the likelihood of falling into persistent poverty. In addition to highly vulnerable groups, a large amount of people are affected by poverty experiences. It has also been shown that persistent poverty is not directly connected to actual poverty rates. This was made possible by

*Table 3.3   Effects on the risk of being persistently poor compared to
temporary poor people*

	2006–2009	2007–2010	2008–2011	2009–2012
	Risk of being persistently poor			
Social expenditure	−0.051***	−0.029***	−0.024*	−0.039***
	(−4.80)	(−3.55)	(−2.13)	(−3.92)
Income inequality	0.031*	0.021	−0.008	0.036*
	(−2.24)	(−1.77)	(−0.32)	(−2.55)
Unemployment rate	0.021**	0.001	0.008	0
	(−2.88)	(−0.14)	(−0.6)	(−0.01)
No.	11793	11721	11392	11053
R²	0.483	0.486	0.493	0.503
AIC	14679	14593	14381	14102
BIC	14797	14711	14499	14219
Log-likelihood	−7323.58	−7280.84	−7174.98	−7035.13

Notes: Logistic regression on the risk of being persistently poor in the four-year time span compared to temporary poor people; taking into account the country level; the coefficients are the average marginal effects, confidence intervals in brackets. Individual factors are included in all models (see Table 3A.2), full results are displayed in the appendix at the end of the chapter.
Significance levels: *** ($p < 0.001$), ** ($p < 0.01$), * ($p < 0.05$), + ($p < 0.1$).

comparing country differences in persistent poverty rates. The structure of 'the poor' thus differs between nations, leading to the role of welfare state characteristics. During the crisis the amount of social expenditure increased. This matters especially as an instrument for preventing persistent poverty. Social expenditures seem to be able to shorten individual poverty spells: the higher the amount of social expenditure, the lower the risk of persistent poverty. Monetary inequality was seen as one additional reason for higher rates of persistent poverty. As a consequence of the nation state's failure to compensate for financial disadvantages suffered by the persistently poor, it was assumed that high inequality rates are associated with increasing poverty rates. Regarding this connection, the results of the analysis were ambiguous. The degree of inequality matters in contrast to non-poor people, whereas no difference between the persistent and temporary poor was found. Finally, the unemployment rate only affects the likelihood of permanent poverty for the years 2006 to 2009. The crisis was followed by high unemployment rates and decreasing wages for employed people. As employed people were also affected, the risk of being poor therefore cannot be traced back to the number of unemployed people.

In summary, it is clear that the temporary and permanently poor are similar target groups with regard to individual factors. In the case of institutional influences, the level of inequality does not influence the division between the poverty types. In contrast, cuts in the social expenditures hit the persistently poor harder. Policy actions therefore have to distinguish between reducing temporary or permanent poverty.

REFERENCES

Aassve, A., F.C. Billari and R. Piccarreta (2007), 'Strings of adulthood: A sequence analysis of young British women's work-family trajectories', *European Journal of Population* **23**, 369–388.

Alderson, A. and F. Nielsen (2002), 'Globalization and the great U-turn: Income inequality trends in 16 OECD countries', *American Journal of Sociology* **107**, 1244–1299.

Beck, U. (1986), *Risikogesellschaft: auf dem Weg in eine andere Moderne*. Edition Suhrkamp, Bd. 1365. Frankfurt am Main: Suhrkamp.

Behrendt, C. (2002): 'Holes in the safety net? Social security and the alleviation of poverty in a comparative perspective', in R. Sigg and C. Behrendt (eds), *Social Security in the Global Village, International Social Security Series*, Volume 8, New Brunswick/London: Transaction Publishers, 333–358.

Bowles, S., S.N. Durlauf and K. Hoff (eds) (2006), *Poverty Traps*. Princeton, NJ: Princeton University Press.

Brady, D. (2003), 'The poverty of liberal economics', *Socio-Economic Review* **1**, 369–409.

Brzinsky-Fay, C. and U. Kohler (2010), 'New developments in sequence analysis', *Sociological Methods & Research* **38**, 359–364.

Buhr, P. and S. Leibfried (2009), 'Ist die Armutsbevölkerung exkludiert?', in R. Stichweh and P. Windolf (eds), *Inklusion und Exklusion. Analysen zur Sozialstruktur und sozialen Ungleichheit*, Wiesbaden: VS Verlag für Sozialwissenschaften, 103–122.

Caminada, K. and K. Goudswaard (2012), 'The relationship between alternative measures of social spending and poverty rates', *International Review of Business and Social Sciences* **1**(5), 8–25.

Caminada, K., K. Goudswaard and F. Koster (2012), 'Social income transfers and poverty: A cross-country analysis for OECD countries', *International Journal of Social Welfare* **21**, 115–126.

Cantillon, B., I. Marx and I. Van den Bosch (2003), 'The puzzle of egalitarianism. The relationship between employment, wage inequality, social expenditure and poverty', *European Journal of Social Security* **5**, 108–127.

Carter, M.R. and C.B. Barrett (2006), 'The economics of poverty traps and persistent poverty: An asset-based approach', *The Journal of Development Studies* **42**(2), 178–199.

Checchi, D. and C. García-Peñalosa (2008), 'Labour market institutions and income inequality', *Economic Policy* **23**, 602–649.

Corcoran, M. (1995), 'Rags to rags: Poverty and mobility in the United States', *Annual Review of Sociology* **21**, 237–267.

Dafermos, Y. and D. Papatheodorou (2013), 'What drives inequality and poverty in the EU? Exploring the impact of macroeconomic and institutional factors', *International Review of Applied Economics* **27**, 1–22.

Damioli, G. (2010), 'How and why the dynamics of poverty differ across European countries', Paper presented at the 31st General Conference of The International Association for Research in Income and Wealth, St. Gallen.

Deaton, A. and C. Paxson (1997), Poverty among children and the elderly in developing countries, mimeo, Research Programme in Development Studies, Princeton University.

Defina, R.H. and K. Thanawala (2001), 'The impact of transfers and taxes on alternative poverty indexes', *Review of Social Economy* **59**, 395–416.

Dennis, I. and A.-C. Guio (2003), 'Armut und soziale Ausgrenzung in der EU nach Laeken', Part 1 and 2, Eurostat: *Statistik kurz gefasst*, Thema 3-21/2003, Brüssel.

Dijkstra, W. and T. Taris (1995), 'Measuring the agreement between sequences', *Sociological Methods & Research* **24**, 214–231.

Duiella, M. and A. Turrini (2014), 'Poverty developments in the EU after the crisis: A look at main drivers', *ECFIN Economic Brief*, No. 31.

Duncan, C.M. (1996), 'Understanding persistent poverty: Social class context in rural communities', *Rural Sociology* **61**(1), 103–124.

Duncan, G.T. and W. Rodgers (1991), 'Has children's poverty become more persistent?', *American Sociological Review* **56**, 538–550.

Foster, J., J. Greer and E. Thorbecke (1984), 'A class of decomposable poverty measures', *Econometrica: Journal of the Econometric Society* **52**(3), 761–766.

Fouarge, D. and R. Muffels (2000), 'Persistent poverty in the Netherlands, Germany and the UK', MPRA Paper 13297, University Library of Munich, Germany.

Fusco, A., A.C. Guio and E. Marlier (2011), 'Income poverty and material deprivation in European countries', CEPS Working Papers.

Gallie, D., S. Paugam and S. Jacobs (2003), 'Unemployment, poverty and social isolation: Is there a vicious circle of social exclusion?', *European Societies* **5**, 1–32.

Gardiner, K. and J. Millar (2006), 'How low-paid employees avoid poverty: An analysis by family type and household structure', *Journal of Social Policy* **35**, 351–369.

Gießelmann, M. and H. Lohmann (2008), 'The different roles of low-wage work in Germany', in H.-J. Andreß and H. Lohmann (eds), *The Working Poor in Europe: Employment, Poverty and Globalization*, Cheltenham, UK and Northampton, MA, USA: Edward Elgar, pp. 96–123.

Groh-Samberg, O. (2005), *Armut, soziale Ausgrenzung und Klassenstrukturen*, Wiesbaden: VS-Verlag für Sozialwissenschaften.

Grootaert, C. and J. Braithwaite (1998), 'Poverty correlates and indicator-based targeting in Eastern Europe and the Former Soviet Union', World Bank Policy Research Working Paper No. 1942, Washington, DC.

Gustafsson, B. and M. Johansson (1999), 'In search of smoking guns: What makes income inequality vary over time in different countries', *American Sociological Review* **64**, 585–605.

Headey, B., P. Krause and R. Habich (1994), 'Long and short term poverty: Is Germany a two-thirds society?', *Social Indicators Research* **31**, 1–25.

Hoechle, D. (2007), 'Robust standard errors for panel regressions with cross-sectional dependence', *Stata Journal* **7**, 281.

Jahoda, M., P. Lazarsfeld and H. Zeisel (2002), *Marienthal: The Sociography of an Unemployed Community*, New Brunswick, NJ: Transaction Publishers.

Jenkins, S.P. (2000), 'Modelling household income dynamics', *Journal of Population Economics* **13**, 529–567.

Jenkins, S.P. and J.A. Rigg (2001), *The Dynamics of Poverty in Britain*, Department for Work and Pensions Research Report No. 157. Leeds: Corporate Document Services.

Jenkins, S. and P. van Kerm (2011), 'Patterns of persistent poverty evidence from EU-SILC', Working Paper 2011-30. Institute for Social and Economic Research, University of Essex, UK.

Karanikolos, M., P. Mladovsky, J. Cylus, S. Thomson, S. Basu, D. Stuckler, J.P. Mackenbach and M. McKee (2013), 'Financial crisis, austerity, and health in Europe', *Lancet* **381**, 1323–1331.

Kenworthy, L. (1999), 'Do social-welfare policies reduce poverty? A cross-national assessment', *Social Forces* **77**, 1119–1139.

Kim, H. (2000), 'Anti-poverty-effectiveness of taxes and income transfers in welfare states', *International Social Security Review* **53**, 105–129.

King, G. and M.E. Roberts (2014), 'How robust standard errors expose methodological problems they do not fix, and what to do about it', *Political Analysis* **23**(2), 159–179.

Korpi, W. and J. Palme (1998), 'The paradox of redistribution and strategies of equality. Welfare state institutions, inequality, and poverty in Western countries', *American Sociological Review* **63**, 661–687.

Leibfried, S., L. Leisering, P. Buhr, M. Ludwig, E. Mädje, T. Olk, W. Voges and M. Zwick (1995), *Zeit der Armut. Lebensläufe im Sozialstaat*, Frankfurt a. M.: Suhrkamp.

Maas, C.J.M. and J.J. Hox (2004), 'Robustness issues in multilevel regression analysis', *Statistica Neerlandica* **58**, 127–137.

Maas, C.J.M. and J.J. Hox (2005), 'Sufficient sample sizes for multilevel modeling', *Methodology* **1**, 86–92.

Maître, B., H. Russell and D. Watson (2011), *Persistent At-Risk-of-Poverty in Ireland: An Analysis of the Survey on Income and Living Conditions 2005–2008*, Dublin: Department of Social Protection.

Marx, I. and G. Verbist (1998), 'Low-paid work and poverty: A cross-country perspective', in S. Bazen, M. Gregory and W. Salverda (eds), *Low-Wage Employment in Europe*, Cheltenham, UK and Lyme, NH, USA: Edward Elgar, 63–86.

Moller, S., E. Huber, J. Stephens, D. Bradley and F. Nielsen (2003), 'Determinants of relative poverty in advanced capitalist economies', *American Sociological Review* **68**, 22–61.

Mood, C. (2010), 'Logistic regression: Why we cannot do what we think we can do, and what we can do about it', *European Sociological Review* **26**(1), 67–82.

Muffels, R., D. Fouarge and R. Dekker (2000), 'Longitudinal poverty and income inequality. A comparative panel study for the Netherlands, Germany and the UK', OSA-Working Papers, 6, Tilburg University.

Richardson, D. (2010), 'Child and Family Policies in a Time of Economic Crisis', *Children & Society* **24**(6), 495–508.

Richardson, D. (2011), 'Child poverty and family policies in a time of economic crisis', in *The Impact of the Economic Crisis on Children: Lessons from the Past Experiences and Future Policies*. The proceedings of the ChildONEurope

Seminar on the Impact of the Economic Crisis on Children, Italian Childhood and Adolescence Documentation and Analysis Centre, 19–30.

Richardson, D. and J. Bradshaw (2012), 'Family-oriented anti-poverty policies in developed countries', Background paper for United Nations Department for Economic and Social Affairs.

Snijders, T.A.B. (2005), 'Power and sample size in multilevel linear models', in B.S. Everitt and D.C. Howell (eds), *Encyclopedia of Statistics in Behavioral Science*, Volume 3, Chichester: Wiley, 1570–1573.

Stegmueller, D. (2013), 'How many countries for multilevel modeling? A comparison of frequentist and Bayesian approaches', *American Journal of Political Science* **57**, 748–761.

Stevens, A.H. (1999), 'Climbing out of poverty, falling back', *Journal of Human Resources* **34**(3), 557–588.

Thompson, S. (2011), 'Simple formulas for standard errors that cluster by both firm and time', *Journal of Financial Economics* **99**, 1–10.

Tilak, J.B.G. (2002), 'Education and poverty', *Journal of Human Development* **3**, 191–207.

Verick, S. (2009), 'Who is hit hardest during a financial crisis? The vulnerability of young men and women to unemployment in an economic downturn', IZA Discussion Papers 4359, Institute for the Study of Labor.

Whelan, C.T. and B. Maître (2012), 'Understanding material deprivation in Europe: A multilevel analysis', *UCD Geary Institute Discussion Paper Series*.

Whelan, C.T., R. Layte and B. Maître (2003), 'Persistent income poverty and deprivation in the European Union: An analysis of the first three waves of the European Community Household Panel', *Journal of Social Policy* **32**(1), 1–18.

APPENDIX

Table 3A.1   Effects on the risk of being persistently poor compared to non- poor people

	2006–2009	2007–2010	2008–2011	2009–2012
	Risk of being persistently poor			
Women	−0.009***	−0.005**	−0.003	−0.002
	(−3.35)	(−2.58)	(−1.70)	(−0.54)
Age group				
15 to 24 years	−0.041***	−0.037***	−0.033***	−0.033***
	(−3.70)	(−3.74)	(−4.80)	(−3.89)
55 years +	−0.034**	−0.037***	−0.031***	−0.027***
	(−6.55)	(−10.20)	(−5.88)	(−4.60)
Main activity				
Unemployed	0.220***	0.241***	0.191***	0.195***
	−10.89	−13.45	−11.38	−11.01
Retired	0.033+	0.024	0.023+	0.01
	−1.74	−1.37	−1.73	−0.95
Other inactive	0.128***	0.129***	0.127***	0.131***
	−6.84	−9.72	−11.49	−10.5
Educational level				
Low	0.129***	0.125***	0.109***	0.120***
	−9.7	−14.36	−11.04	−10.89
Medium	0.061***	0.054***	0.052***	0.056***
	−6.21	−8.05	−5.83	−5.5
Household type				
One person	−0.130***	−0.116***	−0.131***	−0.136***
household	(−8.03)	(−7.14)	(−10.82)	(−9.39)
Adults. no child	−0.133***	−0.118***	−0.138***	−0.144***
	(−7.58)	(−6.92)	(−8.56)	(−7.62)
Single parent	−0.079***	−0.064***	−0.081***	−0.070***
household	(−7.02)	(−5.69)	(−5.74)	(−3.46)
Not classified	−0.124***	−0.118***	−0.133***	−0.135***
	(−8.46)	(−7.97)	(−9.80)	(−9.44)
Social expenditure	−0.024***	−0.015*	−0.011*	−0.019***
	(−3.67)	(−2.51)	(−2.12)	(−4.33)
Income inequality	**0.028****	**0.029*****	**0.027*****	**0.038*****
	−3.19	−3.96	−3.66	−4.76
Unemployment rate	**0.023*****	0.008	0.005	0.003
	−4.47	−1.4	−0.81	−0.63
No.	41 137	42 255	43 050	42 820
R²	0.210	0.206	0.208167	0.203
AIC	22 402	22 515	22 452	22 611
BIC	22 540	22 653	22 591	22 750
Log-likelihood	−11 185.49	−11 241.54	−11 210.18	−11 289.70

Notes: Logistic regression on the risk of being persistently poor in the four-year time span compared to never poor people; taking into account the country level, the coefficients are the average marginal effects, confidence intervals in brackets.
Significance levels: *** (p < 0.001), ** (p < 0.01), * (p < 0.05), + (p < 0.1).

Table 3A.2   *Effects on the risk of being persistently poor compared to temporarily poor people*

	2006–2009	2007–2010	2008–2011	2009–2012
	Risk of being persistently poor			
Women	−0.029***	−0.015**	−0.013*	−0.012
	(−6.30)	(−2.71)	(−2.07)	(−1.47)
Age group				
15 to 24 years	−0.056*	−0.066***	−0.063***	−0.060***
	(−2.46)	(−4.55)	(−4.84)	(−3.57)
55 years +	−0.028	−0.062***	−0.021	0.003
	(−1.51)	(−6.74)	(−1.23)	−0.23
Main activity				
Unemployed	0.193***	0.240***	0.169***	0.183***
	(−7.63)	(−9.85)	(−9.08)	(−7.04)
Retired	0.086**	0.093*	0.092**	0.008
	(−2.84)	(−2.1)	(−3.12)	(−0.27)
Other inactive	0.158***	0.167***	0.160***	0.179***
	(−7.21)	(−9.95)	(−11.92)	(−11.3)
Educational level				
Low	0.189***	0.174***	0.143***	0.170***
	(−6.91)	(−7.52)	(−5.67)	(−6.45)
Medium	0.103***	0.072***	0.076***	0.081**
	(−4.92)	(−3.88)	(−3.82)	(−3.18)
Household type				
One person	−0.118***	−0.080***	−0.106***	−0.115***
household	(−5.99)	(−3.44)	(−5.72)	(−4.90)
Adults. no child	−0.118***	−0.054**	−0.084***	−0.091**
	(−7.70)	(−2.75)	(−4.25)	(−3.20)
Single parent	−0.089***	−0.035	−0.083**	−0.008
household	(−3.72)	(−1.90)	(−3.07)	(−0.25)
Not classified	−0.099***	−0.069*	−0.118***	−0.105***
	(−5.20)	(−2.16)	(−4.13)	(−3.69)
Social expenditure	−0.051***	−0.029***	−0.024*	−0.039***
	(−4.80)	(−3.55)	(−2.13)	(−3.92)
Income inequality	0.031*	0.021	−0.008	0.036*
	(−2.24)	(−1.77)	(−0.32)	(−2.55)
Unemployment	0.021**	0.001	0.008	0
rate	(−2.88)	(−0.14)	(−0.6)	(−0.01)
No.	11 793	11 721	11 392	11 053
R^2	0.483	0.486	0.493	0.503
AIC	14 679	14 593	14 381	14 102
BIC	14 797	14 711	14 499	14 219
Log-likelihood	−7323.58	−7280.84	−7174.98	−7035.13

Notes: Logistic regression on the risk of being persistently poor in the four-year time span compared to temporary poor people; taking into account the country level, the coefficients are the average marginal effects, confidence intervals in brackets.
Significance levels: *** ($p < 0.001$), ** ($p < 0.01$), * ($p < 0.05$), + ($p < 0.1$).

4. The segmentation of the European labour market – the evolution of short- and long-term unemployment risks during the eurozone crisis[1]

Martin Heidenreich

4.1 INTRODUCTION: THE RETURN OF LONG-TERM UNEMPLOYMENT IN THE CURRENT CRISIS

From the 1970s until the end of the 1990s, high long-term unemployment (LTU) had been a major plague affecting the regulated European labour markets, as the Eurosclerosis debate has shown (Boeri and Garibaldi 2009). High LTU levels have been analysed as an outcome of rigid labour markets, i.e. of markets characterized by strict employment protection legislation, strong unions, high unemployment benefits, long benefit duration and a high tax wedge between take-home pay and labour costs (Nickell 1997; Siebert 1997). LTU is a major risk for growth and competitiveness because it reduces the available labour force and is thus highly correlated with low employment rates. This can be explained by the erosion of skills, motivation and general attachment to the labour market during longer periods of unemployment, which Blanchard (2006) has termed the hysteresis effect of LTU. Thus, even a short crisis may have long-term, structural consequences for the labour market because unemployed people often cannot return to their previous career step or levels of pay, job satisfaction and life satisfaction, even when they find a new job. High LTU rates therefore reflect a profound divide between insiders and outsiders; they indicate that a significant part of the labour force is durably excluded from the labour market.

In the decade before the beginning of the current financial, economic and sovereign debt crisis (the so-called 'Great Recession'), the European labour markets became more inclusive. This was partly the result of reforms of national benefit and labour market policies, but especially the result of activation policies proposed by international organizations such as the OECD, the ILO or the EU (Weishaupt 2011). In this way, structural unemployment could be reduced and employment rates increased in many countries – a phenomenon Boeri (2011: 1203) described as the honeymoon effect of labour market reforms: due to increased labour market flexibility, employers more easily create jobs during a cyclical upswing. In the economic slump since 2009, however, the move towards more flexible labour markets, higher employment rates and lower (long-term) unemployment rates seems to have been reversed (Emmenegger et al. 2012; Rueda 2014). Younger and less skilled persons, migrants and especially unemployed persons are once again strongly excluded from the labour market – a result Rueda (2007) and Tepe and Vanhuysse (2013) explain by the political preferences of social democratic parties and/or unions defending the interests of labour market insiders. The current crisis might therefore indicate the end of the honeymoon phase of European labour market reforms. After a significant reduction of the LTU share, i.e. the share of long-term unemployed (12 months or more as a percentage of total unemployment) in the decade before the crisis (2000: 46.4 per cent of the unemployed; 2009: 33.3 per cent of the unemployed), LTU has once again risen to currently 47.4 per cent (2013) in the EU-28. In Slovakia, Greece, Croatia, Ireland, Bulgaria, Italy, Portugal and Slovenia, this figure even exceeds 50 per cent. *The question is whether this (at first sight only cyclical) increase in unemployment and LTU rates is related to the return and deepening of different forms of labour market segmentation between insiders and outsiders.* In this case, the increasing LTU shares since 2009 could effectuate the durable exclusion of a significant proportion of the labour force from employment.

It should be noted, however, that LTU rates are not a sufficient indicator for an increasing segmentation of the labour market because they are strongly influenced by cyclical effects. The low level of the LTU rate in 2009 is the result of a very large inflow of newly unemployed persons, just as the increase in LTU until 2013 can be partly explained by the outflow of unemployed persons into either employment or inactivity. Yet not only LTU rates but also declining transition rates from unemployment into employment indicate a return of persistent unemployment (Figure 4.1 and OECD 2013). The increasing share of unemployed who remain in unemployment could thus indicate that 'the disappearance of European structural unemployment' (Boeri and Garibaldi 2009: 412) and the shift to a more flexible, more open and more dynamic labour market where losing a job signifies only a transitional phase has been reversed in the current crisis.

As indicators of the possible return of segmented labour markets, this chapter discusses the social distribution of the risks to becoming unemployed and remaining unemployed. These risks are not equally distributed, as the debate on insider–outsider divisions and dualization processes has shown (Emmenegger et al. 2012). The question is whether the current crisis and the related increase of unemployment and LTU rates are related to an increasing labour market polarization and dualization alongside an increasing marginalization of already vulnerable groups – three dimensions of labour market segmentation.[2] The *polarization* of labour markets consists of the differentiation between good and bad jobs due to institutional rules that impede mobility between the various labour market segments (Saint-Paul 1996). A second dimension of segmentation processes can be termed *dualization*, referring to organizational and occupational differences between qualified and less qualified employees and occupations, and also between permanent and temporary contracts. A third segmentation dimension can be termed *marginalization*, a concept that refers to 'the process of individuals being relegated to the margins of society' due to broader societal discrimination processes (Emmenegger et al. 2012: 11–12). In the case of labour markets, marginalization implies the durable exclusion of disadvantaged groups from the labour market. These three, empirically related, facets of labour market segmentation can be interpreted as the result of different national institutions (labour market policies, industrial relations, welfare systems), organizational and occupational policies, and broader societal discrimination processes.

In the following we will discuss which groups are mainly affected by the risk of becoming and remaining unemployed, whether these risks have increased for some groups in the current financial and debt crisis, and which institutional contexts and personal and occupational characteristics can explain these dynamics. *In particular, we will examine to what extent the risk of becoming and remaining unemployed is the result of three different facets of labour market segmentation: firstly, the institutionally stabilized polarization between protected labour market insiders and less protected outsiders (often with temporary contracts; cf. Boeri 2011; Bentolila et al. 2012); secondly, the occupational dualization between high- and low-skilled employees and occupations (Schwander and Häusermann 2013); and, thirdly, the marginalization of specific social groups defined on the basis of ascriptive criteria (e.g. age, gender, migration, private living conditions).* After a discussion of the state of the art and the methodological approach of this study, this research question is discussed on the basis of EU-SILC data 2005–2013, covering four years before and five years during the European employment crisis. The chapter concludes with a short summary and discussion of the posited return of segmented labour markets.

4.2 INSTITUTIONAL, OCCUPATIONAL AND INDIVIDUAL DETERMINANTS OF SHORT- AND LONG-TERM UNEMPLOYMENT RISKS

Labour markets are 'arenas in which workers exchange their labor power in return for wages, status, and other job rewards' (Kalleberg and Sørensen 1979: 351). While neoclassical approaches analyse labour market dynamics as determined by supply and demand, institutional approaches in labour economics focus on the institutional regulation of labour market processes. From a neoclassical perspective, such institutions are merely considered market distortions or 'rigidities' that prevent an equilibrium between the demand and supply of labour (Siebert 1997). Examples of such 'rigidities' are social benefits, high unemployment replacement rates, minimum wages, trade unions, wage bargaining systems, and reduced wage differentials combined with a low educational level at the bottom of the labour market (Nickell 1997; Blanchard 2006). The level of unemployment and also long-term unemployment has been explained by these institutional factors which stabilize the relative advantages of labour market insiders in comparison to outsiders, i.e. the *polarization* of the labour market (cf. Boeri 2011 for a comprehensive overview). Thus, according to leading representatives of a neoclassical labour market perspective:

- *stricter employment protection legislation* 'will tend to reduce the inflow into unemployment and, because they make firms more cautious about hiring, will also reduce the flow out of unemployment into work' (Nickell 1997: 66). Bentolila et al. (2012) have highlighted the importance of the difference between the employment protection legislation (EPL) for fixed-term and permanent contracts, since larger gaps between dismissal costs for permanent and temporary jobs might increase the unemployment risks, especially for temporary workers. In addition to the EPL summary indicator, differences between the employment protection legislation for regular and temporary workers will be included in the following models. A higher EPL level should be correlated with higher unemployment, while a higher gap should lower the risk of long-term unemployment for people with a fixed-term contract because firing costs are lower (Boeri 2011).
- An essential claim of the neoclassical analysis of 'labour market rigidity' is that *high social expenditures, high unemployment benefits and long entitlement periods* decrease financial incentives for taking up a new job and may therefore contribute to prolonged unemployment. Gangl (2004) adds that higher unemployment benefits reduce

the long-term negative effects of unemployment on employment histories.

- Negative impacts can be expected especially when *job search requirements* (so-called conditionality) are low. This refers to the role of *inclusive employment regimes*, which increase the obligation, possibility and interest in taking up a new job by abolishing barriers to labour market entry and by various enabling and demanding measures (Heidenreich and Aurich-Beerheide 2014). An indicator of inclusive employment regimes is employment rates.

It can therefore be expected that the risks of becoming and remaining unemployed are lower in countries with inclusive employment regimes and weaker social protection, weaker unions and lower income replacement rates. Less strict employment protection legislation and a smaller difference between employment protection for permanent and temporary workers might increase the risk of becoming unemployed, but decrease the risk of remaining unemployed, i.e. to become long-term unemployed (H1) (cf. Table 4.1).

As distinct from neoclassical and institutional approaches, a different explanation of labour market segmentation processes has been proposed by studies focusing on the exclusion of outsider groups from attractive employment opportunities. In this perspective, labour market outsiders can be defined as 'individuals who incur a particularly high probability of being in atypical employment and/or unemployment' (Schwander and Häusermann 2013: 252). The dualization approach focuses not so much on institutional labour market regulations but rather on the dynamics of internal labour markets. Thus, at the company level, insider–outsider differences will be established when labour turnover costs are high (Lindbeck and Snower 1988). Labour turnover costs therefore operate as entry barriers to inner-organizational, privileged employment opportunities. Although high labour turnover costs may also be the result of institutional regulations, for example strict employment protection, this approach focuses mainly on the organizational requirements and costs associated with making outsiders productive. Examples of such costs are higher drop-out rates or high hiring and training costs, high costs for monitoring and control, and high repair and quality costs or higher (perceived) costs of absenteeism due to health problems that may prevent employers from employing outsiders in spite of lower wages having to be paid for them (Kalleberg 2009: 9). An important source of production-related costs is the tacit knowledge of employees, which is hard to replace and tends to be closely linked to the qualification and occupational level of employees. Therefore, employees who have managed to accede to internal labour markets have the opportunity to accumulate company-specific skills, competences and contacts, and to evade wage competition on the external, secondary labour market characterized by higher unemployment risks (Doeringer and Piore 1971). According to the *dualization* approach, labour market segmentation processes and the related unemployment risks can therefore be explained by processes of social closure between different organizational, occupational and skill groups.

However, a high unemployment rate does not necessarily imply a high LTU rate because unemployment risks could also be equally distributed among different groups. It is therefore necessary to analyse precisely which unemployed remain in unemployment. According to Lindbeck (2001: 15956), the persistence of some groups in unemployment can be explained by 'the loss of skill among individuals who have been unemployed for a long time; (by) endogenous changes in preferences in favor of leisure or household work; and (by) the breakdown of social norms in favor of work and hence the emergence of unemployment cultures . . . Long spells of unemployment may also function as a negative signal to prospective employers about the quality of individual workers.' *Thus, it can be expected that lower-skilled employees in less demanding occupations with non-standard employment contracts and difficult health conditions will have a higher risk of short- and long-term unemployment than others (H2).*

Besides the institutional, organizational and occupational dynamics of labour market segmentation, current studies (Palier and Thelen 2010; Emmeneger et al. 2012; Schwander and Häusermann 2013; Rueda 2014) refer to a third dimension of segmentation processes, which can be designated as marginalization. This debate focuses on the relationship between insider–outsider divisions in the population at large and the labour market more specifically. Already the founding fathers of segmentation theory, Doeringer and Piore (1971) expected that women, young people, and foreigners and people with a different ethnic background have considerably worse opportunities for acceding to privileged positions in internal labour markets. In the current crisis, older, male and migrant workers seem to have a higher risk of staying unemployed for at least a year (European Commission 2012: 80–89). Therefore, in addition to institutional and occupational explanations for the risk of becoming long-term unemployed, ascriptive characteristics of the workforce have to be taken into account. What I prefer to call 'marginalization' (Emmenegger et al. 2012: 11–12), Kalleberg (2012: 433) terms 'polarization' and argues that segmentation processes take place not only between high- and low-skilled occupations, but also 'among individuals with particular characteristics' such as 'education and skill' but also 'gender and race'. This form of segmentation thus refers to the differential treatment of social groups not only in the labour market but also in the educational system and the welfare state, i.e.

discrimination (Kalleberg 2009: 10). From such a viewpoint, the impact of individual characteristics on unemployment and LTU risks is not only limited to achievement-based criteria (skills, occupational status), but also refers to ascriptive criteria, i.e. migration status, age, gender, or private living conditions. *I therefore expect that the risks of becoming and remaining unemployed vary significantly by individual age, migration background, gender and even private living and household conditions. Older persons, single parents, women and employees with a migration background will be more strongly affected by long-term unemployment than others (H3).*

4.3   DATA AND METHODS

The LTU level of a country can be conceived as the result of two different types of flows. Firstly, it is determined by flows from employment to short-term unemployment (STU). High transition rates from employment into unemployment contribute *ceteris paribus* to high unemployment and later to a high long-term unemployment rate. Secondly, the LTU level is *ex negativo* determined by the flows out of unemployment, i.e. into inactivity or employment. High exit rates from unemployment into new jobs, training, early retirement, inability, or unpaid domestic and care work will reduce the share of short-term unemployed (i.e. those unemployed less than a year) while *ceteris paribus* increasing the share of long-term unemployed. Hence, the higher the transition rates from unemployment into employment or inactivity, the lower the persistence rate, i.e. the share of persons remaining in unemployment (OECD 2011).

Entry rates into unemployment have clearly increased since the beginning of the crisis (all data based on the Eurostat table ilc_lvhl30). Before the crisis, in 2007, 2.7 per cent of all employed Europeans lost their job during one year. In 2012, this rate increased to 3.9 per cent in the EU-27 (and to 10.5 per cent in Spain, 7.6 per cent in Latvia and 11.3 per cent in Greece in 2011). A similar increase has been registered for transitions from inactivity to unemployment (3.4 per cent in 2007, 5.0 per cent in 2012) – with a peak of 13 per cent in Spain in 2012. These rising entry rates into (initially short-term) unemployment are a first explanation for increasing LTU rates. The second explanatory factor is the increasing share of unemployed who remain in unemployment because exiting from unemployment into employment became more difficult during the crisis. While exit rates into inactivity decreased or remained stable in most EU countries, transitions from unemployment into employment decreased in most European countries – especially in Bulgaria, Latvia, Greece, Spain and Lithuania. As a result of declining transitions into employment and inactivity, the

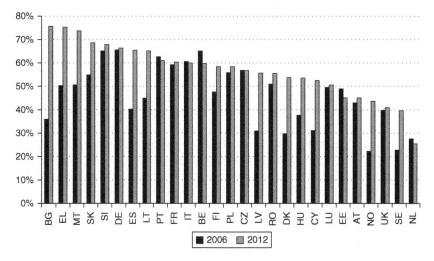

Source: Eurostat on the basis of the Labour Force Survey (table_ilc_lvhl30), accessed 6 August 2014.

Figure 4.1   Rate of persistently unemployed (in % of unemployed; 2006 and 2012)

share of unemployed who remained in unemployment increased in nearly all European countries (with the exception of the Netherlands, Belgium and Austria) – for example, in Spain from 40 per cent (2006) to 65 per cent (2012) and in Greece from 50 per cent to 75 per cent (cf. Figure 4.1). In addition to the high and increasing inflows into unemployment, this explains increasing LTU levels in Europe.

Statistically, the entry rate into unemployment can be approximated by the share of short-term unemployed in relation to the employed (excluding entries from inactivity into unemployment because the inactive are a very broad category whose motives to enter the labour force are extremely heterogeneous). This indicator will be termed STU risk below. The persistence rate can be estimated by the share of long-term unemployed as a percentage of all unemployed (LTU risk). Those two risks will be used as the dependent variables of the following models.

The three previously developed hypotheses will be discussed on the basis of the latest available version (August 2015) of the cross-sectional EU-SILC data for the years 2005–2013 for (in general) 26 European countries.[3] EU-SILC (Statistics on Income and Living Conditions) is an EU-wide survey on income, poverty and living conditions in Europe which started in 2004, initially in 13 countries. EU-SILC tries to unify and harmonize the employed concepts and survey methods; it is based on uniform definitions and methodological minimum standards. The data are obtained from a household questionnaire and an individual questionnaire for household members aged 16 years. The employment, living and income conditions of individuals and households in Europe are covered in detail. Both in the sampling and the data collection, the SILC data are still afflicted by considerable problems. In Germany, for example, Hauser (2007) points to sampling problems caused by the under-representation of poorly integrated foreigners (especially Turks), younger children and lower-skilled residents. Households with employed persons are likewise under-represented, while house and apartment owners are over-represented. This is the same as for non-representative samples (Frick and Krell 2010: 36). Despite the aforementioned methodological limitations in terms of representativeness, accuracy, comparability and coherence, the EU-SILC data are currently the most comprehensive data source for comparative analyses of income and employment conditions in Europe. They will therefore be used below in order to analyse the social distribution of STU and LTU risks. The impact of the national institutional context is taken into account on the basis of data provided by Eurostat and the OECD (cf. Table 4.1). In addition to the variables mentioned in the hypotheses, one control variable, the real growth rate of the respective country, is included.

The previously developed research hypotheses raise the question of which individual and institutional factors affect the probability that an employed person will become STU and that an unemployed person is long-term unemployed. Both variables are binary, for which reason the adequate method to be used is binary logistic regressions. Since the three research hypotheses focus on the individual and the national level, multi-level models and more specifically the logistic two-level random intercept models which can be calculated with the xtmelogit algorithm of STATA 13 will be used (Hox 2010: chapter 6):

$$logit \: [p_{ij} / (1 - p_{ij})] = \beta_0 + \beta_1 X_{ij} + \beta_1 Z_j + \varepsilon_{ij} + \mu_j \qquad (1)$$

where p_{ij} is the probability that a person i in a country j becomes short- or long-term unemployed. X_{ij} is an individual explanatory variable and Z_j is a variable on the country level. The probability p_{ij} that the outcome equals one, i.e. that an individual becomes or remains unemployed, is modelled using a logistic link function. The multi-level model decomposes the error variance into a proportion associated with the individual level (ε_{ij}) and one associated with the national level (μ_j). The between-nation variance or intra-class correlation (ICC) shows how similar the risk of becoming or remaining unemployed is in a country – measured against the risk for the whole sample population.

Table 4.1 The variables used, their operationalization and their expected and observed effects

Hypothesis	Variable	Operationalization	Data source	Expected	Observed
	Dependent				
	Short-term unemployment risk of employed	Unemployed persons (less than one year) who were employed at least one month in the previous year (in relation to all persons who were employed at least one month in the previous year) (1: short-term unemployed (STU); 0: not STU).	EU-SILC (pl030, pl031, pl080, pl073-pl076)		
	Long-term unemployment risk of unemployed	Unemployed for 12 months in the previous year (in relation to all unemployed) (1: long-term unemployed (LTU); 0: not LTU).	EU-SILC (pl030, pl031, pl080)		
	Independent	*Micro-level*			
H3	Gender	1: 'male' (ref. category); 2: 'female'	EU-SILC (rb090)	+/+	–/+
H3	Age class	1: 15–24 years; 2: '25 to 54 years'; ref. category; 3: '55 years and older'	EU-SILC (rx020)	Old: +/+	Old: –/+
H3	Household type	1: 'one person household'; 2: 'adults, no children'; 3: 'single parent household'; 4: 'adults with children'; (ref. category)	EU-SILC (hx060)	Single parent: +/+	+/+
H3	Migration status	Foreign nationality or born abroad (0: domestic origin (ref. category); 1: foreign origin)	EU-SILC (pb210 (a))	+/+	+/0
H2	Health	Self-perceived health (1: 'very good'; 2: 'good'; 3: 'fair'; 4: 'bad'; 5: 'very bad')	EU-SILC (ph010)	+/+	(+)/+

Table 4.1   (continued)

Hypothesis	Variable	Operationalization	Data source	Expected	Observed
H2	Educational level	Highest ISCED level attained (3: Tertiary education – levels 5–6; ref. category; 2: Upper secondary and post-secondary non-tertiary education (3–4); 1: Pre-primary, primary and lower secondary education (0–2)	EU-SILC (pe040)	+/+	+/+
H2	Occupational skill level (ISCO08)	1: 'simple and routine physical or manual tasks'; 2: 'operating machinery and electronic equipment; driving vehicles; maintenance and repair . . . manipulation, ordering and storage of information' (ref. category); 3: 'complex technical and practical tasks'; 4: 'problem-solving, decision-making, creativity.' (ILO 2012: 12–13)	EU-SILC (pl050; pl051)	High: –/–	–/–
H2	Type of contract	1: 'permanent job' (ref. category); 2: 'temporary job'	EU-SILC (pl140)	+/+	+/–
Independent macro-level (lagged by one year)					
Economic growth	Real GDP growth		Eurostat	–/–	–/(+)
Employment level	Employment rates in % of all persons aged 15 to 64 years		Eurostat	–/–	–/–

H1	Social protection	Social protection expenditure includes social benefits, administration costs and other expenditure linked to social protection schemes (% of GDP)	Eurostat (ESSPROS)	+/+	(−)/0
H1	Unemployment replacement	Net replacement rates for a married single-earner couple with two children, average wage in the initial phase of unemployment	OECD	+/+	0/− 0
H1	EPL	Employment Protection Legislation for temporary jobs (v1)	OECD	+/−	+ 0/0
H1	EPL difference	Difference between the Employment Protection Legislation for permanent and temporary employees (eplregi_v1-epltemp_v1)	Venn (2012)	−/−	− +/0
H1	Union density	Trade Union Density Rate: ratio of wage and salary earners who are trade union members, divided by the total number of wage and salary earners	OECD and J. Visser, ICTWSS 4.1	+/+	+ 0/0

Note: The expected and observed effects refer to the short-term unemployment (STU) risk in percentage of the employed (first sign) respective the long-term unemployment (LTU) risk in percentage of the unemployed (second sign). '+' refers to an effect significantly different from zero, '−' refers to an effect significantly lower than zero; '0' to an effect that does not differ significantly from zero.

A high ICC indicates that (long-term) unemployment risks within a country differ considerably from those of other European countries. The coefficients in the following tables are generally average marginal effects (AME) which express the average effect of the respective category of the independent variable on the dependent variable in comparison to the reference category. In 2013, for example, the LTU risk of unemployed persons with a low education was 13.4 percentage points higher than for unemployed persons with a high education (Table 4.2, column 6). In contrast to odds ratios, AMEs can be compared across groups, samples and models (Mood 2010).

A serious problem is the number of countries that are available for the analysis. Bryan and Jenkins (2016: 20) recommend at least 30 countries for logit models: 'Otherwise, estimates of country-level fixed parameters are likely to be estimated imprecisely ... users will conclude too often that a country effect exists when it does not.' If this admonition is taken seriously, multi-level analyses of at the EU level are impossible. Given the fact that 26 countries are not too far away from the lower limit suggested by Bryan and Jenkins, I have decided to continue with this analysis, but to caution the reader against its potential risk (which, however, does not affect individual-level predictors). When analysing the countries most affected by the crisis (Table 4.4), I use logistic regressions with cluster-robust standard errors.

In a first step, the results for 2013 will be discussed in detail. In models (1) and (4) of Table 4.2, the STU risks of the employed and the LTU risks of the unemployed are described without explanatory variables. The next two models (2) and (5) include the occupational, qualificational and ascriptive characteristics of the employed and unemployed in order to determine which individual and household-related factors influence the risk of becoming and remaining unemployed. In addition to these individual factors, models (3) and (6) in Table 4.2 include the previously discussed contextual and control variables in order to determine which aspects of the national context influence the STU and LTU risks of the employed (column 3) and the unemployed (column 6). In the appendix Tables 4A.1 and 4A.2, the results for the complete models for 2005–2013 are shown in order to describe the evolution before and during the crisis.

The between-country variance in Table 4.2 model (1) is 0.947 which corresponds to 22.3 per cent of the total variance of 4.236. Nearly one-quarter of the STU risk can be explained by the included particularities of the 26 countries. The LTU risk of the unemployed is more equally spread among nations: only 11.1 per cent of the variance can be explained by national particularities. Both proportions are much lower than in the years before the crisis, when more than 40 per cent (2005–2007) or more than 12 per cent (2005–2006) of the unemployment risk could be explained by

*Table 4.2   Unemployment risk of the employed, and long-term unemploy-
ment risk of the unemployed in 26 European countries (2013)*

	Short-term unemployment risk of the employed			Long-term unemployment risk of the unemployed		
	Empty model (1)	Individual (2)	Contextual (3)	Empty model (4)	Individual (5)	Contextual (6)
Women		−0.005**	−0.005**		0.015*	0.015*
		(−8.40)	(−8.40)		(2.06)	(2.05)
Age group (ref.: 25 to 54 years)						
15–24 years		−0.002	−0.002		−0.107**	−0.101**
		(−1.62)	(−1.60)		(−7.81)	(−7.51)
55 years +		−0.025**	−0.030**		0.097**	0.088**
		(−37.09)	(−37.09)		(9.26)	(8.86)
Household type (ref.: adults with children)						
One-person household		0.003**	0.004**		0.055**	0.051**
		(3.55)	(3.56)		(4.24)	(4.12)
Adults, no child		0.002**	0.003**		0.028**	0.028**
		(3.80)	(3.80)		(3.46)	(3.52)
Single-parent household		0.006**	0.007**		0.039*	0.038*
		(4.03)	(4.04)		(1.98)	(2.05)
Foreign nationality or born abroad		0.005**	0.006**		0.008	0.008
		(5.16)	(5.17)		(0.63)	(0.69)
Health		0.000	0.000		0.045**	0.041**
		(0.78)	(0.77)		(9.87)	(9.50)
Educational level (ref.: high)						
Low		0.002*	0.002*		0.139**	0.134**
		(2.00)	(1.98)		(10.59)	(10.55)
Medium		0.001	0.001		0.076**	0.074**
		(0.99)	(0.99)		(6.23)	(6.20)
ISCO skill levels (ref.: operating, repair, information processing (2))						
Simple tasks (1)		0.006**	0.007**		−0.023*	−0.022*
		(6.87)	(6.87)		(−2.52)	(−2.48)
Complex tasks (3)		−0.008**	−0.009**		−0.038**	−0.033**
		(−8.58)	(−8.58)		(−2.82)	(−2.59)
Problem-solving, decision-making, creativity (4)		−0.014**	−0.016**		−0.057**	−0.052**
		(−15.59)	(−15.58)		(−3.49)	(−3.33)
Temporary job		0.050**	0.059**		−0.071**	−0.065**
		(59.27)	(59.26)		(−9.10)	(−8.60)
Economic growth			0.001			0.023
			(0.43)			(1.62)
Employment level			−0.002*			−0.021**
			(−2.35)			(−4.19)

Table 4.2   (continued)

	Short-term unemployment risk of the employed			Long-term unemployment risk of the unemployed		
	Empty model (1)	Individual (2)	Contextual (3)	Empty model (4)	Individual (5)	Contextual (6)
Social protection			0.000			0.005
			(0.08)			(1.05)
Unemployment			0.001			−0.003
replacement			(1.52)			(−1.60)
Employment			0.016+			0.047
protection			(1.70)			(0.89)
EPL difference			0.005			0.021
permanent and			(1.07)			(0.91)
temporary jobs						
Union density			0.000			0.001
			(0.71)			(1.09)
No.	260 739	260 739	260 739	19 582	19 582	18 833
chi²	.	7329	7343	.	793	764
Between-country variance	0.947	0.786	0.525	0.412	0.466	0.183
Variance (total)	4.236	4.076	3.815	3.702	3.756	3.473
Intra-class correlation	0.223	0.193	0.138	0.111	0.124	0.053
McFadden pseudo-R²		0.118	0.118		0.638	0.651
AIC	68 886	60 795	60 799	25 804	24 986	24 110
BIC	68 907	60 963	61 040	25 820	25 113	24 291
Log-likelihood	−34 400	−30 400	−30 400	−12 900	−12 500	−12 000

Note: Tables 4.2, 4.3 and 4.4 and the appendix tables show the results of different binary logistic two-level random intercept models with the dependent dichotomous variables 'short- and long-term unemployment' (yes or no). The included populations are either the labour force or the unemployed of 26 European countries (AT, BE, BG, CZ, DE, DK, EE, EL, ES, FI, FR, HU, IE, IT, LT, LU, LV, NL, NO, PL, PT, RO, SE, SI, SK, UK). The coefficients are average marginal effects (cf. Mood 2010). Figures in parentheses: t-values. The AIC (Akaike information criterion) and the BIC (Bayes information criterion) are measures of the relative quality of the statistical models. Legend: + $p < .1$; * $p < .05$; ** $p < .01$.

Source: Own calculations on the basis of EU-SILC UDB UDB_c13_ver 2013-2 from 1 August 2015.

national specificities. The almost general increase in (long-term) unemployment rates has thus reduced heterogeneity among the European countries, especially between 2008 and 2011.

In the next step, the ascriptive, occupational and qualification characteristics of the short-term (model 2) and long-term unemployed (model 5) are taken into account. While the STU risk of *female* employed is significantly lower, the LTU risk of female unemployed is 1.5 percentage points higher than the risk of men. The below-average unemployment risk of women is a new phenomenon that can be observed only since 2008 (Table 4A.1). The crisis thus seems to have accelerated the structural transformation of the economy to a service-based one – at the expense of the male-dominated industrial sector. Given this background, the structurally higher LTU risk of women is surprising and can be considered as indicative of the *marginalization* of female unemployed (H3) – a sharp contrast to the better and improving position of employed women.

In general, the STU risk of *younger persons* (15–24 years) differs not very much from prime-age employees. Exceptions are the years 2006 and 2009–2011. In sharp cyclical downturns, the STU risk of young people is even lower than that of prime-age employees, which illustrates that the high youth unemployment rates of some Mediterranean countries are mostly the result of difficulties in finding a first job. For younger unemployed, however, LTU risks are lower than those of prime-age persons. This at first sight positive observation, however, might disguise increasing inactivity rates of younger people who are completely excluded from the labour market.

The STU unemployment risk of *older employees* (55 years and above) is 3 percentage points lower than that of prime-age employees, while the LTU risk of older unemployed is 8.8 percentage points higher.

These differences were already significant in the years before the crisis, but during the crisis these differences further increased considerably, which illustrates that employment protection for older employees is higher, but once older employees lose their job their situation is much worse than that of younger people, especially in a economic downturn. The examples of female, younger and older people show that the criteria for the dismissal and for the recruitment of these groups differ significantly: women and older employees have a lower STU, but a higher LTU risk. This is exactly contrary to the situation of younger people.

Another group with clearly higher STU risks is *single-parent households* – another sign of marginalization (H3). In comparison to adults with children, their unemployment risk is 0.7 (2013) or even 1.1 percentage points (2009) higher. However, the LTU risk of single parents does not differ significantly from other groups, which might reflect the effects of targeted welfare and childcare policies on the one side and the (slightly) above-average qualifications and occupational positions of single parents on the other side.

Employees with a *migration background* have a higher STU risk – a clear suggestion of marginalization (H3). At the peak of the crisis, this risk was 1.2 percentage points higher. However, the LTU risk of unemployed migrants does not differ significantly from that of native unemployed.

The STU risk of *employees with poor health* was significantly higher before the crisis but (surprisingly) not during the crisis, while the LTU risk of unemployed with poor health is consistently and significantly higher than the corresponding risk of other groups since 2005. The health-related gap has become much bigger during the crisis, which can be interpreted as a sign of an increased labour market dualization (H2).

Important indicators of the expected dualization between different skill, occupational and contractual groups and labour contracts are skill-biased unemployment risks. In comparison to highly skilled persons, the STU and LTU risks of *medium and low-skilled persons* are consistently and significantly higher. During the crisis, these differences even increased. In 2009, for example, the STU risk of low-skilled employed was 0.9 percentage points higher and the LTU risk of low-skilled unemployed was 10.9 percentage points higher than that of academically trained persons.

In a similar vein, the unemployment risk of employees varies with their occupational profile. STU risks for employees with complex tasks (e.g. technicians and associate professionals or retail managers (skill group 3) or with tasks that require problem-solving, decision-making or creativity (e.g. professionals or sales and marketing managers (skill group 4)) are significantly lower than those of employees with simple (skill group 1) or operational, repairing and information-processing tasks (such as clerical support workers, services and sales workers, skilled agricultural workers, craft workers, plant and machine operators and assemblers (skill group 2)). The different STU risks of occupational skill groups 1 and 2 on the one side and skill groups 3 and 4 on the other side confirm the usefulness of the 'dichotomous operationalization of insiders/outsiders' proposed by Schwander and Häusermann (2013: 262). The clear differentiation of the STU and LTU risks of high- and low-skilled employees also confirms the expected dualization of the European labour markets, especially during the crisis (H2). However, a similar differentiation of LTU risks for unemployed with different occupational backgrounds could not be observed. This means that employees with less demanding tasks are more easily laid off, but they are also more easily recruited after the crisis. Only in 2009 and 2010 was this case not true for unemployed who had previously performed simple tasks. Their LTU risk was significantly higher in those years – which might effectuate long-lasting hysteresis effects.

Another and at least quantitatively the most important dualization indicator (H2) is the type of employment contract. Employees with *temporary contracts* have a 5.9 percentage point higher STU risk than permanent employees. They are especially women, younger people and low-skilled employees (De Grip et al. 1997; Kalleberg 2000; Bentolila et al. 2012). However, people with fixed-term contracts are not only dismissed more easily during the crisis (especially since 2008), but they are also hired more easily. Their LTU risk is consistently and significantly lower than that of those unemployed who previously had a permanent contract. This relative advantage was drastically reduced during the crisis however (from 12.5 percentage points in 2008 to 5.5 points in 2009). Temporary employees are important organizational employment buffers.

Indicators of the third type of segmentation discussed in this chapter – the expected polarization between labour market insiders and outsiders – are social and employment protection and union density. Here, higher national *social protection expenditures* reduced STU risks in 2005, 2008 and 2009 because they buffered the crisis (for example via short-time work). The higher LTU risks in 2009 might indicate a reverse causality, as huge increases in the LTU stock require higher social expenditures. In other years, the neoclassical assumption that higher social expenditures increase the willingness to remain unemployed cannot be confirmed. In contradiction to neoclassical assumptions, the *level of unemployment benefits* before the crisis was not correlated with the LTU risk of the unemployed. At least since 2007, countries with stronger unions have neither higher STU nor higher LTU risks. Contrary to neoclassical assumptions, stronger *unions* with more members do not seem to aggravate the insider–outsider problems of the labour market.

Before the crisis (2005–2007) and in 2013, stricter *employment protection legislation* (EPL) increased the unemployment risk of the employed, while a bigger difference between the EPL for temps and permanent employees reduced it in 2006 and 2007. This is in accordance with neoclassical expectations. During the crisis, however, these relations disappeared for nearly all of the years. This can be explained by the end of the 'honeymoon' of labour market policy reforms: a deregulation of labour markets created new job opportunities and reduced unemployment risks. After the honeymoon period, however, this effect was reversed in an economic downturn. From 2009 until 2011, a relatively lower employment protection for temporary workers increased their unemployment risk because temporary workers could be dismissed more easily. As predicted, no effects on LTU risks could be observed.

In line with expectations, an inclusive employment regime characterized by a better inclusion of women, younger people and older employees in the labour market and indicated by high employment rates reduced the STU and the LTU risks of the labour force in all of the years.

The control variable for the economic situation, the economic growth, had no effect in general on the STU and LTU risks (with the exception of the sharp downturn in 2009 and 2010).

For 2013, the individual and national characteristics of the labour force in general and the unemployed in particular respectively explain 11.8 per cent and 65.1 per cent of the initial value of the log-likelihood function, which McFadden interprets similarly to R^2 in regression models as the percentage reduction of the unexplained variance (Rabe-Hesketh and Skrondal 2008). A log-likelihood ratio test shows a significant increase of the model fit by including the contextual variables.

The aim of comparative research is to reduce the variance that is 'explained' by the national idiosyncrasies, i.e. to move from 'research where nation is context' to cross-national research 'where nation is the unit of analysis' (Kohn 1987: 715). The sharp reduction in the between-country variance by 45 per cent (models 1 and 3, Table 4.2) and 56 per cent (models 4 and 6) shows that the contextual variables are relevant for explaining STU and LTU risks in Europe.

In Table 4.3, the cross-sectional data for all years as well as for the years before the crisis (2005–2008) and during the crisis (2009–2013) have been pooled. The annual dummy variables that were included in the models are not reproduced in the table, since they reflect only the strong increase of the STU and LTU risks since 2008 and 2009, respectively. The table allows a comprehensive evaluation of the determinants of the unemployment risk before and during the crisis. At the individual level, the changing situation during the crisis is overall reflected in an increase, but not a reversal of the previous effects: the unemployment risks of males, migrants, younger employees and people with simple tasks have strongly increased since 2009 (models 2 and 3 in Table 4.3). For example, before the crisis, the STU risk for employees with a migration background was 0.6 percentage points higher than that of native employees; during the crisis, this gap increased to 0.8 per cent. In a similar vein, the LTU risks of younger people, singles, single parents, and ill people have increased while the risks of older unemployed with former temporary contracts and high-skilled occupations have decreased (models 5 and 6 in Table 4.3). The LTU risk of the unemployed in poor health increased from 3.4 to 4.8 percentage points during the crisis. These are clear indicators of an increasing dualization and marginalization of the European labour force.

As expected by neoclassical approaches (Siebert 1997), high unemployment benefits and strict employment protection (but not a high union density) were positively correlated with the STU level before the crisis. During the crisis, higher unemployment benefits and strict employment protection have been contributing to the reduction of the unemployment risks of employees; the corresponding coefficients have changed their sign.

A higher difference between the employment protection for permanent and temporary workers was positively correlated with the STU risk, i.e. a more rigid labour market increased the unemployment risks in the crisis. Since the beginning of the crisis, the LTU risk of the unemployed has been lowered by higher employment levels, lower unemployment benefits, better employment protection legislation and a smaller difference between the employment protection legislation for permanent and temporary employees (columns 3 and 6 in Table 4.3).

Additionally, similar logistic models have been calculated for six countries that are mostly hidden by the eurozone crisis (Cyprus, Greece, Ireland, Italy, Portugal and Spain; cf. Table 4.4). In these countries, men, older people, migrants and low-skilled employees have a much higher unemployment risk. The LTU risk of the unemployed is particularly high for older people, migrants and people with a challenging occupation, while it is comparatively lower for younger people, the temporary employed, singles, single parents, migrants, low-skilled people and women (even if it is not clear whether these groups simply leave the labour market and are thus no longer counted as unemployed). Economic growth reduces LTU risks more strongly than in all of the European countries taken into consideration. Social protection reduces STU risks and increases LTU risks. Especially during the crisis, a huge gap between the employment protection of temporary and permanent employees significantly increases the LTU risks of the unemployed. Better protection of employed people often means that the unemployed are durably excluded from the labour market. Unions, however, reduce this risk.

In sum, a comparison of STU risks before and during the current crisis shows that the crisis is characterized by an intensification of marginalization and dualization processes, especially at the expense of low-skilled, single, non-native and younger employees as well as younger employees with fixed-term contracts. Fixed-term contracts are the most important buffer of economic downturns. The unemployment risk of women, professionals and managers declined during the crisis, which shows that services and high-skilled professions are less affected by economic downturns than other industries and groups. The LTU risk has increased for singles, single parents and sick people, while it decreased for older and high-skilled people and people who previously had a fixed-term contract. The crisis thus has increased the gaps between older and younger, male and female, unskilled and skilled, foreign and domestic employees as well as between non-standard and standard employment relationships. Both the occupational and ascriptive characteristics of individuals are decisive for their STU and LTU risks. During the crisis, the effect of the institutional variables often does not correspond to neoclassical assumptions: higher

Table 4.3 Unemployment risk of the employed, and long-term unemployment risk of the unemployed in 26 European countries (2005–2013)

	Short-term unemployment risk of the employed			Long-term unemployment risk of the unemployed		
	2005–2013 (1)	2005–2008 (2)	2009–2013 (3)	2005–2013 (4)	2005–2008 (5)	2009–2013 (6)
Women	−0.004** (−21.05)	−0.001** (−3.56)	−0.006** (−23.78)	0.018** (7.43)	0.020** (4.60)	0.020** (6.06)
Age group (ref.: 25–54 years)						
15 to 24 years	0.002** (6.32)	0.002** (2.59)	0.004** (5.91)	−0.127** (−30.28)	−0.144** (−20.44)	−0.125** (−22.31)
55 years +	−0.026** (−106.23)	−0.035** (−60.71)	−0.031** (−87.73)	0.079** (22.75)	0.105** (14.88)	0.082** (17.68)
Household type (ref.: adults with children)						
One-person household	0.003** (7.68)	0.004** (5.59)	0.003** (5.33)	0.039** (9.20)	0.011 (1.25)	0.055** (9.81)
Adults, no child	0.002** (11.74)	0.003** (7.28)	0.003** (9.31)	0.018** (6.95)	0.014** (2.99)	0.023** (6.44)
Single-parent household	0.008** (14.94)	0.011** (10.33)	0.009** (11.24)	0.012+ (1.91)	0.008 (0.75)	0.016+ (1.86)
Foreign nationality or born abroad	0.006** (18.73)	0.006** (8.56)	0.008** (17.02)	0.001 (0.23)	0.001 (0.12)	−0.002 (−0.33)
Health	0.001** (8.07)	0.002** (9.58)	0.0001* (2.41)	0.040** (27.73)	0.034** (13.38)	0.048** (24.27)
Educational level (ref.: high)						
Low	0.005** (13.44)	0.007** (9.79)	0.004** (9.08)	0.114** (25.26)	0.122** (13.89)	0.123** (20.92)

	(1)	(2)	(3)	(4)	(5)	(6)
Medium	0.002**	0.004**	0.002**	0.065**	0.069**	0.067**
	(8.23)	(6.21)	(5.48)	(15.09)	(8.31)	(12.13)
ISCO skill levels (ref.: operating, repair, information processing (2))						
Simple tasks (1)	0.003**	0.002**	0.003**	0.005	0.008	0.005
	(8.76)	(3.41)	(8.17)	(1.59)	(1.44)	(1.14)
Complex tasks (3)	−0.009**	−0.011**	−0.011**	−0.019**	−0.009	−0.025**
	(−28.41)	(−16.08)	(−23.57)	(−4.20)	(−1.13)	(−4.20)
Problem-solving, decision-making, creativity (4)	−0.015**	−0.019**	−0.018**	−0.026**	−0.010	−0.037**
	(−43.67)	(−23.35)	(−37.00)	(−4.72)	(−0.92)	(−5.21)
Temporary job	0.054**	0.063**	0.063**	−0.076**	−0.103**	−0.071**
	(175.95)	(106.24)	(139.82)	(−29.40)	(−21.76)	(−20.32)
Economic growth	−0.001**	−0.002**	−0.001**	0.005**	0.005**	0.004**
	(−24.34)	(−12.80)	(−19.28)	(10.14)	(2.75)	(5.58)
Employment level	0.0001*	0.000	0.001**	−0.021**	−0.031**	−0.018**
	(2.51)	(1.11)	(9.84)	(−22.68)	(−10.88)	(−13.31)
Social protection	−0.000	−0.000	0.000	0.001	0.001	0.001
	(−1.14)	(−0.89)	(0.04)	(0.61)	(0.16)	(0.40)
Unemployment replacement	−0.0001**	0.001**	−0.0001**	0.002**	0.003+	0.002**
	(−2.66)	(8.24)	(−7.97)	(4.80)	(1.88)	(3.74)
Employment protection	−0.002+	0.080**	−0.015**	−0.018	−0.058	−0.047*
	(−1.86)	(7.24)	(−7.18)	(−1.53)	(−1.03)	(−2.41)
EPL difference permanent and temporary jobs	0.005**	0.003	0.016**	0.010	−0.009	−0.029+
	(7.70)	(0.80)	(8.44)	(1.36)	(−0.35)	(−1.74)
Union density	0.001**	−0.001**	0.001**	−0.008**	0.004*	−0.002
	(16.27)	(−5.25)	(3.01)	(−12.45)	(2.30)	(−1.33)

Table 4.3 (continued)

	Short-term unemployment risk of the employed			Long-term unemployment risk of the unemployed		
	2005–2013 (1)	2005–2008 (2)	2009–2013 (3)	2005–2013 (4)	2005–2008 (5)	2009–2013 (6)
No.	2 297 888	945 030	1 352 858	136 486	45 506	90 980
chi^2	64 600	21 168	41 635	8398	2539	5329
Between country variance	0,844	4,877	1,04	0,878	0,581	0,293
Variance (total)	4,134	8,166	4,33	4,168	3,87	3,583
Intra-class correlation	0,204	0,597	0,24	0,211	0,15	0,082
McFadden pseudo-R^2	0,123	0,116	0,124	0,050	0,046	0,048
AIC	515 000	183 000	329 000	175 000	57 532	117 000
BIC	515 000	184 000	330 000	176 000	57 758	117 000
Log-likelihood	−257 000	−91 600	−165 000	−87 600	−28 700	−58 500

Note: Cf. Table 4.2. Year dummies included in the models, but not reproduced in this table. Contextual variables lagged by one year. Missing contextual variables estimated on the basis of earlier or later values.

Table 4.4 Unemployment risk of the employed, and long-term unemployment risk of the unemployed in six eurozone crisis countries (2005–2013)

	Short-term unemployment risk of the employed			Long-term unemployment risk of the unemployed		
	2005–2013 (1)	2005–2008 (2)	2009–2013 (3)	2005–2013 (4)	2005–2008 (5)	2009–2013 (6)
Women	-0.006** (-4.93)	-0.001 (-0.54)	-0.009** (-7.80)	0.022 (1.18)	0.023 (0.74)	0.021 (1.53)
Age group (ref.: 25–54 years)						
15 to 24 years	0.004 (0.59)	0.002 (0.30)	0.006 (0.90)	-0.065** (-2.64)	-0.075** (-3.07)	-0.058* (-2.42)
55 years +	-0.043** (-9.35)	-0.034** (-4.58)	-0.051** (-19.53)	0.117** (2.84)	0.128** (6.09)	0.112* (2.24)
Household type (ref.: adults with children)						
One-person household	0.002 (0.51)	0.003** (4.48)	0.001 (0.15)	-0.051** (-3.96)	-0.077** (-2.71)	-0.040* (-2.43)
Adults, no child	0.004** (4.93)	0.004** (4.49)	0.004** (3.14)	0.012 (0.69)	-0.001 (-0.07)	0.016 (0.66)
Single-parent household	0.007** (3.33)	0.010** (3.90)	0.005 (1.44)	0.003 (0.17)	-0.037 (-0.83)	0.020 (1.25)
Foreign nationality or born abroad	0.011** (5.41)	0.001 (0.30)	0.017** (9.29)	-0.049** (-2.64)	-0.059* (-1.97)	-0.047** (-3.52)
Health	-0.002 (-1.43)	-0.001 (-0.52)	-0.004* (-2.28)	0.042** (3.26)	0.043* (2.37)	0.042** (4.01)

Table 4.4 (continued)

	Short-term unemployment risk of the employed			Long-term unemployment risk of the unemployed		
	2005–2013 (1)	2005–2008 (2)	2009–2013 (3)	2005–2013 (4)	2005–2008 (5)	2009–2013 (6)
Educational level (ref.: high)						
Low	0.010** (38.67)	0.009** (12.44)	0.010** (21.46)	0.089** (9.01)	0.078** (3.13)	0.092** (26.56)
Medium	−0.001 (−0.43)	0.001 (0.63)	−0.002 (−0.67)	0.066** (13.44)	0.052** (2.79)	0.070** (18.98)
ISCO skill levels (ref.: operating, repair, information processing (2))						
Simple tasks (1)	0.001 (0.26)	0.001 (0.43)	0.001 (0.22)	−0.019 (−1.18)	−0.022 (−1.00)	−0.018 (−1.35)
Complex tasks (3)	−0.010** (−3.02)	−0.009** (−3.66)	−0.011** (−2.68)	−0.020* (−2.43)	−0.000 (−0.03)	−0.028** (−2.67)
Problem-solving, decision-making, creativity (4)	−0.022** (−23.08)	−0.016** (−9.01)	−0.026** (−15.62)	−0.036 (−1.61)	−0.015 (−0.88)	−0.045 (−1.36)
Temporary job	0.074** (64.20)	0.062** (47.91)	0.083** (33.02)	−0.053* (−2.20)	−0.075** (−3.01)	−0.044+ (−1.95)
Economic growth	−0.001 (−0.78)	−0.000 (−0.08)	0.001 (0.26)	−0.010 (−1.35)	−0.011+ (−1.67)	−0.018* (−2.12)
Employment level	0.000 (0.24)	0.002** (2.61)	0.001* (2.13)	−0.011** (−3.26)	−0.025** (−3.02)	−0.009** (−5.20)

Social protection	−0.002**	0.008**	−0.006**	0.015**	−0.033	0.027**
	(−3.19)	(6.03)	(−4.54)	(3.19)	(−1.16)	(7.61)
Unemployment replacement	−0.000	0.000	−0.001*	0.000	−0.003**	0.003*
	(−0.85)	(0.05)	(−2.30)	(0.35)	(−5.64)	(2.45)
Employment protection	0.001	−0.040**	−0.002	−0.131**	0.032	−0.123**
	(0.26)	(−4.24)	(−0.61)	(−5.50)	(0.16)	(−5.97)
EPL difference permanent and temporary jobs	−0.002	0.023*	−0.003	0.121**	0.070	0.100**
	(−0.63)	(2.43)	(−1.18)	(6.86)	(0.41)	(6.28)
Union density	−0.001**	−0.004**	−0.000	−0.008**	0.002	−0.009**
	(−3.02)	(−3.67)	(−0.08)	(−10.84)	(0.11)	(−10.95)
No.	589 559	271 944	317 615	50 860	16 318	34 542
Pseudo-R^2	0.15	0.137	0.153	0.047	0.045	0.045
AIC	196 955 394	72 258 756	124 247 780	75 949 936	22 879 355	52 957 270
BIC	196 955 439	72 258 798	124 247 822	75 949 971	22 879 386	52 957 304
Log-likelihood	−98 477 693	−36 129 374	−62 123 886	−37 974 964	−11 439 673	−26 478 631

Note: This table is the result of six logistic regressions. Cf. Table 4.2. The six euro area countries with high borrowing spreads during the sovereign debt crisis are Cyprus, Greece, Ireland, Italy, Portugal and Spain. Year dummies included in the models, but not reproduced in this table. Contextual variables lagged by one year. Missing contextual variables estimated on the basis of earlier or later values.

unemployment benefits and a stricter employment protection reduce the unemployment risk; a lower gap between permanent and temporary jobs reduces the long-term unemployment risk, but in some years (2010–2011) it also contributed to an increasing unemployment risk (Table 4A.1).

4.4 CONCLUSION AND OUTLOOK

During the financial, public debt and economic crisis in Europe from 2008, unemployment and also LTU rates in Europe have increased strongly, which raised fears of an increasing solidification of patterns of labour market segmentation, especially in Southern and Eastern Europe. This chapter discussed how during the current economic crisis in Europe, the distribution of unemployment risks among different social groups differentiated by gender, age, education and occupation has changed. Two major selection barriers on the way to a durable exclusion from the labour market were analysed: the transition from employment to short-term unemployment and the transition from short-term to long-term unemployment. On the basis of previous literature, it can be expected that the group-specific STU risks of employees and the LTU risk of the unemployed reflect three different forms of labour market segmentation. Firstly, institutionally stabilized insider–outsider divisions between more or less protected groups (*polarization*); secondly, the organizational *dualization* between different educational, occupational and contractual groups; and, thirdly, the *marginalization* of disadvantaged groups differentiated by gender, age, family status and migration status. The empirical analyses of these segmentation processes carried out above are based on EU-SILC data for four years before and five years during the crisis (2005–2013).

The empirical results of this paper can be summarized in three main points. Firstly, the European labour markets are strongly and durably segmented: younger employees, male and low-skilled employees with temporary contracts and simple tasks, migrants, singles and single parents face higher unemployment risks than natives, adults with children and older, female and high-skilled employees with permanent contracts and demanding occupations. This segmentation is even stronger in the six eurozone Member States mostly affected by the crisis. Secondly, the social distribution of STU and LTU risks differs for many groups because the two decisions involved (i.e. the dismissal of an employee and the recruitment of an unemployed person) follow different logics and are regulated in different ways. While the STU risk of female employees is lower than that of male employees, the LTU risk of women is higher than that of men. Hence, gender discrimination in the case of recruitment seems to be easier than in the case of dismissal. For younger and older people, the STU and LTU risks are distributed crosswise. For older people, the STU risk is lower but their LTU risk is higher, which can be easily explained by higher seniority and stricter employment protection rules that protect the employed but are not always an advantage for finding a new job. For younger people, the situation is exactly the other way around. This is also the case for people with a fixed-term contract. Thus, temporary employees have a higher STU and a lower LTU risk, while for permanent employees it is the other way around. Low-skilled people/occupations and people with fragile health generally face both a higher STU and a higher LTU risk. Higher employment rates and a smaller difference between the employment protection for permanent and temporary jobs reduce both the STU and LTU rate. Thirdly, the labour market effects of the crisis can be analysed by comparing segmentation patterns before (2005–2008) and during (2009–2013) the crisis. It appears that the employment situation of employed women, single parents, the low-skilled and natives improves by relative standards during the crisis – at least in comparison to men, couples with children, high-skilled employees and migrants. Strict employment protection was linked with a higher STU risk before the crisis. During the current crisis it is linked to lower STU and LTU risks. The impact of employment protection thus has been reversed during the crisis. This is also true for the impact of higher unemployment benefits which are correlated with lower STU risks during the crisis. A huge difference between employment protection legislation for permanent and temporary employees, i.e. a deregulation of temporary contracts, increased the STU risk during the crisis. This has been interpreted above as the end of the honeymoon period of labour market reforms.

Evidence for the expected institutional forms of segmentation is far from univocal in our analysis. Stronger unions and stricter employment protection showed the expected negative effect on short-term employment risks at least in some years before the crisis, but in general the predictions of neoclassical approaches concerning the effects of social and employment protection could not be supported. Contrariwise, occupational, skill-based and organizational aspects of labour market segmentation could be convincingly demonstrated. Higher educational qualifications, a higher occupational status, a stable contractual link to the organization by a permanent contract and a better health status decisively reduce the risk of becoming (and in general also remaining) unemployed. The increasing differentiation between educational and occupational skill groups indicates a stronger occupational segmentation of the labour market. However, women now face lower unemployment risks, and also their relative LTU risk has declined during the crisis (see Chapter 5 of this volume).

The current crisis may therefore contribute to the return and strengthening of pre-existing forms of labour market segmentation, which may lead to a lasting erosion of skills, motivation and attachment to the labour market while also endangering the inclusiveness and long-term growth potential especially of the Southern and Eastern European economies. A shift to more inclusive employment policies which focus on the inclusion of disadvantaged groups in the labour market is therefore decisive for safeguarding the basis of European integration.

NOTES

1. This is a revised and updated version of an article which was in the *Journal of European Social Policy*, **25** (4), 393–413. In this version I have also included the EU-SILC data for 2013 and have used centred and lagged contextual variables.
2. Labour market segmentation has been defined as 'the historical process whereby political economic forces encourage the division of the labor market into separate submarkets, or segments, distinguished by different labor market characteristics and behavioral rules' (Reich et al. 1973: 359).
3. In 2005 and 2006, 24 countries (EU-28 plus Norway minus Bulgaria, Croatia, Cyprus, Malta and Romania) could be included. Since 2007, the required data for Bulgaria and Romania also has been available, extending the sample to 26 countries (EU-28 plus Norway minus Croatia, Cyprus and Malta).

REFERENCES

Bentolila, S., P. Cahuc, J.J. Dolado and T. Le Barbanchon (2012), 'Two-Tier Labour Markets in the Great Recession: France Versus Spain', *The Economic Journal*, **122** (562), F155–F187.

Blanchard, O.J. (2006), 'European Unemployment: The Evolution of Facts and Ideas', *Economic Policy*, **21** (45), 5–59.

Boeri, T. (2011), 'Institutional Reforms and Dualism in European Labor Markets', in O. Ashenfelter and D. Card (eds), *Handbook of Labor Economics*, Volume 4b. Amsterdam: Elsevier, pp. 1173–1236.

Boeri, T. and P. Garibaldi (2009), 'Beyond Eurosclerosis', *Economic Policy*, **24** (59), 409–461.

Bryan, M.L. and S.P. Jenkins (2016), 'Multilevel Modelling of Country Effects: A Cautionary Tale', *European Sociological Review*, **32** (1), 3–22.

De Grip, A., J. Hoevenberg and E. Willems (1997), 'Atypical Employment in the European Union', *International Labour Review*, **136** (1), 49–71.

Doeringer, P.B. and M.J. Piore (1971), *Labor Markets and Manpower Analysis*. Lexington: Lexington Books.

Emmenegger, P., S. Häusermann, B. Palier and M. Seeleib-Kaiser (eds) (2012), *The Age of Dualization: The Changing Face of Inequality in Deindustrializing Societies*. Oxford: Oxford University Press.

European Commission (2012), *Employment and Social Developments in Europe 2012*. Luxembourg: Publications Office of the European Union.

Frick, J.R. and K. Krell (2010), Measuring Income in Household Panel Surveys for Germany: A Comparison of EU-SILC and SOEP, SOEPpapers 265. Berlin: DIW.

Gangl, M. (2004), 'Welfare States and the Scar Effects of Unemployment: A Comparative Analysis of the United States and West Germany', *American Journal of Sociology*, **109** (6), 1319–1364.

Hauser, R. (2007), Probleme des deutschen Beitrags zu EU-SILC aus der Sicht der Wissenschaft – Ein Vergleich von EU-SILC, Mikrozensus und SOEP, SOEPpapers 69. Berlin: DIW.

Heidenreich, M. and P. Aurich-Beerheide (2014), 'European Worlds of Inclusive Activation: The Challenges of Coordinated Service Provision', *International Journal of Social Welfare*, **23** (S1), 6–22.

Hox, J.J. (2010), *Multilevel Analysis. Techniques and Applications.* Hove: Routledge.

ILO (2012), *International Standard Classification of Occupations. Structure, Group Definitions and Correspondence Tables*, ISCO-08 Volume I. Geneva: International Labour Organization.

Kalleberg, A.L. (2000), 'Nonstandard Employment Relations: Part-Time, Temporary and Contract Work', *Annual Review of Sociology*, **26** (1), 341–365.

Kalleberg, A.L. (2009), 'Precarious Work, Insecure Workers: Employment Relations in Transition', *American Sociological Review*, **74** (1), 1–22.

Kalleberg, A.L. (2012), 'Job Quality and Precarious Work: Clarifications, Controversies, and Challenges', *Work and Occupations*, **39** (4), 427–448.

Kalleberg, A.L. and A.B. Sørensen (1979), 'The Sociology of Labour Markets', *Annual Review of Sociology*, **5**, 351–379.

Kohn, M.E. (1987), 'Cross-National Research as an Analytic Strategy', *American Sociological Review*, **52** (6), 713–731.

Lindbeck, A. (2001), *Unemployment: Structural. International Encyclopaedia of the Social & Behavioral Sciences.* Amsterdam: Elsevier, pp. 15952–15958.

Lindbeck, A. and D.J. Snower (1988), *The Insider–Outsider Theory of Employment and Unemployment.* Cambridge, MA and London: MIT Press.

Mood, C. (2010), 'Logistic Regression: Why We Cannot Do What We Think We Can Do, and What We Can Do About It', *European Sociological Review,* **26** (1), 67–82.

Nickell, S. (1997), 'Unemployment and Labor Market Rigidities: Europe Versus North America', *Journal of Economic Perspectives*, **11** (3), 55–74.

OECD (2011), *Economic Outlook.* Paris: OECD.

OECD (2013), *Employment Outlook.* Paris: OECD.

Palier, B. and K. Thelen (2010), 'Institutionalizing Dualism: Complementarities and Change in France and Germany', *Politics and Society*, **38** (1), 119–148.

Rabe-Hesketh, S. and A. Skrondal (2008), *Multilevel and Longitudinal Modeling Using Stata.* College Station, TX: STATA Press.

Reich, M., D.M. Gordon and R.C. Edwards (1973), 'A Theory of Labor Market Segmentation', *The American Economic Review*, **63** (2), 359–365.

Rueda, D. (2007), *Social Democracy Inside Out.* Oxford: Oxford University Press.

Rueda, D. (2014), 'Dualization, Crisis and the Welfare State', *Socio-Economic Review*, **12** (2), 381–407.

Saint-Paul, G. (1996), *Dual Labor Markets: A Macroeconomic Perspective.* Cambridge, MA: MIT Press.

Schwander, H. and S. Häusermann (2013), 'Who Is In and Who Is Out? A

Risk-based Conceptualization of Insiders and Outsiders', *Journal of European Social Policy*, **23** (3), 248–269.

Siebert, H. (1997), 'Labor Market Rigidities: At the Root of Unemployment in Europe', *The Journal of Economic Perspectives*, **11** (3), 37–54.

Tepe, M. and P. Vanhuysse (2013), 'Parties, Unions, and Activation Strategies: The Context-Dependent Politics of Active Labor Market Policy Spending', *Political Studies*, **61** (3), 480–504.

Venn, D. (2012), 'Eligibility Criteria for Unemployment Benefits: Quantitative Indicators for OECD and EU Countries'. OECD Social, Employment and Migration Working Papers: 131. Paris: OECD.

Weishaupt, J.T. (2011), *From the Manpower Revolution to the Activation Paradigm: Explaining Institutional Continuity and Change in an Integrating Europe.* Amsterdam: Amsterdam University Press.

APPENDIX

Table 4A.1 Short-term unemployment risks of the employed (2005–2013)

	2005	2006	2007	2008	2009	2010	2011	2012	2013
Women	-0.000	-0.000	-0.001	-0.003**	-0.010**	-0.008**	-0.006**	-0.006**	-0.005**
	(-0.25)	(-0.52)	(-1.60)	(-4.99)	(-15.12)	(-11.65)	(-9.08)	(-8.69)	(-8.40)
Age group (ref.: 25–54 years)									
15 to 24 years	0.001	0.003**	0.001	0.001	0.009**	0.005**	0.005**	0.000	-0.002
	(0.80)	(2.88)	(0.73)	(0.56)	(6.31)	(3.47)	(3.77)	(0.12)	(-1.60)
55 years +	-0.024**	-0.022**	-0.017**	-0.024**	-0.037**	-0.034**	-0.031**	-0.030**	-0.030**
	(-29.70)	(-30.42)	(-28.75)	(-33.17)	(-43.64)	(-40.97)	(-37.72)	(-36.72)	(-37.09)
Household type (ref.: adults with children)									
One-person household	0.002+	0.001	0.004**	0.004**	0.003*	0.002*	0.003*	0.002	0.004**
	(1.78)	(1.21)	(4.64)	(3.39)	(2.55)	(2.13)	(2.41)	(1.37)	(3.56)
Adults, no child	0.002*	0.003**	0.002**	0.002**	0.004**	0.003**	0.003**	0.002**	0.003**
	(2.56)	(5.01)	(4.16)	(3.27)	(5.20)	(4.51)	(4.17)	(3.32)	(3.80)
Single-parent household	0.006**	0.008**	0.009**	0.009**	0.011**	0.010**	0.011**	0.007**	0.007**
	(3.45)	(5.12)	(6.67)	(5.39)	(5.65)	(5.51)	(5.91)	(4.05)	(4.04)
Foreign nationality or born abroad	0.005**	0.005**	0.004**	0.003**	0.012**	0.010**	0.009**	0.008**	0.006**
	(4.31)	(4.72)	(5.32)	(2.97)	(9.64)	(8.41)	(7.71)	(6.81)	(5.17)
Health	0.001**	0.002**	0.001**	0.002**	0.001	0.000	0.001+	0.000	0.000
	(3.18)	(5.97)	(3.25)	(6.19)	(1.43)	(0.48)	(1.83)	(0.43)	(0.77)
Educational level (ref.: high)									
Low	0.004**	0.005**	0.004**	0.006**	0.009**	0.004**	0.005**	0.003**	0.002*
	(3.61)	(4.98)	(4.40)	(6.07)	(7.05)	(3.71)	(4.36)	(2.90)	(1.98)

101

Table 4A.1 (continued)

	2005	2006	2007	2008	2009	2010	2011	2012	2013
Medium	0.002	0.002**	0.003**	0.004**	0.004**	0.003*	0.003**	0.002+	0.001
	(1.62)	(2.70)	(3.63)	(4.53)	(3.69)	(2.50)	(2.84)	(1.81)	(0.99)
ISCO skill levels (ref.: operating, repair, information processing (2))									
Simple tasks (1)	0.000	0.000	0.002*	0.003**	0.001	0.000	0.004**	0.006**	0.007**
	(0.33)	(0.00)	(2.41)	(4.17)	(1.20)	(0.00)	(4.26)	(6.54)	(6.87)
Complex tasks (3)	-0.010**	-0.006**	-0.006**	-0.009**	-0.013**	-0.012**	-0.011**	-0.010**	-0.009**
	(-9.57)	(-6.00)	(-7.26)	(-9.07)	(-11.86)	(-11.23)	(-10.42)	(-9.74)	(-8.58)
Problem-solving, decision-making, creativity (4)	-0.015**	-0.011**	-0.008**	-0.013**	-0.021**	-0.020**	-0.017**	-0.018**	-0.016**
	(-13.36)	(-10.64)	(-9.73)	(-12.55)	(-17.67)	(-17.82)	(-15.08)	(-16.88)	(-15.58)
Temporary job	0.047**	0.044**	0.036**	0.053**	0.068**	0.069**	0.068**	0.067**	0.059**
	(52.52)	(52.54)	(50.11)	(56.95)	(61.05)	(62.14)	(64.92)	(65.64)	(59.26)
Economic growth	-0.004	0.003	0.004	-0.000	-0.004**	-0.002**	-0.001	0.002	0.001
	(-0.72)	(0.84)	(1.34)	(-0.23)	(-2.71)	(-3.32)	(-1.42)	(1.03)	(0.43)
Employment level	-0.003*	-0.002	-0.001	-0.001	-0.001	-0.001*	-0.002**	-0.003**	-0.002*
	(-1.98)	(-1.51)	(-0.68)	(-1.18)	(-1.45)	(-2.08)	(-3.07)	(-2.90)	(-2.35)
Social protection	-0.005*	-0.002	0.001	-0.001*	-0.003**	-0.001	0.000	0.001	0.000
	(-2.49)	(-0.98)	(0.77)	(-2.20)	(-3.75)	(-1.03)	(0.01)	(0.56)	(0.08)
Unemployment replacement	-0.000	-0.000	0.000	0.000	0.000	0.000	0.000	0.000	0.001
	(-0.19)	(-0.91)	(0.30)	(0.43)	(0.90)	(1.08)	(1.30)	(1.38)	(1.52)

Employment protection	0.020*	0.020*	0.015*	−0.001	−0.004	−0.001	−0.002	0.017*	0.016+
	(2.04)	(2.53)	(2.32)	(−0.27)	(−0.65)	(−0.26)	(−0.51)	(2.07)	(1.70)
EPL difference permanent and temporary jobs	−0.005	−0.012*	−0.008*	0.000	0.006+	0.006*	0.007**	0.002	0.005
	(−0.81)	(−2.52)	(−2.00)	(0.19)	(1.69)	(2.27)	(2.94)	(0.55)	(1.07)
Union density	0.001**	0.001**	−0.000	0.000	0.000	0.000	0.000	0.000	0.000
	(2.64)	(2.91)	(−0.94)	(0.15)	(0.64)	(0.48)	(0.94)	(1.08)	(0.71)
No.	213048	228615	247844	255523	261682	279121	276908	274408	260739
Chi²	5016	5079	4660	6138	8588	8358	8589	8616	7343
Between-country variance	1,394	1,043	1,282	0,322	0,252	0,138	0,131	0,505	0,525
Variance (total)	4,684	4,333	4,572	3,612	3,542	3,427	3,421	3,795	3,815
Intra-class correlation	0,298	0,241	0,28	0,089	0,071	0,04	0,038	0,133	0,138
McFadden pseudo-R²	0,116	0,114	0,11	0,12	0,128	0,115	0,128	0,132	0,118
AIC	44468	44927	42621	50214	68619	71832	64199	62990	60799
BIC	44704	45165	42861	50454	68860	72074	64441	63232	61040
Log-likelihood	−22200	−22400	−21300	−25100	−34300	−35900	−32100	−31500	−30400

Notes and Source: Cf. Table 4.2.

Table 4A.2   Long-term unemployment risk of the unemployed in 26 European countries (2005–2013)

	2005	2006	2007	2008	2009	2010	2011	2012	2013
Women	0.024**	0.023*	0.026**	0.015	0.048**	0.015*	0.001	0.022**	0.015*
	(2.72)	(2.46)	(2.65)	(1.59)	(6.15)	(2.08)	(0.12)	(3.02)	(2.05)
Age group (ref.: 25–54 years)									
15 to 24 years	−0.148**	−0.177**	−0.141**	−0.130**	−0.121**	−0.123**	−0.147**	−0.126**	−0.101**
	(−10.50)	(−12.30)	(−9.13)	(−8.76)	(−10.31)	(−10.33)	(−11.42)	(−9.62)	(−7.51)
55 years +	0.110**	0.115**	0.103**	0.113**	0.122**	0.066**	0.065**	0.087**	0.088**
	(7.29)	(7.49)	(6.69)	(8.08)	(10.19)	(6.22)	(6.11)	(8.52)	(8.86)
Household type (ref.: adults with children)									
One-person household	0.013	0.028	−0.007	0.008	0.035*	0.059**	0.053**	0.072**	0.051**
	(0.71)	(1.55)	(−0.40)	(0.47)	(2.48)	(4.62)	(4.18)	(5.74)	(4.12)
Adults, no child	0.027**	0.009	0.002	0.021*	0.018*	0.020*	0.021**	0.026**	0.028**
	(2.88)	(0.86)	(0.23)	(2.06)	(2.20)	(2.55)	(2.59)	(3.26)	(3.52)
Single-parent household	0.032	−0.009	−0.005	0.015	0.011	0.013	−0.004	0.015	0.038*
	(1.43)	(−0.38)	(−0.22)	(0.68)	(0.53)	(0.70)	(−0.19)	(0.81)	(2.05)
Foreign nationality or born abroad	−0.008	0.009	−0.013	0.017	−0.026*	0.002	0.006	−0.001	0.008
	(−0.49)	(0.52)	(−0.76)	(1.06)	(−2.06)	(0.16)	(0.53)	(−0.11)	(0.69)
Health	0.039**	0.026**	0.046**	0.033**	0.055**	0.050**	0.047**	0.051**	0.041**
	(7.47)	(4.88)	(8.27)	(6.06)	(11.93)	(11.24)	(10.56)	(11.42)	(9.50)
Educational level (ref.: high)									
Low	0.120**	0.145**	0.119**	0.122**	0.109**	0.136**	0.122**	0.117**	0.134**
	(6.80)	(7.81)	(6.29)	(6.77)	(7.64)	(10.26)	(9.04)	(9.05)	(10.55)
Medium	0.080**	0.094**	0.059**	0.052**	0.055**	0.075**	0.071**	0.059**	0.074**
	(4.74)	(5.36)	(3.30)	(3.06)	(4.12)	(6.15)	(5.61)	(4.85)	(6.20)

ISCO skill levels (ref.: operating, repair, information processing (2))									
Simple tasks (1)	0.009	0.007	0.013	0.004	0.034**	0.034**	−0.002	−0.016+	−0.022*
	(0.86)	(0.62)	(1.07)	(0.40)	(3.66)	(3.71)	(−0.21)	(−1.84)	(−2.48)
Complex tasks (3)	−0.017	−0.026	−0.000	0.005	−0.006	−0.028*	−0.033*	−0.027*	−0.033**
	(−1.04)	(−1.55)	(−0.02)	(0.28)	(−0.43)	(−2.11)	(−2.39)	(−2.03)	(−2.59)
Problem-solving, decision-making, creativity (4)	−0.025	−0.018	−0.019	0.022	−0.020	−0.045**	−0.037*	−0.030+	−0.052**
	(−1.17)	(−0.84)	(−0.85)	(1.00)	(−1.13)	(−2.79)	(−2.34)	(−1.84)	(−3.33)
Temporary job	−0.101**	−0.100**	−0.115**	−0.115**	−0.055**	−0.064**	−0.086**	−0.087**	−0.065**
	(−10.73)	(−10.06)	(−11.02)	(−11.57)	(−6.58)	(−7.97)	(−10.75)	(−11.34)	(−8.60)
Economic growth	−0.004	0.010	0.007	−0.009	0.009	0.004	−0.001	0.002	0.023
	(−0.11)	(0.50)	(0.40)	(−1.11)	(0.95)	(0.69)	(−0.06)	(0.23)	(1.62)
Employment level	−0.017+	−0.013*	−0.013*	−0.015**	−0.019**	−0.020**	−0.015**	−0.019**	−0.021**
	(−1.82)	(−2.02)	(−2.35)	(−2.89)	(−3.75)	(−3.95)	(−2.62)	(−3.61)	(−4.19)
Social protection	0.006	0.002	0.007	0.003	0.008+	0.007	0.003	0.002	0.005
	(0.54)	(0.21)	(0.84)	(0.62)	(1.88)	(1.44)	(0.51)	(0.41)	(1.05)
Unemployment replacement	−0.003	−0.004+	−0.004	−0.003	−0.001	−0.001	−0.002	−0.002	−0.003
	(−0.89)	(−1.67)	(−1.58)	(−1.64)	(−0.52)	(−0.56)	(−0.86)	(−1.21)	(−1.60)
Employment protection	0.010	0.005	−0.029	−0.011	−0.058	−0.057	−0.043	−0.003	0.047
	(0.16)	(0.10)	(−0.67)	(−0.24)	(−1.54)	(−1.56)	(−1.01)	(−0.06)	(0.89)
EPL difference permanent and temporary jobs	−0.009	0.009	0.028	0.048*	0.035	0.022	0.013	0.019	0.021
	(−0.24)	(0.30)	(1.08)	(2.06)	(1.46)	(0.95)	(0.54)	(0.78)	(0.91)

Table 4A.2 (continued)

	2005	2006	2007	2008	2009	2010	2011	2012	2013
Union density	-0.007*	-0.001	-0.001	-0.000	0.000	0.001	-0.000	0.000	0.001
	(-2.44)	(-0.50)	(-0.60)	(-0.29)	(0.30)	(0.40)	(-0.24)	(0.32)	(1.09)
No.	12043	11602	10443	11418	15909	18756	18512	18970	18833
Chi²	642	630	582	586	835	816	796	900	764
Between-country variance	0.463	0.205	0.207	0.21	0.206	0.18	0.221	0.199	0.183
Variance (total)	3.753	3.495	3.497	3.5	3.496	3.47	3.511	3.488	3.473
Intra-class correlation	0.123	0.059	0.059	0.06	0.059	0.052	0.063	0.057	0.053
McFadden pseudo-R²	0.704	0.71	0.722	0.747	0.749	0.698	0.673	0.664	0.651
AIC	14902	14760	13336	14492	19815	24566	24094	24428	24110
BIC	15072	14929	13503	14661	19992	24746	24274	24609	24291
Log-likelihood	-7428	-7357	-6645	-7223	-9885	-12300	-12000	-12200	-12000

Notes and Source: Cf. Table 4.2.

5. Women as the relative winners of the eurozone crisis? Female employment opportunities between austerity, inclusion and dualization[1]

Martin Heidenreich

The eurozone crisis resulted in a sharp increase in EU unemployment rates (March 2008: 6.7 per cent; March 2013: 11 per cent). This labour market crisis led to a double dualization; firstly between European countries (especially between Northern and Southern Europe), and secondly between different occupational groups, as younger people, migrants, temporary and low-skilled employees are mostly hidden by the crisis (cf. Chapter 4). Another social group that usually plays an essential role in secondary labour markets and is therefore often used as a buffer during cyclical downturns is women. Their unemployment rate also increased strongly (from 8.1 per cent to 11 per cent in the same period). Therefore, it can be expected that women are seriously and negatively affected by the eurozone crisis. This is the major thesis of a recent, comprehensive overview on the employment and social situation of women during this crisis:

> Austerity is expected to have negative effects not only on demand for female labour but also on access to services that support women as carers, thereby often compelling them to substitute for cutbacks through increasing unpaid domestic labour ... austerity undermines women's progress towards equality in paid work and economic independence and may provoke an ideological backlash favouring a return to traditional gender roles and backward-looking gender contracts. (Karamessini 2014: 4, 14)

However, other studies reach a much more positive conclusion. Ostner et al. (2013: 70), for example, state that 'Germany has for the most part moved away from the male breadwinner model and its underpinnings.' In a similar vein, Dingeldey (2015: 4) describes the diffusion of a modernized breadwinner model based on the 'combination of male standard employment relationship and female part-time employment' as a 'marriage of flexibility and security on the household level'.

In contrast to pessimistic expectations, I argue that women are on the one hand the relative winners of the eurozone crisis, since their relative employment opportunities have improved considerably during the crisis. Especially in the countries with the most traditional gender relations, namely in the Southern European countries, the crisis has contributed considerably to the erosion of the male breadwinner model because women are increasingly obliged to participate in the labour market. However, this does not imply that women will be employed under the same conditions as men in highly industrialized societies, i.e. enjoying stable jobs, with high, collectively-agreed remuneration and permanent and full-time contracts. New jobs are often part time or temporary and low paid. This can be seen as an indicator of gender inequality, as industrial jobs for low-skilled, often male employees are generally better paid and better protected. However, it is also an indicator of the transformation of the labour market and employment structures, especially in the service sector – a transformation which greatly advantages some women yet disadvantages others due to low-paid, instable and burdensome jobs. While men are often employed in shrinking sectors with stable employment relations and decent wages (e.g. construction and manufacturing), low-skilled women are often employed in growing sectors with low wages and atypical employment relations, for example in trade, hotels or food processing.

In the following section, the debate on the employment situation of European women during the financial, sovereign debt and economic crisis since 2008 is briefly reviewed. On this basis I propose three hypotheses (section 1). The austerity, inclusion and dualization theses are first discussed on the basis of aggregated outcome indicators at the level of the five classical employment regimes in Europe (section 2). As a next step, these hypotheses are re-specified for the micro-level and discussed in the light of micro-data on the flows from unemployment and inactivity to employment and on the composition of low-paid employees (section 3). The chapter concludes with a short summary (section 4).

5.1 FEMALE EMPLOYMENT BETWEEN AUSTERITY, INCLUSION AND DUALIZATION

The eurozone crisis has hit the Mediterranean countries especially, which are characterized by a high degree of familialism, rudimentary welfare and employment regimes (Ferrera 1996), and a high level of segmentation between labour market insiders and outsiders. Even if the crisis has resulted in 'an important reduction in the level of security for labour market insiders both in employment and while unemployed' (Moreira et al. 2015: 219), it can be expected that women will have been particularly affected by the economic recession since 2008. As classical labour market outsiders (Doeringer and Piore 1971; Saint-Paul 1996), in times of crisis women might be relegated to their roles of wives, mothers and carers of their elderly parents (Karamessini 2014: 4; Broschinski 2015) – especially due to the austerity policies which have been imposed on the public sector in order to reduce the public debts of the EU Member States, and more particularly the countries of the eurozone that can no longer rely on monetary devaluation. *Formulated as a hypothesis: The austerity policies that followed the Great Recession and the eurozone crisis have stabilized classical male breadwinner models and resulted in the return of women to their roles within the family. A relative increase in female unemployment rates and a relative decrease in female employment rates can be expected – also due to major cuts in public administration, health, education and social services, which are important employment segments for women (H1).*

Alternatively, it can also be expected that the general pattern of increasing employment rates already observed before the crisis will continue. The trend towards dual-earner models will in particular continue due to women's increasing formal qualifications and labour market orientations and the related cultural changes towards more egalitarian gender models and more individualistic private living forms: '(T)he whole system shifts from a family wage economy to an individual wage economy' (Drobnič and Blossfeld 2001: 380). Paradoxically, gender segregated employment relations can also contribute to such an increase when a cyclical downswing mostly affects the classical employment domains of male employees, for example manufacturing jobs, and the concentration of women in personal and social services, for example education and public administration: 'Segregation may protect women against job loss by shielding them from competition from men' (Rubery and Rafferty 2013: 416). *Thus, it can be expected that educational expansion, changing gender models, increasing service sector employment and continuing gender segregation of the labour market will lead to higher female employment rates. This trend towards inclusive employment regimes will be reflected in high female employment and low unemployment rates (H2).*

However, a shift towards an inclusive employment regime might be associated with a further erosion of stable, well-paid and secure jobs. This has been described as a politically induced *dualization* which deepens the segmentation of the labour market, especially along qualification and occupational lines (Emmenegger et al. 2012; Schwander and Häusermann 2013). This dualization also has a gender dimension, since women both benefit and suffer disproportionately from the diffusion of precarious jobs. This has been demonstrated in the case of Germany, where Dingeldey (2015) observed the emergence of the modernized dual breadwinner model characterized by 'a high level of flexible employment and a high incidence of low wage employment . . . high wage differentials between male and female dominated sectors and professions are accepted to support low-cost and low-wage employment in (social) services' (Dingeldey 2015: 18). The increasing labour market participation of women (often due to the creation of jobs in the service sector), may thus be linked to the creation of more flexible, non-standard employment relations characterized by low pay and higher uncertainty and instability (Blossfeld and Hofmeister 2006). A retrenchment of public services as a consequence of the austerity policies may also contribute to such a dualization: '(T)he deterioration of men's position during the first phase of the crisis may be reversed since the full implementation of austerity is likely to harm women's employment position relatively more' (Karamessini and Rubery 2014b: 16–17). *On the basis of this dualization and precarization debate, it can be expected that the increasing inclusion of women in the labour market is also linked to a dualization of their employment opportunities and conditions. Indicators would be a high share of highly qualified women (often in demanding service jobs) accompanied by a concentration of women in low-paid jobs and non-standard employment relations (H3).*

On the basis of these austerity, inclusion and dualization hypotheses, the patterns and evolutions of female employment and unemployment are discussed in the following section on the basis of aggregated data at the macro-level.

5.2   REGIME-SPECIFIC FEMALE EMPLOYMENT PATTERNS DURING THE EUROZONE CRISIS: AGGREGATED EVIDENCE

In this section, I will discuss the previously developed theses on the basis of aggregated, regime-specific indicators[2] in order to show the weak empirical evidence of the austerity thesis, the mixed evidence for the dualization thesis and the convincing evidence for the inclusion thesis.

The first indicator which could be interpreted as supporting the austerity thesis would be the declining employment rate of women and the growing difference between the employment rates of men and women. In the EU, however, the employment rate of women increased between 2008 and 2014 – even though a clear decline of more than one percentage point could be observed in ten predominantly Mediterranean countries (BG, HR, PT, NL, IE, ES, SI, DK, CY and EL). However, especially in the Southern European countries, a declining difference between male and female employment rates can be observed, even though these countries are the most strongly hidden

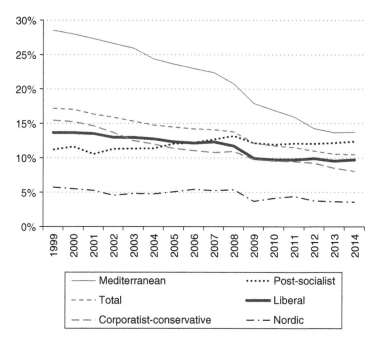

Source: Eurostat, table [lfsa_ergan]; own elaborations.

Figure 5.1 Difference between the male and female employment rate weighted by and in per cent of population from 15 to 64 years (1999–2014, EU-28)

by austerity policies (Figure 5.1). These countries are characterized by more traditional gender relations (Ferrera 1996). The decreasing difference between male and female employment rates indicates a durable cultural and economic modernization, particularly of the Southern European countries. For example, in Spain this gap has been reduced from 31 per cent (1999) to 9.5 per cent (2014). Traditional gender relations and forms of labour market segmentation are thus not only eroded by the previously described secular trends (educational expansion, tertiarization, changing family values), but also by the crisis. Bettio and Verashchagina (2014) recall the 'added worker effect', i.e. the counter-cyclical employment strategies of women, who especially increase their employment offer in times of crisis in order to maintain household income or when the male breadwinner has lost his job. This does not imply that women are completely protected from the employment effects of the economic crisis which has hit the European countries since 2009. On the contrary, female employment rates are still lower in Southern

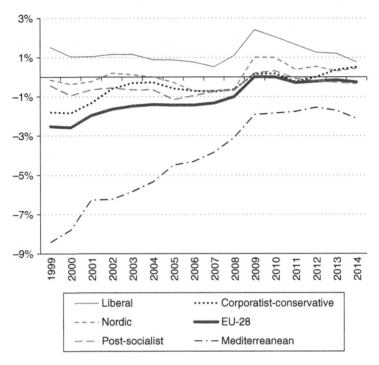

Source: Eurostat, table [lfsa_urgaed]; own elaborations.

Figure 5.2   *Difference between the unemployment rates of men and women (as a percentage of the labour force, 1999–2014, EU-28)*

Europe than in the rest of Europe (for example 46.8 per cent in Italy and 41.1 per cent in Greece in 2014 – in contrast to 59.5 per cent in the EU-28) and they have declined since 2008. But since the introduction of the euro and despite the eurozone crisis, female employment rates increased in, for example, Spain by 13 per cent and Italy by 8.7 per cent.

   The gap between the gender-specific unemployment rates, which especially decreases in Southern Europe, shows a similar pattern (Figure 5.2). The continuing reduction of the employment and unemployment gaps between men and women indicates a secular cultural and institutional modernization process which is facilitating the inclusion of women into the labour market due to higher qualifications, a higher employment share of service activities and the evolution of gender roles and stereotypes. Rubery (2014: 32–33), for example, observes a 'long-term and persistent change in both women's aspirations and labour market activities and in the

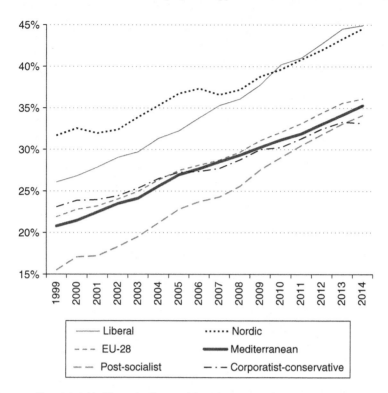

Source: Eurostat, table [lfsa_egised]; own elaborations.

Figure 5.3 *Women with a tertiary education as a percentage of total female employment (15–64 years)*

associated organization of the family economy and relations'. This indicates that the shift from a male breadwinner model to a dual-earner career of men and women has also continued during the eurozone crisis (cf. also Bettio and Verashchagina 2014: 70).

A major reason for the continuing inclusion of women in the labour market (especially in the Southern European countries most strongly hidden by the crisis) is the higher qualification of women. While in the EU-28, 30 per cent of male employees had a tertiary education in 2014, the corresponding share of women was 35.9 per cent. This share increased in all the European welfare regimes (Figure 5.3). However, this does not mean that all highly skilled women in Southern European countries find a job; in fact, their employment rate is also declining.

One indicator for the compensatory increase of the labour supply is an

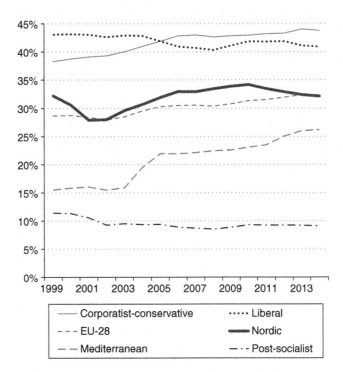

Note: Female part-time employment as percentage of the total female employment (15 to 64 years), weighted by the level of female employment.

Source: Eurostat, table [lfsa_ eppga]; own elaborations.

Figure 5.4   Female part-time employment (%; EU-28; 1999–2014)

increasing share of female part-time employment especially in the countries which have been most strongly hit by the crisis. The 'added worker thesis', which predicts an increasing labour supply when the (usually male) head of a household loses his job (Bettio and Verashchagina 2014), can be especially observed in Southern European countries, where the share of female part-time workers is strongly increasing (Figure 5.4). At the same time, women in Southern Europe increasingly say that they are working part time because they are unable to find full-time work. This indicates both the economic necessity for the comprehensive inclusion of women in the labour market and the changing gender roles and expectations of women. More than 60 per cent of the Greek, Spanish and Italian women who are currently employed on a part-time basis are looking for a full-time job (Figure 5.5). The decreasing difference between the aspirations of men

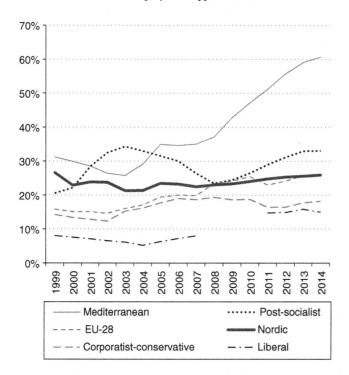

Note: The data are weighted by number of female part-time employees. People working on an involuntary part-time basis are those who declare that they work part time because they are unable to find full-time work.

Source: Eurostat, table [lfsa_eppgai]; own elaborations.

Figure 5.5 Involuntary female part-time employment as percentage of the total female part-time employment (1999–2014; EU-28)

and women show that the shift from a male breadwinner model to a dual-earner career of men and women is especially continuing in the Southern European countries – despite the declining employment rates of women.

The continuing inclusion of women in the labour market is also the outcome of a sectoral shift towards service activities (Karamessini and Rubery 2014b: 21). Two of the most important sectors with declining employment – the manufacturing and construction industries – are dominated by male employees, while growing sectors are characterized by a high share of female employees. Women account for 47.7 per cent of employees in professional and administrative work, 72 per cent in education and 74.3 per cent in health and social work (Table 5.1). In the

Table 5.1 Employment by sex and economic activity (2008–2014; EU-28)

EU-28	Sectoral share in % of total employment		Employment change	Share of women in sectoral employment		Sectoral share in % of male employment		Sectoral share in % of female employment	
Year	2008	2014	2008–2014	2008	2014	2008	2014	2008	2014
Manufacturing, agriculture, mining, water, electricity	23.8	21.9	-4.1	31.1	29.8	29.8	28.4	16.5	14.2
Construction	8.4	6.8	-20.9	9.1	9.8	13.9	11.4	1.7	1.5
Wholesale and retail trade; repair of motor vehicles and motorcycles	14.2	14.0	-3.9	49.6	49.3	13.0	13.2	15.7	15.0
Transportation, accommodation	9.5	9.7	0.0	37.3	37.5	10.8	11.3	7.8	7.9
Communication, finance, real estate	6.6	6.7	0.2	43.6	42.2	6.7	7.2	6.4	6.2
Professional, administrative and technical activities	8.3	9.5	11.5	48.4	47.7	7.8	9.2	8.9	9.8
Public administration, defence, social security, exterritorial org.	7.6	7.7	-1.3	45.7	46.4	7.5	7.6	7.7	7.7
Education	7.0	7.6	6.0	71.4	72.0	3.6	4.0	11.1	11.9
Health, social work, entertainment, households, other	14.7	16.1	6.9	74.0	74.3	6.9	7.7	24.1	25.9
Total	100	100	-2.5	44.9	46.1	100	100	100	100

Source: Eurostat, table [lfsa_egan2], own elaborations.

case of public administration, Karamessini and Rubery (2014b) expect a shrinking share due to European-wide austerity policies. Empirically, however, the employment share of this sector in which 46.4 per cent of employees are women remains broadly stable, at least when all of the EU countries are viewed together (–1.3 per cent from 2008 to 2014). The most important sector in which a quarter of all employed women are working – health and social work – is in fact growing (6.9 per cent between 2008 and 2014). Approximately 35 per cent of all employed women in Scandinavia, 29 per cent in continental European and liberal countries, 24 per cent in Southern European countries and 15 per cent in Eastern European countries are working in this sector. This shows that women are not affected above average by the negative labour market effects of austerity policies.

Previous studies have demonstrated convincingly that the shift from a male breadwinner model to a dual-earner career of men and women is accompanied by gender-related segmentation of the labour market. Women are often employed in the secondary labour market, which might imply a concentration in low-paid and low-level jobs (Blossfeld and Hakim 1997; Blossfeld and Hofmeister 2006). This is still true. According to Eurostat [earn_ses_pub1s], 13.3 per cent of all male and 21 per cent of female employees earned two-thirds or less of the national median gross hourly earnings in 2010. This shows that despite the high qualification of women and their privileged access to expanding economic activities, women are still over-represented in low-wage jobs. The reasons for this puzzling phenomenon which is at the core of the dualization thesis cannot be discussed sufficiently on the basis of aggregated data. Therefore, in the following section this issue is analysed on the basis of micro-data.

In sum, women are increasingly included in the labour market. The declining gender gap between the employment and unemployment rates of men and women has continued during the current crisis (also due to the expansion of further education, increasing care facilities for children and elderly people and changing gender roles). This transformation into an inclusive employment regime has also been accelerated by the crisis in Southern Europe, which has been a laggard in the transformation from a male breadwinner to a dual-earner model. Rather than being simply a short-term reaction to increasing pressures to take up a job when another household member becomes unemployed, the increasing share of involuntary part-time workers in the Mediterranean countries may perhaps indicate a far-reaching transformation of gender relations, especially in Greece, Spain and Italy.

Up to now I have discussed the employment situation of women on the basis of the aggregated employment data provided by Eurostat in order to test the austerity, the inclusion and the dualization theses. However, such an approach has three shortcomings. Firstly, the interaction of the different individual and job-related variables (age, citizenship and migration background, private living forms, level of education, sectoral employment, employment and contractual forms, wages, etc.) cannot be thoroughly analysed on the basis of aggregated data alone. For example, private living conditions, which shape the decisions to take up a job and/or to accept low wages and their interactions with other factors relating to the demand side of the labour market can hardly be analysed on the basis of aggregated data. Secondly, the reported employment figures for one year are the result of dynamic processes in which inactive and unemployed people take up a job ('inflows') while other people take up a new job ('mobility') or are dismissed and become unemployed or inactive ('outflows'). Thirdly, the relationship between aggregated supply and demand-side indicators and contextual factors is often analysed by correlation analyses or scatterplots on the macro-level. However, the interpretation of correlations between macro-data usually implies ecological fallacies, i.e. assumptions about causal relations on the individual or household level which cannot be deduced from correlations at the macro-level. Therefore, in the following I will discuss two questions on the basis of micro-data: Which previously unemployed or inactive women have decided and have been able to take up a new job before and during the financial and sovereign debt crisis? And which women have had to accept low-wage jobs?

5.3   EMPLOYMENT AND EARNINGS OPPORTUNITIES OF WOMEN BEFORE AND DURING THE CRISIS

5.3.1   Hypotheses, Data and Methods

The employment situation of women is first of all determined by individual job searches and by organizational recruitment decisions, i.e. by the decisions of women to look for paid employment and by employers to offer them a job. An important indicator of these decisions is the flows from inactivity and unemployment to employment; another would be the flows from one job to another, which, however, cannot be directly measured on the basis of EU-SILC. The characteristics of the people who enter the employment system after having been unemployed or inactive are an indicator of the types of jobs in which women are interested and for which they can successfully apply. In addition, this reflects the recruitment criteria of employers. These movements from unemployment and inactivity to employment reflect very different situations. It might reflect the transition from one job to another (interrupted by a short unemployment spell); it may be one phase in an unstable working life characterized by temporary jobs, seasonal work and self-employment; it may indicate the entrance of a previously inactive person into the labour market after school, the birth of a child or other forms of home work, or it may reflect the successful job search of an unemployed person. As a group of reference I chose employed women (and not inactive, unemployed or all women) because I am interested in the question of which women successfully enter the labour market – and not which women with which characteristics can be success- fully activated for the labour market. In this way the characteristics of the employees who have successfully applied for a job can be established. In particular, their qualifications, a possible migration background and their private living situations (type of households, age of the youngest child) as indicators of possible care responsibilities and the characteristics of the jobs they attain (permanent or temporary, part or full time, occupational level, economic sector) are taken into account.

An essential dimension of these employment opportunities is the quality of the job. Even though this quality is a complex and multidimensional phenomenon, there is broad agreement that the level of remuneration is an essential criterion. Low wages are considered to be essential characteristics of bad jobs (Kalleberg 2011: 10). Therefore, in a second step, I analyse in more detail which women with which individual, household-related and occupational criteria influence the likelihood of receiving low pay.

Both the employment opportunities and the likelihood of having a low-paid job are determined by the characteristics of the employed women (demand side of the labour market) as well as by the particularities of the job (supply side of the labour market). By transferring the previously developed inclusion and dualization theses H2 and H3 to the micro-level, the following two hypotheses can be formulated: *Firstly, it can be expected that higher-skilled, native and healthy women in the core age group (25–54 years) with no young children have better employment and earnings opportunities than low-skilled, ill women with a migration background and burdensome care responsibilities. Single parents with younger children will be particularly handicapped (demand-side hypothesis H2'). Most of the jobs will be offered in administrative, social and personal services, which will also offer – with the exception of public services – the highest share of low-paid and atypical jobs for both high- and low-skilled women (supply-side hypothesis H3').*

In addition, the national context is important for shaping both the employment opportunities of women and their wage level. In the exist- ing literature it has been pointed out that labour market regulations (Dingeldey 2015), equal pay and fair hiring regulations (Card et al. 2015), unions, family and care policies (cf. Christofides et al. 2013) and more generally the level of social security – which may be threatened by austerity policies (Karamessini and Rubery 2014a) – are important determinants of female labour market opportunities. In order to specify the initially developed austerity thesis H1 for the micro-level, *it can be expected that high social expenditures, good childcare facilities and a low level of austerity will have a positive effect on the employment opportunities and a negative effect on the likelihood of being low paid (H1')*.

These three hypotheses will be discussed on the basis of the latest available version (August 2015) of the cross-sectional EU-SILC data 2006–2013 for at least 24 European countries.[3] The impact of the three national context factors is taken into account on the basis of data provided by Eurostat (cf. Table 5.2). As the two dependent variables – the likelihood of unemployed and inactive women finding employment (in relation to all employed women) and the likelihood of employed women receiving low wages, i.e. wages lower than two-thirds of the average hourly earnings – are binary variables, a binary logistic regression is the suitable method of analysis (cf. Chapter 4 for more detail). Although the number of European countries for which relevant data are available is below 30 – the recommended minimum level for multi-level analysis (Bryan and Jenkins 2016: 18) – I will perform a multi-level logistic regression in order to exploit the potential of this method for analysing context effects. Similar to Chapter 4, the coefficients in the following tables are average marginal effects (AME) which express the average effect of the respective category of the independent variable on the dependent variable in comparison to the reference category (Mood 2010). Only in Table 5.4 are odds ratios used because they are more suited for dealing with the multiplicative logic of interaction effects (Buis 2010).

The first step looks at the characteristics of employed women who have successfully looked for a job in the previous year (Table 5.3), while the second step analyses the likelihood of having a low-paid job (Table 5.5) – both times in relation to all the employed women. In both cases the likelihood of getting a job or being unemployed is calculated on the basis of the years from 2006 to 2013, i.e. three years before and five years during the crisis. In addition, the models were also calculated for men (only for 2013; column 9) and for the six countries most strongly affected by the financial, economic and sovereign debt crisis (only for 2013; column 10). These 'crisis countries' (CC) are the five members of the eurozone that had to accept bailout programmes (Cyprus, Greece, Ireland, Portugal and Spain) and Italy. According to the IMF (2015), these countries have been characterized by high borrowing spreads during the European sovereign debt crisis. Following the suggestions of Bryan and Jenkins (2016),

Table 5.2 *The variables used, their operationalization and their expected and observed effects*

Hypothesis	Variable	Operationalization	Data Source	Expected		Observed	
				Em	Lo	Em	Lo
(dep.)	Entry into employment	Likelihood of inactive and unemployed women to find a new job: employed women who were unemployed or inactive for at least one month in the previous year (in relation to all currently employed women (1: previously unemployed or inactive; 0: employed 12 months in the previous year)	EU-SILC (pl030, pl031, pl080, pl090, pl073-pl076)				
(dep.)	Low pay	Two-thirds of the hourly median gross cash income for workers for which the number of hours usually worked per week is available (without apprentices, in relation to all employed women) (1: low pay; 0: higher wage).	EU-SILC (py010g, py010n, pl060, pl100, pl030, pl031, pe010)				
H2'	Age class	1: '15-24 years'; 2: '25 to 54 years' (ref. category); 3 '55 years and older'	EU-SILC (rx020)	+(1)	+(1)	+(1)	+(1)
H2'	Young child	0: 'No child'; 1: 'Younger than 7 years'	EU-SILC (rx020, rb210)	–	+	0	(+)
H2'	Household type	1: 'One person household'; 2: 'Adults, no children'; 3: 'Single parent household'; 4: 'Adults with children'; ref. category	EU-SILC (hx060)	–(3)	+(3)	0(3)	–(3)
H2'	Unemployed in household	At least one unemployed person in household	EU-SILC (pl030, pl031)		+		+
H2'	Migration status	Foreign nationality or born abroad (0: domestic origin (ref. category); 1: foreign origin)	EU-SILC (pb210 (a)	–	+	0	+
H2'	Health	Self-perceived health (1: 'very good'; 2: 'good'; 3: 'fair'; 4: 'bad'; 5: 'very bad')	EU-SILC (ph010)	–	+	0	+

Table 5.2 (continued)

Hypothesis	Variable	Operationalization	Data Source	Expected		Observed	
				Em	Lo	Em	Lo
H2'	Educational level	Highest ISCED level attained (3: Tertiary education – levels 5–6; 2: Upper secondary and post-secondary non-tertiary education (3–4); 1: Pre-primary, primary and lower secondary education (0–2; ref. category)	EU-SILC (pe040)	+(3)	−(3)	+(3)	−(3)
H3'	Occupational skill level (ISCO08)	1: 'simple and routine physical or manual tasks'; 2: 'operating machinery and electronic equipment; driving vehicles; maintenance and repair, manipulation, ordering and storage of information' (ref. category); 3: 'complex technical and practical tasks'; 4: 'problem-solving, decision-making, creativity' (ILO 2012: 12–13)	EU-SILC (pl050; pl051)	+(4)	−(4)	−(4)	−(4)
H3'	Economic activity	Economic activity of the local unit of the main job for respondents who are currently at work (NACE Rev. 1.1/2 since 2008). 1: 'manufacturing, agriculture, mining, water, electricity, construction' (ref.); 2: 'trade, accommodation and food service activities' 3: 'transportation and storage; information and communication' 4: 'finance and insurance; real estate, professional, scientific and technical, administrative and support services'; 5: 'public administration, education, health and social work; arts, entertainment and recreation'	EU-SILC (pl110, pl111)	+(5)	+(5)	−(5)	−(5)

122

Hyp.	Variable	Description	Data source			
H3'	Part-time employment	1: 'full-time job' (ref. category); 2: 'part-time job'	EU-SILC (pl030, pl031)	+	+	+
H3'	Type of contract	1: 'permanent job' (ref. category); 2: 'temporary job'	EU-SILC (pl140)	+	+	+
H1'	Social protection	National social protection expenditure includes social benefits, administration costs and other expenditure linked to social protection schemes (% of GDP) (contextual variable)	Eurostat (ESSPROS)	–	–	–
H1'	Fiscal austerity	Change of national primary public balance in comparison to previous year (in % of GDP)	Eurostat [gov_10a_main]	–	+	0
H1'	Family benefits in kind	Social protections expenditures for families and children in kind (in % of GDP)	Eurostat [spr_exp_ffa]	+	–	0

Note: 'dep.' refers to the dependent variables. The expected and observed effects refer to the likelihood of finding an employment (column: em) respective of having a low wage (column: lo) – in both cases in relation to all employed women. '+' refers to an effect significantly different from zero, '–' refers to an effect significantly lower than zero; '0' to an effect that does not differ significantly from zero.

the last model was calculated as a logistic regression with cluster-robust standard errors.

5.3.2   Results

The models in Table 5.3 first of all show the clear *age* bias of employment opportunities. Younger women have a much higher likelihood of finding a job than older women – with the exception of 2009 and 2010 when production sharply declined in nearly all the EU countries. The ninth column indicates that this is not a gender-specific phenomenon; younger men also have much better employment opportunities than men in the core age groups. The comparison of models 8 and 10 shows that the (re-)employment opportunities of younger women are higher in the 28 EU countries than in the six crisis countries (10.8 in contrast to 6.5 percentage points), while the employment chances of *older women* are much lower in the EU-28 and in the crisis countries (−2.4 respective 3.5 percentage points). In comparison with the employment opportunities of *couples with children*, single women and adults without children (but surprisingly not single parents) have lower employment opportunities – an indicator of the strong economic necessity for this type of family to find a job. Single men (and the few male single parents) have better employment opportunities than single women. The employment opportunities in the countries most affected by the crisis are significantly worse for all household types beyond the classical constellation of couples with children – an indicator of the primacy of the male breadwinner model. Surprisingly, the employment opportunities of *migrants* are not worse than that of the native population – perhaps because migrants are prepared to accept all types of jobs or because their fluctuation is higher (I am observing flows, not stocks).

For *highly skilled women* it has been easier to find a new job in most of the years since the crisis began (with the exception of the years 2008 to 2010). The better employment opportunities of highly skilled women before and during the crisis reflect the dualization of the labour market, especially along educational lines (Emmenegger et al. 2012; Schwander and Häusermann 2013) (H3'). This effect is much stronger than the corresponding effects for men. This indicates a more meritocratic and thus more 'modern' occupational and qualification-related profile of women, who are mostly employed in service activities in which collective forms of employment status and income protection are less important. Surprisingly, medium-skilled women generally have worse employment opportunities than low-skilled women – perhaps an additional indicator of the dualization of female employment opportunities. This would also explain the relative difficulties of women in attaining positions with complex and problem-solving tasks. Furthermore, due to the higher fluctuation, it is much easier to find simple jobs.

Another question is in which *industrial sectors* women find their new jobs. The answer is surprising: it is not the sectors with the highest share of female employees – community, social and personal services or trade, restaurants and hotels – in fact, the manufacturing and construction industries are the sectors in which women most easily find a new job. This result can also be confirmed by a more detailed sectoral disaggregation of these results (not shown here). Only agriculture, construction, accommodation and professional services offer relatively better employment opportunities for women (always in relation to the number of women already employed in the sectors). Given the considerable employment growth of personal and social services even during the crisis (cf. Table 5.1) this result is completely unexpected and hard to explain. A possible explanation could only be a high fluctuation of female employees in the manufacturing industry who are often assigned to unattractive, stressful and burdensome secondary-market jobs. In crisis countries, the employment opportunities of younger women in community, social and personal services are clearly lower than in the other EU countries – perhaps an indicator of the negative employment effects of austerity policies, as expected by Karamessini and Rubery (2014a).

With the exception of 2009 and 2010, women who were prepared to accept *temporary and part-time jobs* had much higher employment opportunities (16.2 respective 3.2 percentage points in comparison to women who received a permanent contract respective to a full-time job). The reverse side of the inclusion of women in the labour market seems to be the acceptance of *part-time or fixed-term contracts*. In sum, these results can be interpreted as a specification of the conditions under which women are successfully included in the labour market (H2'): it is in particular younger and highly-skilled women that find a new job (especially a part-time or temporary job for simple tasks in the manufacturing industry and also in hotels). These results do not differ fundamentally from the employment opportunities of men.

Social expenditures only had a positive effect in some years (2006, 2009 and 2012) and austerity policies have had no effect on the employment opportunities of women – a result which clearly contradicts H1'. Surprisingly, family benefits in kind, i.e. childcare, likewise have no impact on these opportunities.

In addition, interaction effects between the age and type of contract have been included in the models reported in Table 5.3 (cf. Table 5.4). One result is a negative relationship between young age and temporary contracts (with the exception of 2009 and 2010), showing the clear negative

Table 5.3 Employment opportunities of women (and also men in 2013) previously unemployed or inactive (2006–2013; 24–28 European countries)

Entry employment	2006 (1)	2007 (2)	2008 (3)	2009 (4)	2010 (5)	2011 (6)	2012 (7)	2013 (8)	2013 (men; 9)	2013 (CC; 10)
Age group (ref.: 25–54 years)										
15 to 24 years	0.127**	0.121**	0.122**	0.006	0.001	0.110**	0.108**	0.108**	0.087**	0.065**
	(43.27)	(40.87)	(40.88)	(1.33)	(1.44)	(39.56)	(37.15)	(36.12)	(37.72)	(14.51)
55 years +	−0.031**	−0.036**	−0.026**	0.000	−0.000	−0.031**	−0.027**	−0.024**	−0.015**	−0.035**
	(−4.63)	(−6.87)	(−6.10)	(−0.28)	(−0.92)	(−8.20)	(−7.12)	(−5.99)	(−5.19)	(−4.87)
Young child	0.031*	0.012	0.046**	0.001	0.000	0.018	0.009	−0.003	−0.011	−0.008
	(2.36)	(0.85)	(4.06)	(0.45)	(0.09)	(1.47)	(0.70)	(−0.18)	(−0.88)	(−0.07)
Household type (ref.: adults with children)										
One-person household	−0.014**	−0.013**	−0.024**	0.001	0.001	−0.027**	−0.027**	−0.019**	0.011**	−0.022**
	(−3.25)	(−3.13)	(−5.59)	(1.58)	(1.21)	(−7.06)	(−7.01)	(−5.11)	(3.42)	(−2.94)
Adults, no child	−0.025**	−0.025**	−0.027**	−0.000	0.001*	−0.029**	−0.028**	−0.026**	0.005**	−0.013*
	(−9.80)	(−9.98)	(−10.86)	(−0.22)	(2.21)	(−12.54)	(−12.10)	(−11.37)	(2.65)	(−2.34)
Single-parent household	0.004	−0.007	−0.003	−0.000	0.000	−0.009*	−0.001	0.000	0.018+	−0.015*
	(0.75)	(−1.40)	(−0.54)	(−0.72)	(0.18)	(−2.08)	(−0.35)	(0.07)	(1.79)	(−2.27)
Foreign nationality or born abroad	−0.006	0.006	0.000	−0.000	−0.000	0.001	0.002	−0.006+	0.005	0.003
	(−1.53)	(1.49)	(0.09)	(−0.00)	(−0.68)	(0.26)	(0.49)	(−1.80)	(1.50)	(0.64)
Health	−0.001	0.001	0.003*	0.000	0.000	−0.001	0.002	0.003*	0.007**	0.002
	(−0.43)	(0.77)	(1.96)	(1.57)	(0.41)	(−0.82)	(1.63)	(2.11)	(5.08)	(0.34)

Educational level (ref.: low)

Medium								
−0.01**	−0.015**	0.001**	−0.000	−0.009**	−0.010**	−0.014**	−0.017**	−0.009*
(−3.13)	(−4.83)	(2.76)	(−0.20)	(−2.95)	(−3.25)	(−4.55)	(−6.61)	(−2.46)
High								
0.010*	0.003	0.000	0.000	0.016**	0.009*	0.008*	−0.004	0.010
(2.55)	(0.72)	(0.67)	(0.55)	(4.31)	(2.53)	(2.09)	(−1.13)	(0.43)
ISCO skill levels (ref.: operating, repair . . .)								
Simple tasks								
0.025**	0.016**	0.000	0.001*	0.014**	0.018**	0.023**	0.027**	0.033**
(7.74)	(4.85)	(0.45)	(2.23)	(4.61)	(5.95)	(7.37)	(9.89)	(10.37)
Complex tasks								
−0.019**	−0.013**	−0.000	0.000	−0.020**	−0.018**	−0.017**	−0.014**	−0.010
(−5.75)	(−4.08)	(−0.25)	(0.36)	(−6.40)	(−5.75)	(−5.40)	(−4.48)	(−0.47)
Problem-solving								
−0.029**	−0.030**	−0.000	−0.001+	−0.031**	−0.027**	−0.024**	−0.032**	−0.001
(−7.74)	(−7.78)	(−0.07)	(−1.88)	(−9.23)	(−8.03)	(−7.12)	(−9.25)	(−0.06)
Economic activity (ref. industry)								
Trade, restaurants, hotels								
0.016**	0.016**	−0.000	−0.000	0.003	0.011**	0.009**	0.006*	−0.005
(4.80)	(4.84)	(−1.16)	(−1.12)	(1.02)	(3.60)	(2.68)	(2.21)	(−0.48)
Transport, storage, communication								
−0.008	−0.008	−0.001*	−0.000	−0.009+	−0.005	−0.009+	−0.005	−0.006
(−1.27)	(−1.41)	(−2.03)	(−0.87)	(−1.78)	(−1.01)	(−1.72)	(−1.43)	(−0.95)
Financial and business services								
−0.006	0.007	−0.001	−0.000	−0.008*	−0.006	−0.005	0.004	−0.045**
(−1.46)	(1.63)	(−1.25)	(−0.26)	(−2.00)	(−1.61)	(−1.35)	(1.11)	(−8.03)
Community, social and personal services								
−0.029**	−0.016**	−0.000	0.000	−0.025**	−0.021**	−0.018**	−0.022**	−0.042**
(−9.22)	(−4.73)	(−0.34)	(0.22)	(−8.32)	(−7.04)	(−5.97)	(−7.90)	(−2.87)

Table 5.3 (continued)

Entry employment	2006 (1)	2007 (2)	2008 (3)	2009 (4)	2010 (5)	2011 (6)	2012 (7)	2013 (8)	2013 (men; 9)	2013 (CC; 10)
Part-time employment	0.050** (18.68)	0.044** (16.62)	0.044** (16.30)	-0.000 (-0.44)	-0.000 (-0.32)	0.039** (15.74)	0.037** (15.16)	0.032** (13.23)	0.041** (13.17)	0.013** (2.88)
Temporary job	0.173** (66.81)	0.166** (65.64)	0.160** (61.28)	-0.000** (-3.21)	-0.002** (-5.75)	0.162** (67.90)	0.163** (68.30)	0.162** (67.08)	0.148** (64.86)	0.182** (35.56)
Social protection	-0.003* (-2.19)	-0.001 (-0.58)	-0.002 (-1.38)	-0.000+ (-1.71)	-0.000 (-1.11)	-0.002 (-1.20)	-0.003* (-2.17)	-0.002 (-1.06)	-0.000 (-0.31)	0.005 (1.30)
Austerity	0.006 (0.84)	-0.006 (-0.69)	-0.005 (-1.28)	-0.000 (-0.39)	-0.000 (-0.05)	0.001 (0.69)	-0.001 (-0.64)	-0.000 (0.18)	-0.001 (-0.25)	0.001 (1.02)
Family benefits in kind	0.035* (2.31)	0.006 (0.32)	0.023 (1.15)	0.001 (0.77)	0.001 (0.79)	0.016 (1.02)	0.025+ (1.72)	0.026 (1.51)	0.015 (0.92)	0.073 (1.21)
No.	70640	76088	71184	74278	79096	77157	77913	73920	73264	17159
Chi²	8766	8492	7629	41	61	8370	8689	8138	8380	
Between-country variance	0.082	0.167	0.18	1.274	1.2	0.199	0.157	0.272	0.333	

Variance (total)	3.371	3.456	3.47	4.564	4.49	3.489	3.447	3.562	3.623	
Intra-class correlation	0.024	0.048	0.052	0.279	0.267	0.057	0.046	0.076	0.092	0.245
McFadden pseudo-R^2	0.187	0.172	0.169	0.017	0.014	0.18	0.191	0.188	0.221	
AIC ('000)	44	46	42	3	4	42	41	39	34	8680
BIC ('000)	44	46	42	4	4	43	42	39	34	8680
Log-likelihood ('000)	-22	-23	-21	-2	-2	-21	-21	-19	-17	-4340

Note: This table shows the results of different binary logistic regressions with the dependent dichotomous variables 'employed (after at least one month of inactivity or unemployment in the previous year' (yes or no). The included populations are the employed women in at first 24 and finally 28 European countries (AT, BE, BG, CY, CZ, DE, DK, EE, EL, ES, FI, FR, HR, HU, IE, IT, LT, LU, LV, MT, NL, PL, PT, RO, SE, SI, SK, UK). Data for Bulgaria, Romania, Malta and Croatia are gradually included. The coefficients are average marginal effects (cf. Mood 2010). Figures in parentheses: t-values. The nested structure of the data – individuals live in nation-states and are therefore exposed to similar institutional contexts and economic structures – are controlled by contextual factors. Cluster-robust standard errors have been calculated. Data in the last column (10) refer to the countries mostly affected by the crisis (CC: Cyprus, Greece, Ireland, Italy, Portugal and Spain). The AIC (Akaike information criterion) and the BIC (Bayes information criterion) are measures of the relative quality of the statistical models. Legend: + p < .1; * p < .05; ** p < .01.

Source: Own calculations on the basis of EU-SILC UDB UDB_c13_ver 2013-2 from 1 August 2015 and previous years.

Table 5.4 *Employment opportunities of women previously unemployed or inactive (2006–2013; 24–28 European countries): interaction effects*

	2006 (1)	2007 (2)	2008 (3)	2009 (4)	2010 (5)	2011 (6)	2012 (7)	2013 (8)	2013 (men;9)	2013 (CC;10)
Women in public sector/austerity	1.04 (1.59)	1.00 (−0.04)	1.04* (2.38)	1.04 (0.52)	0.92 (−1.08)	1.00 (−0.44)	1.00 (−0.43)	0.96* (−2.52)	0.97 (−1.30)	0.75** (−2.61)
Young child/family benefits in kind	1.32 (0.60)	0.44 (−1.25)	0.69 (−0.87)	13.54 (0.57)	19.69 (0.96)	0.64 (−0.80)	0.83 (−0.29)	0.59 (−0.84)	0.48 (−1.03)	0.31 (−1.43)
Young/temporary contract	0.36** (−16.58)	0.40** (−14.35)	0.42** (−12.86)	0 (0.03)	1.40 (0.64)	0.35** (−14.87)	0.38** (−13.53)	0.35** (−13.52)	0.28** (−17.15)	0.36** (−12.60)
Old/temporary contract	0.88 (−1.10)	1.09 (0.77)	1.26* (2.21)	1.69 (0.69)	1.44 (0.73)	1.33** (2.72)	1.18+ (1.68)	1.03 (0.32)	1.17 (1.63)	1.07 (0.15)

Note: The coefficients in this table are odds ratios. Only the coefficients of the interaction terms are represented; the rest of the models is represented in Table 5.3 (which however uses AMEs). Figures in parentheses: t-values. Legend: + p < .1; * p < .05; ** p < .01.

impact of these combined indicators on employment opportunities. The interaction between the share of women employed in the public sector and austerity policies was only negative in 2013 (both in all 28 EU countries and in the countries mostly affected by the crisis). This can be seen as providing limited support for the austerity thesis (H1').

I will now discuss a specific feature of the jobs successfully applied for by women – low remuneration. The background is the well-known gender pay gap of 16.3 per cent (2013) between the average gross hourly earnings of male and female paid employees. This gap raises the question of what characteristics do the women exhibit who have to accept a low-paid job? And what are the characteristics of these jobs? These questions are discussed on the basis of the models in Table 5.5, which are nearly identical to the models in Table 5.3 (I only added an indicator of the presence of unemployed people in the household in order to take into account the related economic pressures).

The models in Table 5.5 show that low-paid women are mostly younger. The chance of *younger women* (and also men, as shown in the last column but one) being low paid is 14 percentage points higher than in the core age group. The previously formulated expectation that *women with younger children* (6 years and younger) are less mobile and less flexible and thus are obliged to accept lower wages can be confirmed for some years during (2009, 2011 and 2012) the crisis. The best earnings opportunities are enjoyed by singles and couples without children. In comparison with couples with children, *single parents* have a worse chance of avoiding low-paid jobs. *Foreigners, people with health restrictions, low-skilled employees with simple tasks, part-time workers and temporary workers have a significantly higher likelihood of being in a low-paid job.* These are clear indicators of the dualization of the labour markets on both the demand and the supply side. These results clearly show that better-paid jobs are characterized by more challenging tasks, requiring higher skills, and are held by native, healthy persons with full-time jobs and permanent contracts. Men with a low-skilled job have a lower chance of being low-paid than women in less demanding occupations. The skill premium for women, i.e. the likelihood of being low paid for women with qualified and simple tasks, is much higher than for men. These results clearly support the dualization thesis H3'.

Trade, restaurants and hotels are the sectors with the lowest wages. This is not only true for women but also for men. In comparison with the manufacturing industry, the percentage of low-paid women is clearly lower in transport, storage, communication and financial services. On average, the share of low-paid women in community, social and personal services is identical to or even lower than in manufacturing. A more detailed analysis

Table 5.5 Employed women's risk of being in a low-paid job (2006–2013; 24–28 European countries)

	2006	2007	2008	2009	2010	2011	2012	2013	2013 (men)	2013 (CC)
Age group (ref.: 25–54 years)										
15 to 24 years	0.14**	0.15**	0.16**	0.16**	0.14**	0.16**	0.15**	0.14**	0.14**	0.20**
	(21.11)	(21.94)	(22.39)	(22.40)	(20.19)	(22.16)	(20.91)	(16.87)	(23.91)	(19.63)
55 years +	-0.02**	-0.02**	-0.01	-0.03**	-0.02**	-0.03**	-0.02**	-0.01**	-0.02**	-0.05**
	(-3.24)	(-3.05)	(-1.24)	(-5.21)	(-3.69)	(-4.87)	(-4.51)	(-3.42)	(-4.13)	(-6.27)
Young child	0.01	0.03	0.00	0.05*	0.02	0.05*	0.03+	0.02	0.07**	-0.01
	(0.37)	(1.51)	(0.03)	(2.44)	(1.31)	(2.50)	(1.77)	(0.99)	(4.32)	(-0.23)
Household type (ref.: Adults with children)										
One-person household	-0.04**	-0.05**	-0.05**	-0.05**	-0.04**	-0.04**	-0.03**	-0.03**	0.03**	0.06**
	(-6.38)	(-7.44)	(-8.19)	(-7.97)	(-6.34)	(-7.04)	(-5.65)	(-5.63)	(6.50)	(5.82)
Adults, no child	-0.01*	-0.01**	-0.02**	-0.02**	-0.01**	-0.01**	-0.01**	-0.01**	0.02**	0.03**
	(-2.31)	(-4.22)	(-6.47)	(-7.04)	(-3.39)	(-4.24)	(-2.90)	(-3.37)	(8.21)	(3.19)
Single-parent household	-0.01+	-0.01	-0.02**	-0.03**	-0.02*	-0.02*	-0.02**	-0.01*	-0.02	0.05**
	(-1.82)	(-1.41)	(-2.82)	(-3.97)	(-2.51)	(-2.46)	(-3.18)	(-2.33)	(-1.55)	(2.78)
Unemployed in household	0.03**	0.03**	0.02**	0.03**	0.03**	0.02**	0.01**	0.01*	0.02**	0.03
	(5.43)	(5.34)	(3.10)	(4.95)	(6.38)	(3.81)	(3.11)	(2.43)	(4.10)	(1.27)
Foreign nationality or born abroad	0.07**	0.07**	0.08**	0.08**	0.08**	0.080**	0.08**	0.07**	0.07**	0.13**
	(12.16)	(12.65)	(13.68)	(14.65)	(15.22)	(15.56)	(16.24)	(14.14)	(14.23)	(5.27)
Health	0.02**	0.01**	0.02**	0.02**	0.01**	0.02**	0.01**	0.01**	0.01**	-0.01
	(8.48)	(6.48)	(11.28)	(8.44)	(6.63)	(7.98)	(6.91)	(7.07)	(7.18)	(-1.49)
Educational level (ref.: low)										
Medium	-0.06**	-0.07**	-0.06**	-0.07**	-0.07**	-0.06**	-0.06**	-0.05**	-0.05**	-0.05**
	(-13.68)	(-14.74)	(-13.22)	(-14.97)	(-15.66)	(-13.74)	(-12.62)	(-10.66)	(-12.75)	(-6.08)
High	-0.12**	-0.13**	-0.12**	-0.13**	-0.13**	-0.13**	-0.12**	-0.11**	-0.08**	-0.07**
	(-19.91)	(-22.78)	(-19.87)	(-21.76)	(-23.12)	(-22.50)	(-21.96)	(-19.76)	(-15.77)	(-4.99)

ISCO skill levels (ref.: Operating, information processing)

	(1)	(2)	(3)	(4)	(5)	(6)	(7)	(8)	(9)	(10)
Simple tasks	0.13** (22.41)	0.12** (21.48)	0.13** (21.99)	0.13** (21.75)	0.13** (22.51)	0.14** (23.66)	0.13** (23.17)	0.15** (24.28)	0.07** (13.48)	0.11** (5.13)
Complex tasks	−0.13** (−26.30)	−0.15** (−30.78)	−0.13** (−28.41)	−0.14** (−30.45)	−0.13** (−29.35)	−0.13** (−29.53)	−0.14** (−30.29)	−0.13** (−28.33)	−0.07** (−17.94)	−0.09** (−6.65)
Problem-solving, decision-making, creativity	−0.17** (−30.31)	−0.19** (−33.26)	−0.18** (−31.20)	−0.18** (−32.43)	−0.17** (−33.25)	−0.16** (−32.76)	−0.17** (−35.16)	−0.17** (−33.77)	−0.09** (−21.17)	−0.13** (−10.63)
Part-time employment	0.03** (6.64)	0.03** (7.77)	0.02** (4.68)	0.01* (2.43)	0.02** (6.23)	0.02** (4.75)	0.02** (5.05)	0.03** (6.63)	0.07** (11.19)	0.04* (2.18)
Temporary job	0.14** (27.67)	0.15** (30.01)	0.16** (29.69)	0.15** (28.95)	0.16** (30.11)	0.15** (30.49)	0.17** (33.13)	0.17** (32.44)	0.15** (30.99)	0.17** (8.96)
Economic Activity (ref. Industry)										
Trade, restaurants, hotels	0.07** (13.92)	0.07** (15.04)	0.07** (15.40)	0.07** (15.24)	0.07** (14.22)	0.05** (11.96)	0.06** (13.30)	0.05** (11.36)	0.06** (15.54)	0.03+ (1.87)
Transport, storage, communication	−0.06** (−7.02)	−0.05** (−6.24)	−0.02** (−3.53)	−0.05** (−6.78)	−0.06** (−8.59)	−0.06** (−7.94)	−0.04** (−5.74)	−0.05** (−6.45)	−0.00 (−0.66)	−0.03 (−0.66)
Financial and business services	−0.03** (−5.37)	−0.04** (−6.67)	−0.03** (−4.83)	−0.02** (−2.83)	−0.02** (−4.80)	−0.02** (−2.98)	−0.01** (−2.60)	−0.01* (−2.42)	0.03** (5.96)	0.02 (1.11)
Community, social and personal services	−0.03** (−7.65)	−0.02** (−5.05)	−0.01** (−2.69)	−0.01* (−2.39)	−0.02** (−5.45)	−0.01** (−2.61)	0.00 (0.50)	0.00 (0.72)	−0.01+ (−1.77)	0.03+ (1.91)
Social protection	−0.01** (−3.11)	−0.01** (−3.03)	−0.01** (−3.28)	−0.01** (−2.79)	−0.01+ (−1.85)	−0.01* (−2.53)	−0.01** (−2.82)	−0.01** (−2.78)	−0.00* (−2.22)	0.00 (0.90)
Austerity	−0.02+ (−1.83)	−0.00 (−0.33)	−0.00 (−0.49)	−0.00 (−0.44)	−0.003 (−0.51)	0.001 (0.34)	−0.00 (−1.00)	−0.00 (−0.23)	−0.01+ (−1.83)	−0.01 (−1.41)
Family benefits in kind	−0.01 (−0.20)	−0.01 (−0.18)	0.04 (1.10)	−0.00 (−0.08)	0.003 (0.10)	0.009 (0.34)	−0.01 (−0.20)	0.01 (0.28)	0.01 (0.93)	0.09 (1.48)

Table 5.5 (continued)

	2006	2007	2008	2009	2010	2011	2012	2013	2013 (men)	2013 (CC)
No.	61 924	67 131	62 919	65 787	67 501	68 257	68 663	65 275	64 506	15 407
Chi²	7846	8819	8173	8646	8929	8873	9115	8404	5594	.
Between-country variance	0.138	0.146	0.18	0.169	0.204	0.185	0.194	0.209	0.12	
Variance (total)	3.428	3.435	3.47	3.458	3.494	3.475	3.484	3.499	3.409	
Intra-class correlation	0.04	0.042	0.052	0.049	0.058	0.053	0.056	0.06	0.035	
McFadden pseudo-R²	0.159	0.161	0.16	0.164	0.171	0.169	0.174	0.167	0.134	0.146
AIC ('000)	55	62	57	59	58	58	59	56	43	13 600
BIC ('000)	55	62	57	59	59	59	59	56	44	13 600
Log-likelihood ('000)	−27	−31	−28	−29	−29	−29	−29	−28	−22	−6820

Note: See Table 5.3.

(not reproduced here) shows the heterogeneity of this sector: the share of low-paid jobs is clearly lower in public administration, but since 2012 it has been higher in education and in arts and entertainment. The share of low-paid jobs used to be lower in health and social work, but this has changed since 2009. In sum, the main explanation for the gender pay gap seems to be the high female employment share in trade and accommodation (Table 5.1) as well as the over-representation of women in part-time jobs (one-third of all female employees, but less than one-tenth of all male employees).

Finally, I will discuss the impact of the three contextual variables analysed. Contrary to the previous models shown in Table 5.3, a higher level of *social expenditures* significantly reduces the risk of having a low-paid job in all the years. A possible explanation could be the availably of publicly financed childcare facilities, which reduces the need to take up every offer of employment, even low-paid jobs. However, expenditures on family benefits in kind have no systematic impact on low-pay risks. Therefore, another explanation is more likely: higher social expenditures also mean higher social benefits for unemployed people and poor households. However, a higher minimum income increases the reservation wage, i.e. the lowest wage rate at which an employee is willing to take a job. Thus, higher social expenditures contribute indirectly to lower shares of low-paid jobs.

5.4   CONCLUSION AND OUTLOOK

The financial, economic and sovereign debt crisis has also had major effects on the employment and earnings conditions of women. On the basis of macro- and micro-data, it was discussed whether this crisis and the austerity policies have had a negative effect on the employment and wage conditions of women, especially in the countries most affected by the crisis (*austerity*), whether the *inclusion* of women in the labour market has continued and whether the *dualization* of the labour market also affects the employment and earnings situation of women and in which dimensions. These three hypotheses were discussed on the basis of aggregated and micro-data on the employment and remuneration opportunities of women in Europe. The austerity hypothesis can generally be refuted. However, when examined in detail, some observations also support this thesis – for example the deterioration in female employment opportunities in the social and personal services in the countries most affected by the crisis. Further examples are the interaction between the share of women employed in the public sector and austerity policies or the negative interaction between the share of women employed in the public sector and austerity policies in 2013.

Secondly, the evolution of more inclusive employment patterns has continued during the crisis – and women are the (relative) winners of this secular transformation. The gender gaps in employment and unemployment rates have continued to shrink, especially in the Southern European countries, which have been the bulwark of the male breadwinner model in Europe. Paradoxically, the high unemployment rates particularly in Southern Europe have contributed to the erosion of traditional gender relations because women are forced to take up a job – and not only a part-time job, as the high share of involuntary part-time work shows.

Thirdly, the employment profiles of women differ in some aspects from their male counterparts. Employed women are generally more highly qualified, mostly employed in the service sector and are over-represented in atypical and low-paid jobs. This highlights a dualized form of the labour market inclusion of women. On the one hand, highly-skilled women with flexible, often part-time jobs are particularly employed in educational, administrative and social services. On the other hand, younger, less skilled women with younger children are employed in trade, hotels or food processing where they have to accept low pay. In principle, this dualization between low- and high-skilled women can also be found in the case of men, but the differences between the extremes seem to be higher in the case of women. The low-skilled industrial jobs are better paid due to the strength of collective forms of interest representation in many European countries, and the prospects of highly-skilled women with complex tasks in the growing public, educational, health and social services are excellent – also in comparison to the declining industrial sectors and their male employees. These results show the fictitious basis of gender mainstreaming policies, which ignore the dualization of female as well as male employment and earnings opportunities.

NOTES

1. I thank Irene Dingeldey, Stefanie Kley, André Ortiz, Ilona Ostner and Norbert Petzold for insightful comments on earlier drafts and important substantial and methodological suggestions.
2. The five regimes distinguished are an enhanced version of the three employment and welfare regimes described by Esping-Andersen (1990; Gallie and Paugam 2000; Blossfeld and Hofmeister 2006). 1: 'Liberal' (UK, IE); 2: 'Corporatist-conservative' (AT, DE, FR, LU, NL) (ref. category); 3: 'Mediterranean' (ES, IT, MT, PT, CY, EL); 4: 'Post-socialist' (BG, CZ, EE, HR; HU, LT, LV, PL, RO, SI, SK); 5: 'Nordic countries' (DK, FI, SE).
3. Cf. Chapter 4 of this volume for a more detailed explanation of the EU-SILC dataset. In 2006, 24 countries (EU-28 minus Bulgaria, Croatia, Malta and Romania) were able to be included. Since 2007, the required data for Bulgaria and Romania have also been able to be added; since 2008, the data for Malta; and, since 2010, the data for Croatia.

REFERENCES

Bettio, F. and Verashchagina, A. (2014), 'Women and men in the "great European recession"', in M. Karamessini and J. Rubery (eds), *Women and Austerity: The Economic Crisis and the Future for Gender Equality*, London: Routledge, pp. 57–81.

Blossfeld, H.P. and Hakim, C. (1997), *Between Equalization and Marginalization: Women Working Part-time in Europe*, Oxford: Oxford University Press.

Blossfeld, H.P. and Hofmeister, H. (eds) (2006), *Globalization, Uncertainty and Women's Careers*, Cheltenham, UK and Northampton, MA: Edward Elgar.

Broschinski, S. (2015), *Zwischen Refamiliarisierung und Kompensation. Die Auswirkungen der Eurokrise auf die weibliche Arbeitsmarktpartizipation*, Oldenburg: unpublished masters thesis.

Bryan, M.L. and Jenkins, S.P. (2016), 'Multilevel modelling of country effects: A cautionary tale', *European Sociological Review*, **32** (1), 3–22.

Buis, M.L. (2010), 'Stata tip 87: Interpretation of interactions in non-linear models', *The Stata Journal*, **10** (2), 305–308.

Card, D., Cardoso, A.R. and Kline, P. (2015), 'Bargaining, sorting, and the gender wage gap: Quantifying the impact of firms on the relative pay of women', *The Quarterly Journal of Economics*. doi: 10.1093/qje/qjv038 (online).

Christofides, L.N., Polycarpou, A. and Vrachimis, K. (2013), 'Gender wage gaps, "sticky floors" and "glass ceilings" in Europe', *Labour Economics*, **21**, 86–102.

Dingeldey, I. (2015), 'Gender inequality as part of a new family model: A case study on policy changes and institutional dualization in a conservative welfare state', Paris: *Contribution to the Council for European Studies* (CES).

Doeringer, P.B. and Piore, M.J. (1971), *Labor Markets and Manpower Analysis*, Lexington: Lexington Books.

Drobnič, S. and Blossfeld, H.P. (2001), 'Careers of couples and trends in inequality', in H.P. Blossfeld and S. Drobnič (eds), *Careers of Couples in Contemporary Societies: From Male Breadwinner to Dual-Earner Families*, Oxford: Oxford University Press, pp. 371–386.

Emmenegger, P., Häusermann, S., Palier, B. and Seeleib-Kaiser, M. (eds) (2012), *The Age of Dualization: The Changing Face of Inequality in Deindustrializing Societies*, Oxford: Oxford University Press.

Esping-Andersen, G. (1990), *The Three Worlds of Welfare Capitalism*, Cambridge, UK: Polity Press.

Ferrera, M. (1996), 'The "Southern model" of welfare in social Europe', *Journal of European Social Policy*, **6**, 17–37.

Gallie, D. and Paugam, S. (eds) (2000), *Welfare Regimes and the Experience of Unemployment in Europe*, Oxford: Oxford University Press.

ILO (2012), 'International Standard Classification of Occupations. Structure, group definitions and correspondence tables', *ISCO–08* Volume I. Geneva: International Labour Organization.

IMF (2015), *World Economic Outlook*, Washington: IMF.

Kalleberg, A.L. (2011), *Good Jobs, Bad Jobs. The Rise of Polarized and Precarious Employment Systems in the United States, 1970–2000s*, New York: Russell Sage Foundation.

Karamessini, M. (2014), 'Introduction: Women's vulnerability to recession and austerity', in M. Karamessini and J. Rubery (eds), *Women and Austerity:*

The Economic Crisis and the Future for Gender Equality, London: Routledge, pp. 3–16.

Karamessini, M. and Rubery, J. (eds) (2014a), *Women and Austerity: The Economic Crisis and the Future for Gender Equality*, London: Routledge.

Karamessini, M. and Rubery, J. (2014b), 'The challenge of austerity for equality', *Revue de l'OFCE*, **133** (2), 15–39.

Mood, C. (2010), 'Logistic regression: Why we cannot do what we think we can do, and what we can do about it', *European Sociological Review*, **26** (1), 67–82.

Moreira, A., Domínguez, Á.A., Antunes, C., Karamessini, M., Raitano, M. and Glatzer, M. (2015), 'Austerity-driven labour market reforms in Southern Europe: Eroding the security of labour market insiders', *European Journal of Social Security*, **17** (2), 202–225.

Ostner, I., Kurz, K. and Schulze, K. (2013), 'Coping with the crisis – How have German women fared?', AG About Gender, *International Journal of Gender Studies*, **2** (4), 60–75.

Rubery, J. (2014), 'From "women and recession" to "women and austerity": A framework for analysis', in M. Karamessini and J. Rubery (eds), *Women and Austerity: The Economic Crisis and the Future for Gender Equality*, London: Routledge, pp. 17–36.

Rubery, J. and Rafferty, A. (2013), 'Women and recession revisited', *Work, Employment & Society*, **27** (3), 414–432.

Saint-Paul, G. (1996), *Dual Labor Markets: A Macroeconomic Perspective*, Cambridge, MA: MIT Press.

Schwander, H. and Häusermann, S. (2013), 'Who is in and who is out? A risk-based conceptualization of insiders and outsiders', *Journal of European Social Policy*, **23** (3), 248–269.

6. Temporary employment and labour market segmentation in Europe, 2002–2013

Christian Reimann

6.1 INTRODUCTION

Since the 1970s/1980s, social and economic changes have led to an increasing number of temporarily employed workers in nearly all European countries. In France and Spain, for example, the temporary employment rate doubled between 1985 and 1996 (Kalleberg 2000). In Belgium and Ireland, the number of temporary employed increased during this period while full-time permanent jobs decreased (Cahuc and Postel-Vinay 2002). About 80 per cent of new recruitments in France and over 90 per cent in Spain were jobs characterized by temporary contracts at this time (ibid.). The situation in other European countries was hardly any better: in Germany, the Netherlands and Luxembourg at least 50 per cent of new hires were characterized by fixed-term contracts in the 1980s (Delsen 1991). Nowadays, the highest share of temporary employed can be found in Poland (24.6 per cent), Spain (20 per cent) and Portugal (17.5 per cent) (own calculations on the basis of Eurostat).

The increased use of temporary employment has led to greater segmentation of labour markets by 'creating a division between organizational insiders and outsiders' (Kalleberg 2003: 156) – a common trend observed in many European countries (Häusermann and Schwander 2012). The outsiders are not only insecurely employed but are also paid less and removed from training opportunities (Kalleberg 2003; Schmid 2010). Although large country differences with respect to the probability of becoming temporarily employed and transitioning into permanent jobs have been observed (Kahn 2010; European Commission 2012), a number of tendencies are common across EU countries. In particular, similar social groups are at risk of being affected by temporary employment. Throughout the EU, it is particularly women, younger people, low-skilled workers or migrants who are more likely to be temporarily employed with fewer prospects of an unlimited contract (Barbieri 2009; European Commission 2012; Kalleberg 2012).

Following the widespread literature on labour market segmentation, national policymakers and firms in search of greater labour market flexibility are responsible for this development. Firstly, due to stagnating job growth and persistent high unemployment rates in Europe, deregulation measures for fixed-term employment were implemented in the hope that this would create new jobs (De Grip et al. 1997; Kalleberg 2000; Eichhorst 2014). While these reforms ease the use of temporary jobs through lower restrictions, for example in terms of defining specific tasks and employment duration, they do not help to increase employment rates and instead 'encourage a substitution of temporary for permanent work' (Kahn 2010: 14). Secondly, due to increased international competition on product and financial markets with corresponding higher uncertainty among firms, employers are more and more interested in fixed-term contracts. Such contracts can operate as a buffer to protect the organizational core segment against economic shocks, serve as a screening instrument to lengthen probationary periods avoiding skill-mismatch and are much more cost-effective in terms of wages, firing-costs and other workplace-related expenditures (Kalleberg 2000, 2003).

The process of Europeanization with the creation of the world's biggest common market could also be seen as responsible for the growing share of flexible employed and labour market segmentation. To make the EU the most competitive and dynamic knowledge-based economy worldwide (European Council 2000), firms' flexibility through individual employability is seen as the main precondition for successfully positioning the European common market in the globalized economy (Ebner 2007). Since the 1990s, this perspective of economic competitiveness has been a core element of the European Employment Strategy (EES) (ibid.), increasing the pressure on national institutions towards greater efficiency and effectiveness (Münch 2001). This has led to the priority of aligning policies with market principles, whereby 'the EES has supported a shift to activation policies and a preventive approach' (Heidenreich and Zeitlin 2009: 5), e.g. in Poland, Spain, Denmark and the UK. Following the recommendations of the EES, changing national employment as well as social policies implies increasing privatization of individual labour market risks (Ebner 2007). Even though nation states are the most important arenas for regulating social inequalities (Heidenreich 2003), the creation and deepening of the common market is resulting in a convergence of national social policies. It is also leading to increasing inner-country differences, where social positions are increasingly allocated by individual characteristics such as educational attainment (Münch 2001).

On the basis of Münch's (2001) thesis of transnational spaces and inspired by Parsons' distinction of ascription versus achievement as the fundamental principles of social stratification in traditional versus modern societies (Parsons 1970), it is to be expected that territorial differences of social inequalities have become less important in comparison to individual achievements in the economically and politically integrated Europe. This can be termed *de-territorialization of social inequalities*. An indicator of such de-territorialization is the dependence of individuals' welfare on their socio-economic characteristics as well as on their successful market participation (Heidenreich 2003, 2006). This article develops a similar thesis for the use of fixed-term contracts before and during the Great Recession and the subsequent sovereign debt crises in Europe (2008 to date). In particular, it raises the question of whether the probability of being temporarily employed in Europe is becoming more and more dependent on individual characteristics and individual labour market chances than on national welfare and labour market regimes. The thesis of this chapter is that the insider–outsider divide is increasingly based on gender, age and educational attainment while national framework conditions are becoming less important in explaining the probability of being temporarily employed. De-territorialization of social inequalities can thus be interpreted as an indication of the extent to which Europeanization processes are affecting labour market segmentation and social inequalities.

This chapter is structured as follows. Firstly, labour market segmentation together with its individual and institutional determinants is presented in order to explore which social groups are most affected and which national institutional and economic framework conditions might have an impact on the probability of being temporarily employed. The relationship between Europeanization and an assumed de-territorialization of social inequalities is subsequently examined to elaborate the hypotheses. After presenting the data and methods, the results are then finally discussed.

6.2 LABOUR MARKET SEGMENTATION – INDIVIDUAL AND INSTITUTIONAL DETERMINANTS

In the 1970s, the segmentation of labour markets and their relationship with different institutional arrangements was intensively discussed. Reich et al. (1973), and also Piore and Doeringer (1971), made a distinction between internal and external labour markets.[1] Internal labour markets are defined as institutionally regulated markets, characterized by jobs with permanent contracts, a higher income, training opportunities and career possibilities, which altogether ensure security for employees. The existence of permanent jobs can be mainly explained by employers' interests in binding their employees to the company, as transaction costs are lowered when firm-specific tasks and internal knowledge exist. To increase internal company flexibility, firms can internally adapt working time arrangements. The external labour market consists of jobs that do not require a tight relationship between employers and employees due to limited requirements regarding firm-specific tasks and knowledge. Firms' requirements of gaining more flexibility in this segment are mostly reached via external flexibilization instruments such as hire and fire. This is often associated with a higher use of temporary employment due to the lower employment protections implied in these kinds of employment. This labour segment especially consists of jobs which are characterized by fixed-term contracts, a lower income, lower training possibilities, poorer working conditions and higher labour turnover with an increased risk of becoming unemployed (Piore and Doeringer 1971; Keller and Seifert 2008; Jakštienė and Beržinskienė 2011). However, country and welfare regime differences with respect to the outcome between insiders and outsiders have been observed (Häusermann and Schwander 2012).

Not all social groups are affected to the same extent by labour market segmentation. Previous studies have shown that with regard to gender, age and skill level, it is particularly women, younger people and poorly-educated workers who are more likely to be temporarily employed (Polavieja 2006; Barbieri 2009; European Commission 2012; Kalleberg 2012; O'Conner 2013). The greater share of women in temporary employment can be explained by occupational and sectoral segregation. While women are more often employed in the low-skilled service sector, men are still more likely to work in industry, where historically more permanent jobs are available. Nevertheless, as a result of the ongoing de-industrialization and the reduction of standard work arrangements in the industrial sector, men are increasingly affected by fixed-term employment due to outsourcing processes and the increasing role of temporary agency work. A higher proportion of younger workers in temporary jobs can be attributed to the fact that temporary contracts for this age group are often used as an entry position into the labour market. This form of employment is used by employers as a screening instrument and a probationary period to avoid skill-mismatch (De Grip et al. 1997; Baranowska and Gebel 2008; Gebel and Giesecke 2011). However, among young workers the risk of becoming temporarily employed is much higher in countries with high unemployment rates (De Grip et al. 1997; European Commission 2012). As a last group, the poorly-skilled are more likely to be less securely employed (De Grip et al. 1997; DiPrete et al. 2005; Maurin and Postel-Vinay 2005), which can be attributed to the fact '[that] European labor markets have observed-skill-biased technological change by allocating an increasingly large share of unskilled workers to flexible jobs' (DiPrete et al. 2005: 14). The continuing shift towards knowledge-intensive services is increasing the demand for higher skill levels in Europe and lowering the prospects of low-qualified workers (European Commission 2012).

The use of temporary employment by companies has been facilitated since the 1970s, when as a response to high unemployment rates 'many European governments made a simultaneous use of two apparently diverging policy instruments' (Cahuc and Postel-Vinay 2002: 63f.). On the one hand, existing permanent contracts were strongly protected to avoid the destruction of jobs. On the other hand, the relatively high legal regulations of fixed-term employment were deregulated, for example in terms of duration, defining specific tasks or restrictions on the number of renewals in order to increase the flexibility of the labour market (ibid.). Aimed at protecting permanent workers and facilitating the use of temporary employment, this partial deregulation was implemented as a labour market policy answer to high unemployment rates and the increasing flexibilization[2] needs of firms due to increased international competition and market insecurities (De Grip et al. 1997; Kalleberg 2000; for Central and Eastern European Countries (CEECs) cf. Baranowska and Gebel 2008). These double-faced policies triggered the dualization of labour markets instead of a general liberalization, especially in Continental and Southern Europe, but also in Central and Eastern European countries (Emmenegger et al. 2012; Palier and Thelen 2010; for CEECs cf. Baranowska and Gebel 2008).

As recent studies have shown, the use of fixed-term contracts depends in particular on the differences between the employment regulations for permanent and fixed-term contracts. 'Employment protection regulations . . . set conditions under which it is possible to lay off an employee (fair dismissal) and the sanctions in the case of breach of these provisions (unfair dismissal)' (Bassanini et al. 2008: 3). This means that high regulation of regular contracts causes employers to shift to non-standard employment in order to maintain their flexibility. The segmentation of labour markets by rigid employment protection legislation for permanent workers and the partial deregulation of fixed-term contracts is causing workers in Europe to be increasingly affected by temporary jobs (Kahn 2010; for young employees cf. European Commission 2012). Furthermore, Gebel and Giesecke (2011) showed that low-skilled workers are more affected by segmentation if levels of employment protection for permanent contracts are high and the level of regulation regarding fixed-term contracts is simultaneously low. 'Obviously, when confronted with strict dismissal regulations and high firing costs for permanent contracts, employers tend to resort to temporary contracts, particularly in the case of low-skilled workers' (Gebel and Giesecke 2011: 36). Additionally, the transition from a fixed-term to a permanent job depends significantly on the degree of employment protection for permanent contracts. Higher protection of permanent jobs causes a lower level of transition from temporary employment into open-ended jobs. It also increases the risks of unemployment and fixed-term employment as a trap in a person's life course (Giesecke and Groß 2002; European Commission 2012; for CEECs cf. Babos 2014; for age-based effects of employment protection legislation (EPL) cf. Dieckhoff and Steiber 2012).

Nonetheless, other national determinants can also lead to higher rates of fixed-term employment and therefore to a widening insider–outsider divide in labour markets. Firstly, positive economic prospects expressed through a growing gross domestic product can have a positive influence on the probability of working under a temporary contract. This is conceivable because one requirement for dynamic economies is a higher diversity of employment forms – which are a precondition to the high flexibility needs of firms to adjust their workforce to volatile economic conditions (Schmid 2010). A contrary explanation was provided by Gebel and Giesecke (2011) with reference to Holmlund and Storrie (2002), who 'show that depressed labor market conditions will create incentives for firms to use – and to exert pressure on individuals to accept – temporary contracts' (Gebel and Giesecke 2011: 26).

Secondly, high unemployment rates may lead to more workers with temporary contracts, especially for labour market entrants. A higher unemployment rate leads to greater 'power' of employers, who in this situation prefer to provide fixed-term contracts. Moreover, the causality can also be the other way around: a higher occurrence of temporary employment leads to higher unemployment rates (Blanchard and Landier 2001; Cahuc and Postel-Vinay 2002). This can be explained by large differences between the employment regulations of regular contracts and the employment regulations of fixed-term contracts. Having analysed the unemployment rates in Spain and France during the crisis, Bentolila et al. (2012) show that 'a larger gap between the dismissal costs of workers with permanent and temporary contracts and a much lower regulation of the use of the latter in Spain than in France . . . could explain up to 45 per cent of the much higher rise of Spanish unemployment' (Bentolila et al. 2012: 155). The higher the differences, the lower the probability of fixed-term workers transitioning to a permanent contract and therefore the higher the average unemployment rates (ibid.).

Thirdly, active labour market policies (ALMP) can have a negative effect on forms of employment. As Heidenreich (2014) shows, spending on ALMP measures has a positive effect on labour market participation and long-term unemployment. However, it can be assumed that policies promoting labour market entry go hand in hand with re-commodification tendencies (Bonoli and Natali 2011). This produces higher demands for the unemployed to take jobs which may be beneath their qualifications or below their perception of sufficient wages. Therefore, it can be expected that higher ALMPs can lead to higher fixed-term employment relations, as these employment forms are aimed at creating jobs – also by urging the unemployed to take up jobs (also with fixed-term contracts). To answer the research question of whether national structural and institutional determinants have a lower impact on temporary employment and whether individual characteristics shape increasingly individual labour market risks, the next section discusses labour market segmentation in the context of a politically and economically more integrated Europe.

6.3   HOW EUROPEANIZATION COULD DEEPEN INSIDER–OUTSIDER DIVISIONS OF LABOUR MARKETS

The EES 'contributed to broad shifts in national policy orientation and thinking, involving the incorporation of EU concepts and categories into domestic debates' (Zeitlin 2005: 451). This shift implies the realignment of these policies with markets and international competitiveness (Ebner 2007). Following the concepts of 'activation' and 'flexicurity' (Weishaupt 2011), national institutions need to achieve more institutional efficiency and effectiveness to make labour markets more flexible in order to meet the challenges of increased market competition and insecurities (Münch 2001; Bauer et al. 2007). National institutions were deregulated to pursue the course of liberalization, leading to negative implications for national welfare institutions (Münch 2001; Ferrera 2014). Thus, some 'extensively reformed (social policies) in many countries may have subsequently lost some of their redistributive capacities' (Emmenegger et al. 2012: 8), which has led to more social inequalities on labour markets. At the same time, however, the market-oriented realignment of national institutions implies restructuring processes on the company level to create more flexibility, leading to the emergence of non-standard forms of employment (Münch 2001). Streeck (2013) and Beckfield (2009) stated that this process of creating a European common market has led to a liberalization of national labour markets, which implies a re-commodification of labour. Employees in non-standard employment forms are increasingly dependent on individual negotiation processes oriented towards market rules, which leads to more social inequalities e.g. in terms of income inequalities (Beckfield 2009).

As a result of the impact on national policies and economic decisions due to the process of Europeanization and the creation of the world's largest single economic area,[3] we can expect to see increasing *de-territorialization of social inequalities* (Münch 2001; Heidenreich 2003, 2006). De-territorialization of social inequalities in this context means that in the economically and politically integrated Europe, territorial differences of social inequalities have become less important compared to individual achievements. Due to the creation of the common market with deepened economic interrelations and dependencies through an increased exchange of goods, capital, services and information between the European nation states, the commonalities between countries have increased. Simultaneously, the single nation state has become more heterogeneous and differences within countries have increased (Münch 2001). Just as with the emergence of modern nation states, a shift from achieving social positions through ascription (via birth or economic capital) to achieving social positions through educational achievements within a pluralized occupational system has taken place (Parsons 1970). We assume that the processes of European market integration have similarly led to a shift from the ascription of social risks on the macro-level through national institutions to the achievement of social positions through individual characteristics – due to a shift from mechanical to organic solidarity through an economic differentiation by a European division of labour (Münch 2001). This raises our research question of whether the probability of being temporarily employed is increasingly influenced by individual characteristics. It is assumed that individual characteristics such as gender and age as well as individual educational attainment level increasingly determine the individual probability of being temporarily employed. At the same time, the assumption of a de-territorialization of social inequalities implies a decreasing impact of particular national institutions on labour market structures. Therefore we expect that national labour market institutions will have a lower influence on individual labour market risks.

These hypotheses will be explored by comparing the years before and during the international financial and European currency and economic crises, as it is assumed that with the onset of the crisis in 2007/2008 two different trends can be identified. *Firstly, following the thesis of a de-territorialization of social inequalities, the risk of being temporarily employed increasingly depends on the individual determinants of gender, age and educational attainment for the years before the crisis. Women and younger and lower-educated employees will be increasingly affected by fixed-term contracts compared to their reference groups. Simultaneously, the influence of national factors determining this risk should be declining (H1). Secondly, due to different national experiences since the onset of the crisis, it is expected that in the years following the crisis the national institutional context compared to the individual characteristics has once again become more important for the likelihood of being employed on a temporary contract (H2).*

In the following section the underlying data are discussed together with the operationalization of the variables and the method used.

6.4   DATA AND METHODS

The following analyses are based on the European Union Labour Force Survey for the period 2002 to 2013 (database EU-LFS 2015 release).[4] The EU-LFS provides detailed information on employment and labour market participation on micro-data for 28 EU countries plus Switzerland, Norway and Iceland and is a good database for a European-wide analysis of labour markets. Due to data limitations on the micro- as well as on the macro-level, only 17 countries in this study can be considered.[5] The micro-data are supplemented by macro-data from Eurostat, OECD and data from the Database on Institutional Characteristics of Trade Unions, Wage Setting, State Intervention and Social Pacts (ICTWSS) to analyse the institutional influence.

The analyses concentrate on dependent employees aged 20 to 64 years. People under 20 years of age are excluded because they could cause an overestimation of temporary employment due to the higher share of apprentices in this age group, especially in countries with a dual education system. Furthermore, the analyses are limited to full-time employees and therefore exclude part-time workers even if they are fixed-term employed.[6]

To analyse the influence on the binary dependent variable (being full-time permanent or full-time temporary employed[7]), binary logistic regression models are used. To investigate the effects of the individual as well as the contextual level and their development over the period of investigation, average marginal effects are calculated (Mood 2010). Considering the nested structure of the data, as individuals are part of nation states and hence exposed to similar institutional frameworks, the country level has to be controlled for. Since only 17 countries are included in the analyses, multi-level analyses should not be performed because at least 30 countries are needed when using logit models (Bryan and Jenkins 2013). Therefore, the option *vce (cluster 'country variable')* is used to achieve cluster-robust standard errors (Cameron and Miller 2011).

The individual and institutional determinants, their operationalization and the expected effects on the probability of being temporarily employed are presented in Table 6.1.

*Table 6.1 Dependent and independent variables, their operationalization,
data sources and the expected effects*

Variable	Operationalization and data source	Expected
Dependent		
Temporary employment	Full-time temporary employment (0: permanent full-time employed; 1: temporary full-time employed) (source: EU-LFS 2014)	
Independent	*Micro-level*	
Gender	1: male (ref. group); 2: female (source: EU-LFS 2014)	+
Age groups	1: 20 to 34 years;	+
	2: 35 to 49 years (ref. group);	.
	3: 50 to 64 years (source: EU-LFS 2014)	–
Educational attainments	1: Pre-primary, primary and lower secondary education – ISCED 0–2 (ref. group);	.
	2: Upper secondary and post-secondary non-tertiary education – ISCED 3–4;	–
	3: Tertiary education – ISCED 5–6; (source: EU-LFS 2014)	–
Independent	*Macro-level*	
Economic growth	Growth of the gross domestic product in % to the previous year (source: Eurostat)	+
Unemployment rate	Unemployment rate in % of active persons aged 20 to 64 years (source: Eurostat)	+
Active labour market policies	Active labour market policy measures in % of GDP (categories 2–7, source: Eurostat)	+
EPL regular	'This indicator is the weighted sum of sub-indicators concerning the regulations for individual dismissals (weight of 5/7) and additional provisions for collective dismissals (2/7) (for permanent contracts). It incorporates 12 detailed data items.' The present study uses version 2 (EPRC_V2) to cover the period of study (source: OECD)	+
Difference between EPL regular and EPL temporary	Difference between EPL for permanent and EPL for temporary contracts.	+
	'The indicator for temporary employment measures the strictness of regulation on the use of fixed-term and temporary work agency contracts. It incorporates 6 data items.' The present study uses version 1 (EPT_V1) to cover the period of study (source: OECD)	

Note: The higher the expression of an independent variable, the higher (+) and respectively the lower (−) the expected individual risk of being fixed-term employed. Operationalization of the control-variable (industries: NACE-classification) not displayed.

6.5 RESULTS

Before discussing the determinants of the risk of being temporarily employed, the evolvement of the full-time temporary employment rate in the analysed European countries between 2002 and 2013 will be briefly presented (Figure 6.1).

In 2002, the highest share of full-time temporary employed in Europe was observed in Spain. Due to labour market reforms in the 1980s, the flexibility of the Spanish labour market was increased in order to combat high unemployment rates. An outcome of these reforms has been the creation of more temporary jobs (Lang 2000; Sola et al. 2013). Despite the 'Pact for Employment Stability' in 1997, which reduced dismissal costs for individuals with permanent contracts and was supposed to 'restore the "causality principle" (a temporary contract requiring correspondence to a temporary task)' (Sola et al. 2013: 67) to reduce the high fixed-term employment rate, the temporary employment rate remained the highest in Europe at 28.7 per cent of all full-time employees in 2002 (own calculations). Furthermore, the regulation of standard forms of employment was softened in 2002,[8] but without any effect on reducing temporary employment (ibid.). Portugal, Finland, Poland and Slovenia also had relatively high rates of full-time employees with temporary contracts in 2002, which can be explained partly by major differences between the EPL for permanent and temporary employees. In Portugal and Poland, for example, the EPL for permanent employees was 4.095 and 2.557 compared to 2.813 and 0.75 for the temporarily employed, which partly explains the extensive use of fixed-term contracts as a cheaper and more flexible form of employment.

In 10 out of 17 countries,[9] the share of full-time temporary employees was higher in 2013 than in 2002, albeit to a very different extent. The largest increase as well as the highest rate of temporary employment in Europe in 2013 was in Poland, where '[n]on-standard employment is the most prevalent form of employment' (Buchner-Jeziorska 2013: 117). From 12.7 per cent in 2002, full-time temporary employment nearly doubled to 24.6 per cent in 2013. Poland has the most flexible European labour market due to mass substitution of permanent contracts by temporary jobs in the post-socialist decades, especially for lower-educated people. Otherwise, an anti-crisis act introduced in 2008 which deregulated the maximum duration of temporary employment eases a firm's use of this employment form, which explains why temporary employment has not significantly decreased since the onset of the crisis (ibid.). Italy is the second country with a much higher share in 2013 than in 2002. Temporary employment increased by 4.1 percentage points and by nearly 60 per cent from 7.4 to 11.6 per cent, which also can be explained by deregulation measures in recent years. 'A first-time fixed-term

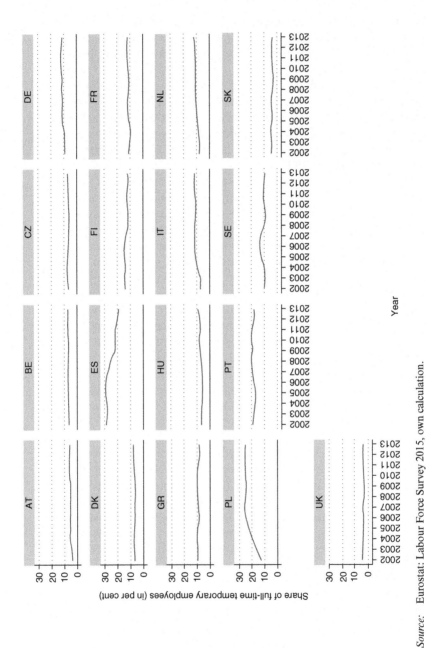

Source: Eurostat: Labour Force Survey 2015, own calculation.

Figure 6.1   Development of full-time temporary employees as percentage of all full-time employees by country between 2002 and 2013

contract can now be concluded with no particular reason, with the limitation that it can then only last for a maximum of 12 months' (Lang et al. 2013: 11), which leads to the assumption that temporary employees in Italy are more often trapped in a circle of 'unemployment follows fixed-term employment'. The EPL for temporary employees decreased from 2.375 to 2.

In 13 out of 17 countries, full-time temporary employment decreased with the onset of the financial and economic crisis in 2007/2008 – albeit very moderately in nearly all countries. The exception again is Spain, where the full-time temporary employment rate decreased between 2006 and 2013 by 10.3 percentage points – or 35 per cent – from 29.3 to 19 per cent. More than in the other European countries, Spanish fixed-term employees were hit by the economic crisis, which led to the destruction of more than 2.5 million jobs (Sola et al. 2013). Temporary employment was the most important buffer in response to the economic downturn.

The individual determinants and their influence on temporary contracts will now be explored (Figure 6.2). With respect to the first hypothesis, the first question is whether an *increase* of employment risks for women, younger people and low-skilled employees can be observed between 2002 and 2007/ 2008. First of all, in 2002 the probability for women is 1.9 per cent higher than for men. The risk for young employees is also higher; they are more affected by temporary contracts (11.4 per cent) compared to prime-age workers. Compared to mid-age workers, the older workers aged 50 to 64 years face fewer risks of holding a fixed-term contract, at 2.1 per cent. As they have a higher average length of job tenure, older people are still more often employed on permanent contracts. In addition to ascriptive criteria, the degree of educational attainment influences the form of employment. Compared to higher-educated workers, the low-skilled faced a higher risk in 2002 with 6.3 per cent compared to medium-educated employees, or 5.8 per cent compared to highly-educated employees.

With regard to the development of the individual determinants, the results show that the risk for the analysed social groups increased between 2002 and 2007/2008. For women, the higher risk of holding a full-time fixed-term contract slightly increased by 0.6 percentage points to 2.5 per cent compared to men in 2007. With 13.6 per cent, employees aged 20 to 34 years were much more affected than in 2002 (+2.2 percentage points). For older workers, with −3.0 per cent the risk is even lower than in 2002 (−0.9 percentage points). The risk for workers aged 35 to 49 years has thus increased in comparison to the older employees. The effect of the educational level has also increased. The risk for lower educated employees in 2007 was 6.3 per cent higher than for the medium educated (+0.5 percentage points compared to 2002) and 7.5 per cent higher compared to the highly educated (+1.7 percentage points compared to 2002).

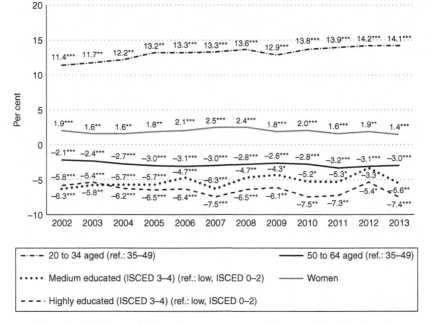

Note: Logistic regression on the risk of full-time temporary employment. The percentage points are the average marginal effects multiplied by 100. Significance levels: *** (p < 0.001), ** (p < 0.01), * (p < 0.05).

Source: Eurostat: Labour Force Survey 2015, own calculation.

Figure 6.2 *Development of the individual risks of being temporarily full-time employed depending on individual ascriptive criteria and the educational attainment level between 2002 and 2013 in Europe*

These developments of the individual determinants between 2002 and 2007/ 2008 confirm our first hypothesis that the individual characteristics of gender, age and educational attainment increasingly determined the risk of being fixed-term employed in the years prior to the crisis.

The second question raised by H2 is whether the institutional determinants of labour markets simultaneously lost their influence in explaining individual labour market risks between 2002 and 2007/2008, as assumed in the thesis of a de-territorialization of social inequalities. The development of the analysed structural and institutional determinants regarding the individual risk of being temporarily employed between 2002 and 2007/2008 is in line with this thesis (Table 6.2). Thus, while the individual characteristics are increasingly influencing the risk of holding a fixed-term

Table 6.2 Structural and institutional determinants on the risk of full-time temporary employment for 2002 to 2013

	2002	2003	2004	2005	2006	2007	2008	2009	2010	2011	2012	2013
Structural determinants												
Economic growth	0.026*	0.016	0.070	0.008	0.029**	0.030*	0.023	0.031***	0.040	0.047**	0.021	0.038**
	(2.50)	(1.28)	(1.81)	(0.60)	**(3.27)**	**(2.51)**	(1.09)	**(4.03)**	(1.85)	**(2.95)**	(1.93)	**(3.22)**
Unemployment rate	0.018***	0.032***	0.018**	0.030***	0.024**	0.021**	0.032***	0.023***	0.029**	0.034***	0.014***	0.030***
	(3.64)	**(4.32)**	**(3.11)**	**(8.23)**	**(3.10)**	**(2.48)**	**(4.40)**	**(6.37)**	**(3.21)**	**(5.72)**	**(4.05)**	**(4.37)**
Institutional determinants												
Active labour market measures (in % of GDP)	0.018*	0.016	0.003	0.017*	0.024**	0.016	0.024	0.021	-0.004	-0.003	-0.009	0.013
	(2.36)	(1.37)	(0.55)	**(2.31)**	**(2.61)**	(1.51)	(1.67)	(1.76)	(-0.24)	(-0.26)	(-0.62)	(1.42)
Employment protection for permanent employees (EPL)	0.015*	0.006	0.034***	0.008*	0.012	0.008	0.007	0.009	0.009	0.017**	0.032***	0.000
	(2.00)	(0.47)	**(3.52)**	**(2.19)**	(1.73)	(1.44)	(0.66)	(1.17)	(1.04)	**(2.63)**	**(3.85)**	(0.02)
Difference between EPL permanent and EPL temporary	-0.015	-0.024	-0.030*	-0.024	-0.020***	-0.013	-0.003	0.012*	-0.013	-0.009	-0.018	-0.002
	(-1.53)	(-1.84)	**(-1.97)**	(-1.50)	**(-3.58)**	(-1.11)	(-0.51)	**(2.08)**	(-1.17)	(-1.63)	(-1.69)	(-0.59)
Pseudo-R^2	0.11	0.12	0.12	0.12	0.13	0.11	0.12	0.12	0.12	0.11	0.10	0.12
AIC	72333312	73201019	75757767	81998694	84435492	87615869	86354114	81032326	82581024	83095137	82425159	79828646
BIC	72509867	73376580	75932911	82191654	84622743	87803338	86541178	81218703	82768571	83281254	82612973	80015589
No.	458038	430461	419357	1277045	893769	906036	883366	846220	910446	832604	925745	876741

Note: Logistic regression on the risk of full-time temporary employment; taking into account the country level; the coefficients are the average marginal effects. Significance levels: *** ($p < 0.001$), ** ($p < 0.01$), * ($p < 0.05$). Controlled for industries (NACE). Variables at the individual level are not displayed in this table. For full model see appendix Table 6A.1.

Source: Eurostat: Labour Force Survey 2015, own calculation.

contract, with the exception of the unemployment rate, the institutional determinants in particular lost their explanatory power prior to the crisis.

This observed development can be interpreted as a de-territorialization of social inequalities in which individual labour market risks are becoming increasingly dependent on the individual characteristics of gender, age and educational attainment and to a lesser extent on national framework conditions. This can be traced back to the process of creating a European common market through processes of re-commodification and the convergence of national institutions, which has led to decreasing between-country differences and increasing inner-country differences. As can be seen in Figure 6A.1 in the appendix to this chapter, the differences between the national expenditures on active labour market policies and between the national levels of employment protection legislation decreased in the years prior to the crisis.

The development of the analysed individual and institutional determinants after the onset of the financial and economic crisis in 2007/2008 will now be explored. Has the national institutional context once again become more important than the individual characteristics in explaining the likelihood of being temporarily employed due to different national experiences during the times of the crisis (H2)? Firstly, the results in Figure 6.2 show that, with the exception of women, the risk increases depending on individual characteristics in the years after the crisis. While the risk for younger employees slightly decreased from 2008 to 2009, at 14.1 per cent, employees aged 20 to 34 years in 2013 faced a higher risk than the prime-age workers – the highest value in the period of investigation and an increase of 0.5 percentage points compared to 2007 and 2.7 percentage points compared to 2002. The risk for the lower-educated at first decreased in the years immediately following the crisis. However, in 2010 their risk compared to highly-educated employees increased again – with a 7.4 per cent higher risk of holding a fixed-term contract compared to the highly-educated employees. The risk of the lower-educated compared to medium-educated employees decreased compared to 2002, but the lower-educated still faced a 5.6 per cent higher risk in 2013. Secondly, the national institutional factors simultaneously become important again in explaining the individual labour market risk of being temporarily employed (Table 6.2). While at the macro-level only the degree of the national unemployment rate determined whether employees were permanently employed or not in 2008, economic growth, the EPL level and the difference between EPL for permanent and temporary jobs have had an impact in the years after the onset of the crisis. Nonetheless, the second hypothesis has to be rejected. Indeed, national factors have become important again in explaining the likelihood of being employed on a temporary contract, but this development has not been accompanied by a decreasing impact of the individual characteristics of age and education on temporary employment. The trend can be explained by the crisis. In times of uncertain economic prospects, firms make greater use of flexible working contracts. The EPL for permanent forms of employment also has a positive effect on the risk of having a fixed-term contract again. Firms make use of temporary employment when employment protection for permanent employees is relatively high, especially in times of major economic downturns and uncertainties.

6.6 CONCLUSION

Temporary employment has become very important for European labour markets over the last decades. One explanation for the increasing share of fixed-term employed is that national policymakers and firms are responsible for this development through their search for greater labour market flexibility. Deregulation measurements due to high unemployment rates and firms' adjustments to growing market insecurities have led to more fixed-term jobs. Country differences in fixed-term employment rates can be explained by national labour market institutions and structures. Higher unemployment rates or high employment protection for permanent contracts accompanied by low restrictions for fixed-term jobs have led to more workers being temporarily employed. This chapter discussed to what extent the process of Europeanization and the creation of the world's biggest common market can be seen as responsible for a higher prevalence of fixed-term employment for women and for younger and lower-educated employees – the 'risk groups' of labour markets.

Firstly, the results show that the individual risk of being temporarily employed has become more dependent on the employee's age. Between 2002 and 2013 the risk for employees aged 20 to 34 years increased from a higher risk of 11.4 per cent compared to the prime-age workers in 2002 to 14.1 per cent in 2013. The higher risk for the prime-age workers compared to the employees aged 50 to 64 years also increased: from 2.1 per cent in 2002 to 3.0 per cent in 2013. Secondly, the level of educational attainment has also become more important in explaining the individual labour market risk of fixed-term contracts. While in 2002 the risk of lower-educated workers was 5.8 per cent higher than highly-educated workers, this risk increased to 7.4 per cent in 2013. Only the fixed-term employment risk for women compared to men hardly varied in the period of investigation. Simultaneous to this increasing risk being dependent on individual characteristics, the influence of national institutional factors decreased in the years prior to the crisis. This increasing risk of temporary employment depending on individual characteristics can be interpreted as the emergence of more flexible labour markets based on occupational and ascriptive criteria.

In a more economically and politically integrated Europe, national institutions were also deregulated by the initiation of the European employment strategy. This was aimed at flexibility and activation with a view to creating flexible labour markets in order to react to global competitiveness. This course of liberalization led to a re-commodification of labour accompanied by more social inequalities on labour markets. In the light of the influences on national policies and economic decisions resulting from the Europeanization process and the creation of the European common market, the observed coincidence of increasing individual risks depending on individuals' characteristics and a simultaneously decreasing dependence on national institutions can be seen as a de-territorialization of social inequalities. Due to the creation of the common market, with deepened economic interrelations and dependencies through an increased exchange between the European nation states, the commonalities between the countries increased while the single nation state became more heterogeneous and therefore differences within the countries increased (Münch 2001). Since the onset of the crisis, the national institutional context compared to the individual characteristics has once again become more important in explaining the likelihood of being employed on a temporary contract. However, this should not be taken as a 're-nationalization' of social inequalities, since individual characteristics determine the individual risk of being temporarily employed to a higher extent. The renewed influence of national context can be explained by the particularities of national labour markets, for example high unemployment rates, economic devastation and high shares of dismissed employees with former temporary contracts since the onset of the crisis.

NOTES

1. By analysing the insider–outsider division between permanent and fixed-term employees this chapter is limited to internal and external labour market segments.
2. Contrary to internal measures of flexibilization, where firms adjust their workforce by numerical or functional instruments (e.g. short-time work, working-time account or redeployment measures), the use of fixed-term contracts as an external instrument makes use of the external labour market by hiring and firing employees when the workforce has to be quickly increased in times of economic booms or rapidly and cost-effectively decreased when economic shocks occur.
3. 'Nearly half of all world trade occurs within the EU' (Beckfield 2009: 492).
4. To account for Germany in the analyses, we start with the year of 2002.
5. AT, BE, CZ, DE, DK, ES, FI, FR, GR, HU, IT, NL, PL, PT, SE, SK and UK.
6. Part-time employment is excluded from the analyses because it is much more voluntary

compared to fixed-term jobs and depends on other institutional factors than those analysed here in the context of temporary employment – e.g. in-kind family benefits, which could have an impact on the prevalence of part-time employment (European Commission 2012).
7. It must be noted that the information given by the EU-LFS with regard to being temporarily employed concerns employees having a contract with a fixed termination date as well as employees who are employed via a temporary employment agency.
8. The EPL for permanent employees was lower than for temporary employees in 2002.
9. AT, BE, CZ, DE, DK, FR, HU, IT, NL and PL.

REFERENCES

Babos, P. (2014), 'Step or Trap? Transition from Fixed-term Contracts in Central and Eastern Europe', *Post-Communist Economies*, **26** (1), 39–52.
Baranowska, A. and M. Gebel (2008), 'Temporary Employment in Central- and Eastern Europe: Individual Risk Patterns and Institutional Context', *Arbeitspapiere – Mannheimer Zentrum für Europäische Sozialforschung Working Paper* **106**.
Barbieri, P. (2009), 'Flexible Employment and Inequality in Europe', *European Sociological Review*, **25** (6), 621–628.
Bassanini, A., L. Nunziata and D. Venn (2008), 'Job Protection and Productivity Growth in OECD Countries', *Forschungsinstitut zur Zukunft der Arbeit, IZA Discussion Paper* **3555**.
Bauer, M.W., C. Knill and D. Pitschel (2007), 'Differential Europeanization in Eastern Europe: The Impact of Diverse EU Regulatory Governance Patterns', *Journal of European Integration*, **29**, 405–423.
Beckfield, J. (2009), 'Remapping Inequality in Europe: The Net Effect of Regional Integration on Total Income Inequality in the European Union', *International Journal of Comparative Sociology*, **50**, 486–508.
Bentolila, S., P. Cahuc, J.J. Dolado and T. Le Barbanchon (2012), 'Two-tier Labour Markets in the Great Recession: France Versus Spain', *The Economic Journal*, **122**, 155–187.
Blanchard, O. and A. Landier (2001), 'The Perverse Effects of Partial Labor Market Reform: Fixed Duration Contracts in France', *NBER Working Paper* **8219**.
Bonoli, G. and D. Natali (2011), 'The Politics of the New Welfare States in Western Europe', *EUI Working Paper, RSCAS*, **17**.
Bryan, M.L. and S.P. Jenkins (2013), 'Regression Analysis of Country Effects Using Multilevel Data: A Cautionary Tale', *ISER Working Paper Series, Research Paper* **7583**.
Buchner-Jeziorska, A. (2013), 'Non-standard Employment in Poland: Option or Necessity?', in M. Koch and M. Fritz (eds), *Non-Standard Employment in Europe. Paradigms, Prevalence and Policy Responses*, Basingstoke: Palgrave Macmillan, pp. 117–131.
Cahuc, P. and F. Postel-Vinay (2002), 'Temporary Jobs, Employment Protection and Labor Market Performance', *Labour Economics*, **9**, 63–91.
Cameron, A.C. and D.L. Miller (2011), 'Robust Inference with Clustered Data', in A. Ullah and D. E. Giles (eds), *Handbook of Empirical Economics and Finance*, Boca Raton, FL: CRC Press, pp.1–28.

De Grip, A., J. Hoevenberg and E. Willems (1997), 'Atypical Employment in the European Union', *International Labour Review*, **136** (1), 49–71.

Delsen, L. (1991), 'Atypical Employment Relations and Government Policy in Europe', *Labour*, **5**, 123–149.

Dieckhoff, M. and N. Steiber (2012), 'Institutional Reforms and Age-graded Labour Market Inequalities in Europe', *International Journal of Comparative Sociology*, **53**, 97–119.

DiPrete, T.A., D. Goux, E. Maurin and A. Quesnel-Vallee (2005), 'Work and Pay in Flexible and Regulated Labor Markets: A Generalized Perspective on Institutional Evolution and Inequality Trends in Europe and the U.S.', accessed 9 April 2015 at http://www.columbia.edu/~tad61/RSSM120705.pdf.

Ebner, A. (2007), 'Die Europäische Beschäftigungsstrategie in der Reform des Wohlfahrtsstaats: aktive Arbeitsmarktpolitik, aktivierende Sozialpolitik und das Leitbild der Wettbewerbsfähigkeit', *Wirtschaft: Forschung und Wissenschaft*, **21**, 203–227.

Eichhorst, W. (2014), 'Fixed-term Contracts. Are Fixed-term Contracts a Stepping Stone to a Permanent Job or a Dead End?', *IZA World of Labor*, **45**.

Emmenegger, P., S. Häusermann, B. Palier and M. Seeleib-Kaiser (2012), 'How We Grow Unequal', in P. Emmenegger, S. Häusermann, B. Palier and M. Seeleib-Kaiser (eds), *The Age of Dualization: The Changing Face of Inequality in Deindustrializing Societies*, Oxford and New York: Oxford University Press, pp. 3–26.

European Commission (2012), *Employment and Social Developments in Europe 2012*, Luxembourg: Publications Office of the European Union.

European Council (2000), 'Presidency Conclusion', accessed 13 September 2014 at http://www.europarl.europa.eu/summits/lis1_en.htm.

Ferrera, M. (2014), 'Ein schlechtgeordnetes Europa: Eine neo-Webersche Perspektive auf die EU und den Wohlfahrtsstaat', in M. Heidenreich (ed.), *Krise der europäischen Vergesellschaftung? Soziologische Perspektiven*, Wiesbaden: Springer VS, pp. 149–184.

Gebel, M. and J. Giesecke (2011), 'Labour Market Flexibility and Inequality: The Changing Skill-Based Temporary Employment and Unemployment Risks in Europe', *Social Forces*, **90** (1), 17–39.

Giesecke, J. and M. Groß (2002), 'Befristete Beschäftigung: Chance oder Risiko', *Kölner Zeitschrift für Soziologie und Sozialpsychologie*, **54** (1), 85–108.

Häusermann, S. and H. Schwander (2012), 'Varieties of Dualization? Labor Market Segmentation and Insider-Outsider Divides across Regimes', in P. Emmenegger, S. Häusermann, B. Palier and M. Seeleib-Kaiser (eds), *The Age of Dualization. The Changing Face of Inequality in Deindustrializing Countries*, Oxford and New York: Oxford University Press, pp. 27–51.

Heidenreich, M. (2003), 'Territoriale Ungleichheiten in der erweiterten EU', *Kölner Zeitschrift für Soziologie und Sozialpsychologie*, **55** (1), 31–58.

Heidenreich, M. (2006), 'Die Europäisierung sozialer Ungleichheiten zwischen nationaler Solidarität, europäischer Koordinierung und globalem Wettbewerb', in M. Heidenreich (ed.), *Die Europäisierung sozialer Ungleichheit*, Frankfurt a. M. and New York: Campus, pp. 17–64.

Heidenreich, M. (2014), 'Europäische Beschäftigungsordnungen in der Krise. Die Rückkehr segmentierter Arbeitsmärkte', in M. Heidenreich (ed.), *Krise der europäischen Vergesellschaftung? Soziologische Perspektiven*, Wiesbaden: Springer VS, pp. 281–309.

Heidenreich, M. and J. Zeitlin (2009), 'Introduction', in M. Heidenreich and J. Zeitlin (eds), *Changing European Employment and Welfare Regimes. The Influence of the Open Method of Coordination on National Reforms*, London: Routledge, pp. 1–9.

Holmlund, B. and D. Storrie (2002), 'Temporary Work in Turbulent Times: The Swedish Experience', *The Economic Journal*, **112**, 245–269.

Jakštienė, S. and D. Beržinskienė (2011), 'Labour Market Segmentation in the Context of Modern Theories', *Changes in Social and Business Environment*, **04**, 80–89.

Kahn, L.M. (2010), 'Employment Protection Reforms, Employment and the Incidence of Temporary Jobs in Europe: 1996–2001', *Labour Economics*, **17**, 1–15.

Kalleberg, A.L. (2000), 'Nonstandard Employment Relations: Part-time, Temporary and Contract Work', *Annual Review Sociology*, **26**, 341–365.

Kalleberg, A.L. (2003), 'Flexible Firms and Labor Market Segmentation: Effects of Workplace Restructuring on Jobs and Workers', *Work and Occupation*, **30**, 154–175.

Kalleberg, A.L. (2012), 'Job Quality and Precarious Work: Clarifications, Controversies, and Challenges', *Work and Occupations*, **39**, 427–448.

Keller, B. and H. Seifert (2008), 'Flexicurity: Ein europäisches Konzept und seine nationale Umsetzung', *WISO-Diskurs*, April 2008, Bonn.

Lang, C., I. Schömann and S. Clauwaert (2013), 'Atypical Forms of Employment Contracts in Times of Crisis', *European Trade Union Institute Working Paper* **03**.

Lang, W. (2000), 'Spanien und Portugal. Die ungleichen Nachbarn der iberischen Halbinsel: Warum ist die Arbeitsmarktbilanz Portugals besser als die Spaniens?', in H.-W. Platzer (ed.), *Arbeitsmarkt- und Beschäftigungspolitik in der EU. Nationale und europäische Perspektiven*, Baden-Baden: Nomos Verlagsgesellschaft, pp. 54–89.

Maurin, E. and F. Postel-Vinay (2005), 'The European Job Security Gap', *Work and Occupations*, **32**, 229–252.

Mood, C. (2010), 'Logistic Regression: Why we Cannot Do What we Think we Can Do, and What we Can Do About It', *European Sociological Review*, **26** (1), 67–82.

Münch, R. (2001), *Offene Räume. Soziale Integration diesseits und jenseits des Nationalstaats*, Berlin: Suhrkamp.

O'Conner, J.S. (2013), 'Non-Standard Employment and European Union Employment Regulation', in M. Koch and M. Fritz (eds), *Non-Standard Employment in Europe. Paradigms, Prevalence and Policy Response*, Basingstoke: Palgrave Macmillan, pp. 46–66.

Palier, B. and K. Thelen (2010), 'Institutionalizing Dualism: Complementaries and Change in France and Germany', *Politics & Society*, **2010** (38), 119–148.

Parsons, T. (1970), 'Equality and Inequality in Modern Society, or Social Stratification Revisited', *Sociological Inquiry*, **40** (2), 13–72.

Piore, M.J. and P. Doeringer (1971), *Internal Labor Markets and Manpower Adjustment*, New York: D.C. Heath and Company.

Polavieja, J.G. (2006), 'The Incidence of Temporary Employment in Advanced Economies: Why is Spain Different?', *European Sociological Review*, **22** (1), 61–87.

Reich, M., D.M. Gordon and R.C. Edwards (1973), 'Dual Labor Markets: A Theory of Labor Market Segmentation', *The American Economic Review*, **63** (2), 359–365.

Schmid, G. (2010), 'Non-Standard Employment and Labour Force Participation: A Comparative View of the Recent Development in Europe', *Institute for the Study of Labour, Discussion Paper* **5087**, Bonn: IZA.

Sola, J., E. Alonso, C.J.F. Rodríguez and R.I. Rojo (2013), 'The Expansion of Temporary Employment in Spain (1984–2010): Neither Socially Fair nor Economically Productive', in M. Koch and M. Fritz (eds), *Non-Standard Employment in Europe. Paradigms, Prevalence and Policy Responses*, Basingstoke: Palgrave Macmillan, pp. 67–102.

Streeck, W. (2013), *Gekaufte Zeit. Die vertagte Krise des demokratischen Kapitalismus*, Berlin: Suhrkamp.

Weishaupt, T.J. (2011), *From the Manpower Revolution to the Activation Paradigm. Explaining Institutional Continuity and Change in an Integrating Europe*, Amsterdam: Amsterdam University Press.

Zeitlin, J. (2005), 'The Open Method of Co-ordination in Action. Theoretical Promise, Empirical Realities, Reform Strategy', in J. Zeitlin and P. Pochet (eds), *The Open Method of Co-ordination in Action. The European Employment and Social Inclusion Strategies*, Brussels: P.I.E.-Peter Land S.A., pp. 447–504.

Table 6A.1 Individual and institutional determinants on the risk of full-time temporary employment for 2002 to 2013

	2002	2003	2004	2005	2006	2007	2008	2009	2010	2011	2012	2013
Individual determinants												
Women	0.019***	0.016**	0.016**	0.018**	0.021***	0.025***	0.024***	0.018***	0.020***	0.016***	0.019**	0.014***
	(3.74)	(3.22)	(2.70)	(3.24)	(3.46)	(5.82)	(4.29)	(4.59)	(7.45)	(7.28)	(3.18)	(5.13)
Age group (ref. 35 to 49 years)												
20 to 34 years	0.114***	0.117***	0.122***	0.132***	0.133***	0.133***	0.136***	0.129***	0.138***	0.139***	0.142***	0.141***
	(15.55)	(13.06)	(12.37)	(10.64)	(10.84)	(11.74)	(9.45)	(7.69)	(10.61)	(8.61)	(8.27)	(11.34)
50 to 64 years	−0.021***	−0.024***	−0.027***	−0.030***	−0.031***	−0.030***	−0.028***	−0.026***	−0.028***	−0.032***	−0.031***	−0.030***
	(−3.57)	(−4.20)	(−3.74)	(−3.90)	(−5.98)	(−4.58)	(−5.54)	(−5.57)	(−4.88)	(−5.72)	(−7.04)	(−8.26)
Educational level (ref.: low, ISCED 0–2)												
Medium (ISCED 3–4)	−0.063***	−0.058***	−0.057***	−0.057***	−0.047***	−0.063***	−0.047**	−0.043*	−0.052*	−0.053*	−0.033	−0.056**
	(−3.81)	(−3.35)	(−3.65)	(−3.52)	(−3.39)	(−3.79)	(−2.77)	(−2.03)	(−2.43)	(−2.46)	(−1.23)	(−2.69)
High (ISCED 5–6)	−0.058***	−0.054**	−0.062***	−0.065***	−0.064***	−0.075***	−0.065***	−0.061***	−0.075**	−0.073***	−0.054*	−0.074***
	(−3.46)	(−3.06)	(−4.13)	(−3.93)	(−4.38)	(−4.23)	(−3.79)	(−2.84)	(−3.20)	(−3.10)	(−2.21)	(−3.35)
Structural determinants												
Economic growth	0.026*	0.016	0.070	0.008	0.029**	0.030*	0.023	0.031***	0.040	0.047**	0.021	0.038**
	(2.50)	(1.28)	(1.81)	(0.60)	(3.27)	(2.51)	(1.09)	(4.03)	(1.85)	(2.95)	(1.93)	(3.22)
Unemployment rate	0.018***	0.032***	0.018***	0.030***	0.024***	0.021*	0.032***	0.023***	0.029***	0.034***	0.014***	0.030***
	(3.64)	(4.32)	(3.11)	(8.23)	(3.10)	(2.48)	(4.40)	(6.37)	(3.21)	(5.72)	(4.05)	(4.37)

Table 6A.1 (continued)

	2002	2003	2004	2005	2006	2007	2008	2009	2010	2011	2012	2013
Institutional determinants												
Active labour market measures (in % of GDP)	**0.018*** **(2.36)**	0.016 (1.37)	0.003 (0.55)	**0.017*** **(2.31)**	**0.024**** **(2.61)**	0.016 (1.51)	0.024 (1.67)	0.021 (1.76)	−0.004 (−0.24)	−0.003 (−0.26)	−0.009 (−0.62)	0.013 (1.42)
Employment protection for permanent employees (EPL)	**0.015*** **(2.00)**	0.006 (0.47)	**0.034***** **(3.52)**	**0.008*** **(2.19)**	0.012 (1.73)	0.008 (1.44)	0.007 (0.66)	0.009 (1.17)	0.009 (1.04)	**0.017**** **(2.63)**	**0.032***** **(3.85)**	0.000 (0.02)
Difference between EPL permanent and EPL temporary	−0.015 (−1.53)	−0.024 (−1.84)	**−0.030*** **(−1.97)**	−0.024 (−1.50)	**−0.020***** **(−3.58)**	−0.013 (−1.11)	−0.003 (−0.51)	**0.012*** **(2.08)**	−0.013 (−1.17)	−0.009 (−1.63)	−0.018 (−1.69)	−0.002 (−0.59)
Pseudo-R^2	0.11	0.12	0.12	0.12	0.13	0.11	0.12	0.12	0.12	0.11	0.10	0.12
AIC	72333312	73201019	75757767	81998694	84435492	87615869	86354114	81032326	82581024	83095137	82425159	79828646
BIC	72509867	73376580	75932911	82191654	84622743	87803338	86541178	81218703	82768571	83281254	82612973	80015589
No.	458038	430461	419357	1277045	893769	906036	883366	846220	910446	832604	925745	876741

Note: Logistic regression on the risk of full-time temporary employment; taking into account the country level; the coefficients are the average marginal effects. Significance levels: *** (p < 0.001), ** (p < 0.01), * (p < 0.05). Controlled for industries (NACE).

Source: Eurostat: Labour Force Survey 2015, own calculation.

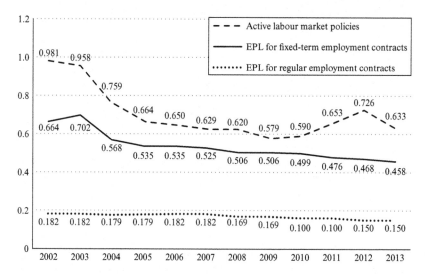

Note: Coefficients are coefficients of variation (standard deviation of unweighted national indicators for 17 countries divided by arithmetic mean).

Source: Own calculation using data from Eurostat and OECD.

Figure 6A.1   Convergent/divergent development of national labour market institutions, 2002 to 2013

7. The Europeanization of social determinants and health in the Great Recession

Sabine Israel

7.1 INTRODUCTION

European integration is becoming a significant factor in delivering and determining health (Chen et al. 1999; Beckfield and Olafsdottir 2009). The EU has a threefold impact on the health of its Member States' population: first through its decisions as a global actor, second by supporting national health systems in terms of best-practice exchange, and third by its direct regulations (Greer and Kurzer 2013). In the aftermath of the global financial crisis in 2008, the impact of the EU on Member States' public health became even more pronounced.

Over the course of the global financial crisis and the subsequent European debt crisis, the countries in the EU were exposed to liquidity, growth and unemployment problems. However, the severity of these issues varied throughout the EU. This led to the re-emergence of a divide between a 'prosperous centre' and an 'instable periphery' (Becker and Jäger 2011), splitting the EU first into countries inside and outside of the eurozone and second into core 'lenders' and periphery 'spenders' (Lapavitsas et al. 2010). For the eurozone periphery, policy responses to the crisis were limited. Without sovereign control over their exchange rates, these countries had no option but to lower debt by real depreciation and reduced governmental spending (Hassel 2006). For the countries outside the eurozone, fiscal consolidation also became a political priority. Increased efficiency in healthcare, as the area taking up the largest part of social expenditures, was included in an increasing number of recommendations in the European Semester process[1] for all but six European countries (see Azzopardi-Muscat et al. 2015). For some of the countries subject to Economic Adjustment Programmes (EAPs), namely Spain, Cyprus, Greece, Ireland and Portugal, reduced healthcare spending was a direct obligation specified in their bail-out agreement (European Commission 2013). Similarly, countries outside of the eurozone, namely Romania, Hungary and Latvia, were assisted by the 'Balance of Payment Programme' (BoP) which imposed budget restrictions. Following these political developments, households in the crisis-affected European periphery (the EAP and BoP countries) have been exposed to a comparable situation of less expenditure on health and social protection – however on different levels. Added to this is the ongoing negative economic growth. By 2012 none of these peripheral states had recovered the level of economic performance they recorded in 2008 (in GDP per capita). For households this implied wage cuts and an increase in long-term unemployment, furthermore reducing income opportunities.

A decrease in household resources is not directly related to poorer health outcomes. Similarly, recessions and healthcare system reforms do not automatically induce higher rates of morbidity and mortality (WHO 2012; OECD 2013a; Burgard and Kalousova 2015). Nevertheless, when a situation of increased need (as given in times of high unemployment) is combined with reduced support for households, a worsening of population health and of health indicators for the most affected population groups is particularly likely (Karanikolos et al. 2013; Stuckler and Basu 2013). In the media, health became a key area of debate, as it strongly reflects the impact of austerity policies on people's lives. In 2011, *The New York Times* bore the headline 'Fiscal Crisis Takes Toll on Health of Greeks' (26 December 2011),[2] describing the dire shortage of all kinds of medical equipment and bureaucratic troubles in obtaining health insurance. In 2013, *The Guardian* stated 'Spanish helpline reports rise in number of callers considering suicide' (3 September 2013).[3] Scientific reports on the crisis have confirmed that the psycho-social effects of the increased strain on households are visible in rising numbers of people with poor mental health (Bartoll et al. 2013), clinical depression (Gili et al. 2012) and cases of suicide (Branas et al. 2015). But also access to medical care was restricted in many European countries, increasing the cases of foregone care (OECD 2013a; Eurofound 2014; Kentikelenis et al. 2014; Kyriopoulos et al. 2014). Physical effects of the eurozone crisis due to the effect of reduced material living standards, e.g. poorer nutrition and poorer housing conditions on health, are also likely (Chzhen 2014; Eurofound 2014) but have not been reported so far. Drawbacks of existing studies are their limitation to psycho-social and medical determinants of health and their reduced coverage of countries. There are few cross-border evaluations of the impact of the eurozone crisis on health, and BoP countries are rarely studied.

The research in this chapter will explore the extent to which the health status of poor individuals worsened throughout the crisis in the European periphery. More specifically, it seeks to analyse the development of physical, psycho-social and medical health determinants which commonly cause ill health among people with a low absolute income. This approach will expose the social conditions which have to be addressed if a worsening of poor health in the European periphery is to be minimized. The analysis will be carried out using EU-SILC data on subjective health and household determinants of health and compare pre-crisis 2006/2007 data to the initial phase of the financial crisis (2009/2010) and the later phase of debt reduction policies (2011/2012). It is structured as follows: first, subjective health will be defined and the development of common causes of ill health traced over the past years. The change in health since the onset of the crisis will then be portrayed and country differences assessed in a regression analysis.

7.2   PRIMARY AND SECONDARY SOCIAL DETERMINANTS OF BAD HEALTH

The WHO defined health in its founding document in 1948 as a 'state of complete physical, mental and social well-being, and not merely the absence of disease or infirmity' (WHO 1948). This statement shows the historic development of the term 'health', which over time went from meaning 'absence of illness' (biomedical definition) or 'functionality' (social definition) to 'balance' (bio-psychological) and 'well-being' (holistic approach). The modern holistic approach can be exemplified by Beckfield and Olafsdottir's (2009) statement: 'Health is about the power, for instance, to live in a neighborhood of one's choice, to take part in political life, to train for and enter an occupation, to opt for a healthy lifestyle, and to claim and access health care' (p. 9). Such a broad definition based on the opportunity structure of an individual, however, is difficult to implement in practice.

Health inequalities, in other words the unequal distribution of good and bad health across the social structure, arise when the opportunity structure of a social group is restricted in the sense that it cannot reach such valuable outcomes easily. With respect to both mortality and morbidity, poorer people are disadvantaged (Marmot et al. 1984). Not only do they live for fewer years, they are more often exposed to cardio-vascular diseases, diabetes and other health problems (Siegrist and Marmot 2006). However, it is not only the very poor who more often report bad health and illnesses. Throughout the social hierarchy it is possible to say that 'the higher you get, the healthier you are' (Marmot et al. 1991; Singh-Manoux et al. 2006). But income is not the only crucial factor. In general, a low socio-economic status (SES), be it for reasons of poor education, a low occupational position or unemployment, has been proven to be related to higher individual health risks.[4] Today, three main theories have been accepted which explain the social gradient of health: the materialist theory, the psycho-social theory and, from a medical point of view, access to healthcare.[5]

7.2.1 Physical Impact of Low Income on Health

The Black Report (Marmot et al. 1984) was the first recorded attempt to find reasons for health inequalities which go beyond lifestyle arguments. It diverted attention away from the 'culture of the poor' towards the importance of money for access to essential goods and services (Bolte and Kohlhuber 2009). Their 'materialist theory' discerned health risks in living conditions which can be avoided when a certain income is available to a household. Physical health effects can be traced back to poor housing conditions (Krieger and Higgins 2002; Braubach and Fairburn 2010). Dampness and rot entail respiratory problems (Braubach and Fairburn 2010) and asthma (Krieger and Higgins 2002). Furthermore, living in housing with insufficient heating is associated with lower general health and recurring illnesses (Evans et al. 2000). Next to substandard living conditions, low income can translate into worse nutrition and in this way impact health (Stafford and McCarthy 2006; Macy et al. 2013). A household's access to healthy food is highly dependent on its economic power, as proven by the Moli-sani study (Bonaccio et al. 2012). Even individuals with high education, who tend to be more aware of nutrition, consume less healthy food when income is low (Bonaccio et al. 2012). The financial crisis is likely to have led to worse living conditions and increased material deprivation. However, the effect on health of recent deteriorations in living standards has been the topic of very few studies.

7.2.2 Psycho-social Impact of Low Income on Health

The psycho-social explanatory model, focusing on the importance of psycho-social health for well-being (see Gee and Payne-Sturges 2004), has gained prominence over the last decades. Both low relative and absolute income have been linked to worse psycho-social health. Relative income is decisive because people tend to compare themselves to their neighbours. 'Status fear' arises when individuals do not feel able to 'keep up' (Wilkinson and Pickett 2009). Absolute income, on the other hand, influences health through higher risk exposure and vulnerability of the poor. First, individual exposure to socio-economic resources and risks is socially stratified, e.g. low-income groups are more likely to be exposed to financial stress, reduced social contacts or difficulties in accessing the labour market. Second, people with a low income often show higher vulnerability to such risk factors due to harmful pre-exposure. Moreover, they tend to lack the social, financial and educational coping resources of other groups (Bolte et al. 2012). In particular, depression is common for reasons of reduced capacity to meet unexpected finances and arrears (Veenstra and Kelly 2007; Burgard et al. 2012). People who are in arrears with their mortgage have been shown to be nine times more likely to develop a clinical depression (Stuckler and Basu 2013). During the eurozone crisis, arrears and evictions from houses were widespread (Novoa et al. 2014). From a sample of people with mental problems visiting primary health care centres in Spain in 2010, one-third could be attributed to the combination of job loss and mortgage payment difficulties (Gili et al. 2012). In Greece, deprivation-related depressions also increased between two to five times during the crisis (from 2005 to 2009) (Kentikelenis et al. 2014), while suicides have increased by 35 per cent since 2011 (Branas et al. 2015).

7.2.3   Difficulties in Accessing the Medical System for Health

Access to the medical system constitutes a third link between low income and bad health. Healthcare offers a chance to identify an illness and treat it before it turns into a chronic disease (Mielck et al. 2007). When access to healthcare is limited, illnesses can become worse and unmet medical need arises. Far more than household income, it is the healthcare system which decides on access to care. European healthcare systems differ regarding healthcare expenditure, financing, service provision and access regulation (Wendt 2009). In turn, these determine the five dimensions of access to healthcare (Penchansky and Thomas 1981): (1) availability of adequate services; (2) geographical accessibility; (3) financial accessibility; (4) accommodation of patients' needs; and (5) acceptability of services for patients. It is thus not only user charges and the coverage of services (affordability dimension) that may play a role for poor individuals in their decision to seek healthcare, but also waiting lists (accommodation dimension) and travel costs (accessibility dimension) which determine their access. Low-income households have a lower probability of accessing healthcare in half of the OECD countries and a lower probability of visiting specialists in all OECD countries (Doorslaer et al. 2006). For the period during the eurozone crisis, the Eurofound (2014) report provides the most detailed analysis of access to care. It finds that even in crisis countries where there were few cuts to the healthcare system, reduced access to healthcare in fact arose. In Greece and Ireland, demand for emergency care rose because of an increase in co-payments for regular doctor visits. Next to co-payments, a lack of insurance was a reason for unmet medical needs in Greece and Cyprus (OECD 2013a). Vulnerable groups encompass individuals with low income, those who lost their job (simultaneously losing insurance) and households in the twilight zone between poor and non-poor. Older people (Kentikelenis et al. 2014) and those with chronic illnesses (Kyriopoulos et al. 2014) were also highly affected in some Member States.

7.2.4 The Impact of the Crisis on Low-income Households in the European Periphery

As shown above, SES and poor health are strongly correlated. However, the link between these two constructs is not a direct one. Lower income does not lead immediately to worse health. Their dynamics are intertwined, but health responses are often lagged as they are mediated by societal factors (referred to as social determinants of health) (Graham 2004). Alongside national arrangements, however, supranational polities like the EU may also contribute to the macro-sociological context in which health is generated (Beckfield and Olafsdottir 2009). While the influence of different European and national policies has often been recognized as part of the multi-level determinants of health (Schulz and Northridge 2004), except for the Eurofound (2014) study, the literature review on the impact of the crisis on morbidity revealed no multi-country impact assessments. The transnational perspective adopted in this chapter aims to fill the void by taking common European influences on population health into perspective. It is assumed that the crisis policy of the EU brought about a new set of rules which not only steer national economic developments but also medical, material and psycho-social individual determinants (see Figure 7.1). The distribution of poor health among the European population can thus be traced back not only to individual and national factors, but also to the process of European integration.

Psycho-social health effects are a probable result of the enduring crisis, given that adverse macro-economic developments affect mental health particularly if they lead to prolonged exposure to high psychological

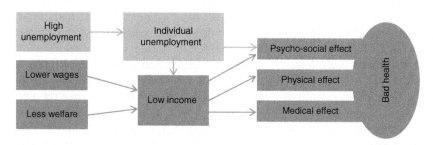

Figure 7.1   Model from income-based social determinants of health to bad health

demands, while possibilities to control the situation are perceived to be limited (Bosma et al. 1997). In addition, physical effects on health stemming from adverse living conditions and financial strain are a likely health outcome of low economic resources. While material deprivation seems to be less responsive to the economic downturn than household income, increases were reported in particular for workless households, lone-parent families and migrant families (Chzhen 2014). When worsened physical and psycho-social conditions exist and access to medical care is difficult, a further deterioration of health can occur. Accordingly, it is expected that *in the period following the financial crisis, a worsening of health and its social determinants arose in the peripheral countries (H1)*.

When speaking about the European periphery during the crisis period, most often solely the EAP countries are being referred to, even though the BoP countries outside of the eurozone have been similarly hit by rising indebtedness (Lapavitsas et al. 2010). They constitute a second European periphery, which is often excluded in public debate. This chapter wants to analyse the impact of the crisis by comparing these two peripheries with each other and with the core countries. Different detrimental social determinants of health will have accumulated in the country clusters depending on the severity of the crisis, its duration and the initial level of health. Given the initial low level of health in the BoP countries and their reduced extent of coping resources (few financial reserves), the vulnerability of these households to the crisis is expected to be particularly high. *It is assumed that in the BoP countries the effects of adverse medical, physical and socio-psychical determinants on health will be more pronounced and that individuals will show a higher deterioration in health than individuals from the EAP countries (H2)*.

Inside the crisis countries, however, the population will not be affected in the same way. A differential impact on income quintiles of the hardship of the financial crisis is likely. In particular, a worsening of the situation among the lower income quintiles can occur, reflecting their higher exposure and vulnerability to cuts. In most crisis countries their wages decreased to a higher extent than those of higher-income individuals (OECD 2013b). In addition, in the second phase of the crisis welfare expenditures were lowered in areas of health and social expenditures. A reduction of such collective resources always affects those at the bottom of the income distribution most, as they rely to a greater degree on governmental support (Blyth 2013). Together with higher health demands, this creates a situation in which negative health responses are particularly likely for poor households. *We therefore expect that the impact of social determinants on health has increased more for lower income quintiles than for higher income quintiles (H3)*.

7.3 METHODS, DATA AND LIMITATIONS

The analysis will be carried out using the cross-sectional surveys from EU-SILC, which is the micro-data set on income and living conditions compiled by the EU. EU-SILC provides detailed information on all EU-28 Member States plus Norway and Iceland from 2005 to 2012. The focus will be set not only on the effects of the recession but also on EU political action. Therefore, the countries under study will be the EAP countries Spain, Cyprus, Greece, Ireland and Portugal, which were assisted by EU emergency measures by the European Financial Stability Mechanism and European Stability Mechanism (EFSM/ESM), plus Hungary, Latvia and Romania (RO in EU-SILC data from 2008 onwards), which were assisted by the BoP programme.

In the EU-SILC the only available variable describing health is self-rated health, which is a subjective rating of 'health in general' from 'very good' to 'very bad' on a 5-point scale. Self-rated health is a frequently used indicator of health, which has shown to be a reliable predictor of morbidity and mortality (Osoba 1999). The reference frame that a person is using in order to answer this question may vary, however, influencing its comparability. Some people assess their health relative to other people of the same age or other people with the same illness, while in other instances a person refers to himself or herself at an earlier point in life (Fayers and Sprangers 2002). Different cultural response styles (Jürges 2007) will be offset by dichotomizing subjective health into good (very good, good) and bad (average, bad, very bad) health status. The operationalization of the above described physical, psycho-social and medical social determinants is as follows: the medical pathway is analysed on the basis of unmet medical needs which arise when a person would have liked to contact a doctor but had only restricted access to medical diagnosis and treatment. First, the individual was asked whether there was any occasion on which he or she really needed to consult a physician during the last 12 months but did not; as a second step different reasons for the unmet need can be given. The reasons 'could not afford (too expensive)', 'waiting list' and 'too far to travel/no means of transportation' are monetary links between access to medical services and poor health (Kentikelenis et al. 2014).

The psychological and physical pathways from low income to bad health can be captured through a multitude of deprivation variables in EU-SILC.[6] A polychoric explanatory factor analysis for binary variables was performed in order to generate latent factors appropriate for the aim of the analysis (see appendix Table 7A.1). Two factors were retrieved: 'difficulty of financing a living' and 'arrears'. The first factor 'difficulty of financing a living' is identified by three variables that cover different parts of substantial physical needs: (1) ability to keep the house warm; (2) ability to afford a proper meal; (3) ability to pay for usual expenses. A lack of any of these variables refers to a serious deprivation of the household with subsequent effects on the physical health. The second factor 'arrears' refers to problems which can have psychological effects if they are long-lasting. This factor is identified by another three variables: (1) arrears on mortgage or rent payments; (2) arrears on utility bills; (3) arrears on hire purchase instalments. Table 7.1 shows the operationalization of the variables, which can all be attributed to the individual level. The analysis applies logistic regressions to the cross-sectional time series data (TSCS) of EU-SILC. TSCS data must be treated with caution because the individuals included in the different waves are not the same. Patterns in the development over time thus cannot be directly related to societal change. They are just as likely to stem from selection effects (Fairbrother 2011). The nesting of households into countries is controlled for by cluster-robust standard errors (Bryan and Jenkins 2013). The effect of single years is not modelled because within their clustering (2006/2007, 2009/2010, 2011/2012) they have revealed no significant difference. The model is constructed with the Stata 13 and the command for binary outcome analysis logit.

7.4   THE DEVELOPMENT OF THE HOUSEHOLD DETERMINANTS OF HEALTH IN THE EUROPEAN PERIPHERY

EU-SILC data (see Table 7.2) shows that Spain, Latvia, Ireland and Cyprus were most affected by negative growth rates in the first years of the economic downturn, spurred by the financial market crisis (2009 and 2010). In the later crisis years in which the debt problems came to the fore (2011 and 2012), the decline of equivalized household income was most pronounced in Greece. Here, the income of the poorest 20 per cent of the population decreased by 28 percentage points. Portugal and Romania also showed increased problems in this phase of the crisis, while Ireland and Spain continued to struggle. Hungary, Cyprus and Latvia had already recovered part of their economic performance at this point of time. The poorest were affected in particular in Greece, Spain and Ireland by a reduction of household income. In Portugal and Latvia, on the other hand, it was the richer people who had to accept the highest cuts. When looking at the income changes, it is interesting to notice that the low macro-economic performance did not translate into wage cuts in all crisis countries.

Where income changes occurred, they translated almost directly into higher deprivation levels and arrears, which had to be accepted by households to afford the usual standard of living. In 2011/2012, 10.7 per cent

Table 7.1   *Operationalization, data sources and the expected effects of variables*

Variable	Operationalization	Data source	Expected
	Dependent		
Health	Subjective health status (0: very good and good, 1: average, bad, very bad)	EU-SILC ph010	
	Control variables		
Sex	1: male (ref. group); 2: female	EU-SILC rb090	+
Age	Age (continuous)	EU-SILC rx020	+
	Individual determinants		
Migrant	0: native; 1: migrant by country of birth or citizenship	EU-SILC pb210, pb220	+
Activity status	0: at work or inactive (ref. group), 1: unemployed	EU-SILC rb210	+
Education	1: high education (ISCED 5–6) (ref. group), 2: middle education (ISCED 3–4), 3: low education (ISCED 1–2)	EU-SILC pe020	+
Poverty	0: non-poor (ref. group), 1: poor. Net equivalized disposable household income below 60% of the EU median (in PPP)	EU-SILC hx090	+
	Social determinants		
Living standard	From 0 to 3 deprivations including 'capacity to keep home adequately warm', 'afford a protein meal', 'face usual expenses'	EU-SILC hs050 hh050 hs120	+
Arrears	From 0 to 3 deprivations including 'arrears on mortgage or rent payments', 'arrears on utility bills', 'arrears on hire purchase instalments or other loans'	EU-SILC hs011, hs021 hs031	+
Unmet medical needs	Unmet need for medical examination or treatment 0: no income-related need, 1: income-related need for reasons of costs, transportation costs; waiting lists	EU SILC ph040, ph050	+

Note: +: effect is positive, expected to increase bad health.

of the population in the EAP countries was exposed to at least one of the three indicators for deprivation (capacity to afford a protein meal, afford usual expenses, and heat the apartment properly), while the incidence of deprivation was 31.1 per cent in the BoP countries. In countries where the

Table 7.2 Latent factors from low income to poor health and exposure to bad health per income quintile

Countries	Income change (%)					Deprivation (%)					Arrears (%)					Access to health (%)				
	Q1	Q2	Q3	Q4	Q5	Q1	Q2	Q3	Q4	Q5	Q1	Q2	Q3	Q4	Q5	Q1	Q2	Q3	Q4	Q5
2006/07 EL	100	100	100	100	100	36	23	13	6	1	53	40	27	16	5	9	7	6	4	1
2009/10 EL	102	102	102	102	100	46	29	14	5	1	48	41	29	22	9	10	7	5	3	2
2011/12 EL	72	81	84	83	86	62	37	20	8	4	60	47	39	24	8	12	10	8	5	4
2006/07 ES	100	100	100	100	100	17	11	7	4	2	11	7	7	5	3	0	1	0	0	0
2009/10 ES	77	94	96	98	101	16	10	6	4	1	22	14	11	7	3	1	0	1	0	0
2011/12 ES	77	90	93	96	98	17	12	7	3	2	21	12	8	5	3	1	1	1	0	0
2006/07 PT	100	100	100	100	10	61	52	42	28	9	12	7	7	5	2	14	9	7	5	2
2009/10 PT	107	106	104	102	96	46	39	33	19	5	16	13	8	5	2	6	3	3	1	0
2011/12 PT	102	104	102	99	97	43	34	27	17	6	19	13	8	7	3	4	3	2	2	0

174

2006/07 IE	100	100	100	100	100	13	7	3	1	0	19	12	6	3	2	3	2	2	2	1
2009/10 IE	90	95	93	92	94	15	10	4	3	0	21*	18*	12*	2*	1*	3	2	2	3	1
2011/12 IE	86	93	90	89	89	17	15	8	3	1	33	33	22	13	8	4	3	3	3	1
2006/07 CY	100	100	100	100	100	57	44	34	22	7	30	33	27	17	7	8	4	3	2	0
2009/10 CY	102	102	101	102	105	40	30	27	18	6	32	35	29	22	10	6	6	4	2	1
2011/12 CY	105	104	104	107	112	50	36	30	19	7	36	40	36	24	13	7	6	4	2	1
2006/07 LV	100	100	100	100	100	64	54	40	28	14	19	14	10	11	10	27	16	10	9	5
2009/10 LV	93	99	93	92	92	58	43	29	21	9	36	24	22	20	13	24	15	11	8	5

Table 7.2   (continued)

Countries	Income change (%)					Deprivation (%)					Arrears (%)					Access to health (%)				
	Q1	Q2	Q3	Q4	Q5	Q1	Q2	Q3	Q4	Q5	Q1	Q2	Q3	Q4	Q5	Q1	Q2	Q3	Q4	Q5
2011/12 LV	103	104	97	96	97	62	49	35	26	13	43	28	23	18	11	25	19	14	9	5
2006/07 HU	100	100	100	100	100	53	40	31	21	11	35	20	14	11	10	5	3	2	2	1
2009/10 HU	106	106	107	108	108	50	39	29	21	9	50	26	21	15	10	5	2	2	1	1
2011/12 HU	113	117	118	120	123	62	43	31	20	9	54	28	21	15	10	7	3	2	1	1
RO 2008* RO	100	100	100	100	100	50	38	34	25	16	38	27	22	22	17	17	15	11	8	4
2009/10 RO	124	121	118	117	109	50	40	33	25	15	40	31	30	24	19	14	13	11	8	4
2011/12 RO	117	119	118	117	107	50	34	27	19	12	42	34	31	25	21	15	16	13	10	5

Note: Own calculation, based on EU-SILC. Displayed are percentage of affected population for different income quintiles from Q1 (poor) to Q5 (rich). Data for pre-crisis arrears in Ireland are based on 2008 numbers, as is all pre-crisis information for Romania.

median household income went below the 2006/2007 level, deprivation rates rose. This was the case for Greece, Ireland and Latvia and to a lesser degree for Spain. In Hungary and Cyprus deprivation also rose, despite stagnating or increasing incomes. Among the population, low-income quintiles showed the highest increase in deprivation. Only in Portugal and Latvia, where income decreased most for the richer, the higher income quintiles were affected most. In general, most countries were more strongly hit by deprivation within the second phase of the crisis, in particular by problems of affording the 'usual expenses' (see appendix Figure 7A.1).

Arrears are a problem with growing importance in all income quintiles. They indicate increased financial stress and problems of keeping up with the living standard. Before, they mostly affected low-income households, but with the advancement of the crisis individuals in the second and third quintiles were also increasingly subject to arrears.

While in 2006/2007 9 per cent of the households from the EAP countries showed at least one out of the three arrear indicators (arrears on rent/ mortgage, arrears on utility bills, arrears on hire purchase instalments), this figure was 11 per cent in 2011/2012. While arrears on utility bills are the most prevalent, in Ireland and Greece arrears on mortgage and rent are also rising (see appendix Figure 7A.2), which is an indicator of severe financial difficulties and highly linked to health problems. In the BoP countries, the problem of arrears rose from 17 per cent in 2006/2007 to 27 per cent in 2011/2012. In Latvia and Hungary, the increase for the lowest income quintile was around 20 percentage points. This change can be mainly attributed to arrears on utility bills, while mortgage and rent problems did not arise to a high extent.

Access to healthcare is the social determinant of health which can be traced back most to a country's political response to the crisis. In Spain, Ireland and Hungary, access to healthcare decreased slightly for lower income quintiles. In Greece, access deteriorated throughout the social strata and by up to three percentage points for the two poorest income quintiles. In contrast, Portugal and also Cyprus show an amelioration of access to healthcare. In Latvia and Romania, the effect of the crisis on access to healthcare varied highly according to income quintile. In both of these countries, an improvement in access for the poor took place, while unmet medical needs worsened for the middle classes by four and two percentage points respectively (see appendix Figure 7A.3). Even a slight deterioration has strong repercussions on population health, as access to healthcare is a fundamental prerequisite for well-being.

This descriptive analysis brings about the conclusion that social determinants of health did worsen as a result of the crisis. The first part of H1 can be confirmed because the extent of arrears and the degree of deprivation are increasing in both EAP and BoP countries. While adequate social and health policies seem to be able to keep the extent of deprivation and healthcare access barriers relatively low despite stark declines in household income (see Spain, Portugal and Ireland), in other places a marginalization of the poor is occurring (Greece and Hungary). Arrears – the social determinant least regulated by policies – are increasing for the poor in all countries. They can therefore be seen as a strong common social determinant of health among peripheral countries.

7.5   THE DEVELOPMENT OF BAD HEALTH IN THE EUROPEAN PERIPHERY

Table 7.3 shows the prevalence of bad health by comparing the period 2006/2007 with the period 2009/2010 and 2011/2012. While in the EAP countries a weighted average of 34 per cent of the population cited bad health in 2006/2007, in 2011–2012 this number had decreased to 30 per cent. The Eastern European BoP countries started from a much higher level of bad health, with an overall exposure rate of 46 per cent in 2008/2009 which decreased in 2011/2012 to 41 per cent. When looking at the lowest income quintile, we see an outright improvement. The incidence of bad health among the poorest increased solely in Greece in 2009/2010 and in Hungary in 2011/2012. This is a surprising result which contradicts the expectation that the poorest are the most exposed and vulnerable to the crisis. In contrast, the other quintiles and in particular the second and third quintile show a worsening of health. This development can be found in Greece for Q2–5, in Ireland for Q2–5, in Cyprus for Q2–5, in Portugal for Q2–3, in Latvia for Q2–4 and in Romania for Q3–5 for at least one of the crisis periods in comparison to 2006/2007. For most countries the probability of bad health for the lowest and middle-income quintiles is converging (see Figure 7.2). In all crisis countries except for Cyprus, the proportion of individuals with ill health in the second income quintile was in fact *above* that of the lowest income quintile in 2011/2012. In Greece, Spain, Hungary and Romania even the middle-income quintile showed a higher or similar incidence of bad health than the poorest. Romania is a clear outlier in the data. Even before the crisis, the lowest income quintile did not conform to the social gradient in health. An explanation for this very good rating (also in terms of health level) of the very poor could be the reference group to which they are comparing themselves.

A similar effect stemming from the subjective nature of the health variable could also be a reason for the improvement in health responses among the low-income quintile, even in countries where their median disposable income dropped with the crisis. A more pronounced decrease in the living

Table 7.3   *Incidence of bad health among different income quintiles in peripheral countries*

	2006/2007 (%)					2009/2010 (%)					2011/2012 (%)				
	Q1	Q2	Q3	Q4	Q5	Q1	Q2	Q3	Q4	Q5	Q1	Q2	Q3	Q4	Q5
EL	**32**	30	24	18	12	**33**	31	27	19	12	27	**31**	27	22	15
ES	**44**	39	33	27	21	**37**	37	31	24	16	27	**35**	28	21	15
PT	**69**	59	53	47	38	**65**	61	51	45	36	59	**62**	54	45	36
IE	**30**	23	14	10	6	24	**25**	16	12	7	21	**25**	17	13	8
CY	**48**	25	19	16	10	**45**	28	21	18	13	**40**	28	20	15	13
LV	**73**	69	58	52	40	**67**	66	52	44	37	59	**68**	56	47	37
HU	56	**60**	57	50	40	46	**51**	48	43	35	47	**51**	47	40	30
RO*	32	**38**	33	30	21	27	**34**	32	31	23	26	**34**	34	34	27

Notes:
Pre-crisis data for Romania from 2008.
Entries in bold indicate the highest incidences for each country and period.

standards of the higher income quintiles will make the poorer relatively better off and lower their relative feeling of deprivation. Thereby the poorer quintile's individual stress level might be reduced, which is a central determinant of vulnerability to detrimental health determinants. This explanation would also be supported by the recent finding of Blásquez et al. (2014), who revealed using similar variables that comparisons with reference groups in terms of financial hardship, basic goods and housing act as a stressor and lead to unhealthy behaviour. Ragnarsdóttir et al. (2012) go even further in their study. They show that in fact no actual relative improvement or deterioration of the standard of living has to take place. Merely the perception that other persons were affected more or less strongly by the crisis than oneself can moderate the health effect of the actual living conditions. Relative deprivation is determined by how just or unjust people judge their situation to be, and can turn into a key reason for depression and anger (Smith et al. 2011). In the Icelandic case, only one-third of the individuals who had seen a drop in their standard of living believed they were worse off than their peers, a situation that lowered the health outcomes in terms of emotional distress. An actual improvement of the subjective health of the lowest income quintile as seen in Table 7.3 could therefore indicate that the poorest in most countries do not judge themselves to be more affected by the crisis than their peers (be they national or transnational reference groups). It should not be forgotten, though, that the objective living conditions of the poor are deteriorating rapidly, which will become a point of concern at the latest when lagged effects on physical health become apparent.

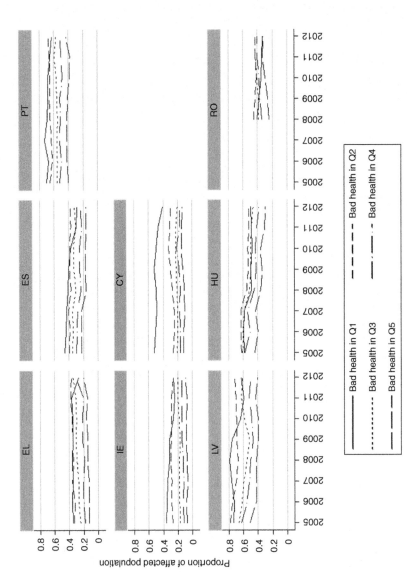

Note: Displayed is the headcount of individuals with average, bad or very bad health per income quintile. Q1 refers to lowest quintile (poorest) and Q5 to highest quintile (richest).

Source: EU-SILC data.

In contrast, the development of poor health among the second income quintile, which shows a worsening in the four EAP countries Greece, Portugal, Ireland and Cyprus and in Latvia in the second crisis phase, corresponds to the objective data on living conditions. In all five countries the second quintile showed high increases in adverse conditions. In Ireland, its increase in deprivation and arrears was even more pronounced than among the poorest quintile. In Cyprus, the level and increase in arrears for the Q2 was higher than for Q1 and their access to healthcare worsened to a higher extent. Latvia also showed higher deprivation exposure and unmet medical needs for the second quintile in the second phase of the crisis. Political exemptions aimed at reducing the burden of the crisis on the poorest can play a role in this result. Often the poorest are eligible (as a result of a means test) for exemptions from service charges, which shifts the weight of the cost burden on to the other income quintiles and in particular on to households just between the 'poor' and the 'non-poor' (Eurofound 2014). While few country studies analysed the effect of the crisis on singular income quintiles, this interpretation of the results is supported at least in the case of Ireland (Kiernan 2014). Findings using the Household Budget Survey show that the second income quintile was the group which most often had to cancel private insurance cover during the crisis, as they were no longer subject to tax reliefs. At the same time, however, this group did not qualify as being 'poor' enough to be granted universal healthcare through the medical card. The case of Ireland also shows that out-of-pocket expenditure for healthcare – that is private health expenditure – increased for all income quintiles except for the lowest one. These are costs which will be felt most by the households just above the poverty line, in turn increasing adverse social determinants such as deprivation and arrears. Nonetheless, a lack of upward mobility which leads to a situation inconsistent with internalized expectations can also play a role in the health effect of the middle classes (Davies 1962). Moreover, the fact that in a middle-class social environment financial difficulties engender responses of exclusion ('falling from grace') (Newman 1999), instead of spurring established support strategies, can be a decisive factor in the diverging health responses of the lower income quintiles (Burgard and Kalousova 2015).

In sum, the descriptive statistics reveal that certain quintiles show a worsening of health in the period following the financial crisis as well as a worsening of social determinants, thus H1 can be confirmed. The evolution of health for the single-income quintiles, however, contradicts the assumption on which H3 is based. Nonetheless, in order to assess the changing impact of the social determinants of health, a regression analysis has to be conducted.

7.5.1 Regression Analysis of Bad Health in the Crisis

The regression model (Table 7.4) enables a comparison of the effect of the social determinants on bad health. A common model is portrayed for all European countries with controls added for the different country types (M1a, M2a, M3a). It compares the EAP countries to the BoP countries, the core countries (Germany, Austria, Belgium, Sweden, Denmark, France, the Netherlands, Luxembourg, Finland and the UK) and the 2004 accession countries which were not so greatly affected by the crisis (Malta, Poland, Bulgaria, the Czech Republic, Estonia, Lithuania and Slovakia). In a second step, interaction terms between country and the social determinants were added (M1b, M2b, M3b).

The analysis shows the expected effect of individual characteristics of health. In general, during the first crisis phase the effect of individual characteristics is most pronounced. Not only migrants and women but also the unemployed and individuals with lower and medium education were exposed to more health problems than their reference groups during this period. In the second phase of the crisis, the risks decreased because a generalization of the crisis took place, shifting the impact on the household level of social determinants. The impact of absolute income on bad health is only significant in 2006/2007 and 2011/2012. This can be taken to mean that the social determinants of health fulfil their function of explaining the pathways between low income and bad health.

Of the social determinants we controlled for, unmet medical needs show the most predictive power. Before the crisis, people without access to healthcare due to economic barriers were 18 per cent more likely to be in bad health than persons with access. With the onset of the crisis its impact increased slightly to 19 per cent, as waiting lists became longer and (transport) costs rose. The capacity to afford the cost of living is the second strongest social determinant of health. However, its impact on health is highest before the crisis. A rise in deprivation in the second phase of the crisis from 2009/2010 levels to 2011/2012 levels is nonetheless discernible, although it is relatively low. Arrears show only a significant impact on bad health before the crisis in the models without country controls. When the country clusters are controlled for, its effect also becomes significant during the crisis years. This implies that only in certain countries will arrears lead to a worsening of health. The countries in which the arrears are mainly mortgage payment difficulties can come to mind.

The location of a household seems to play less and less of a role with the financial crisis in Europe. While EAP countries are still significantly less affected by ill health than Eastern European BoP countries, the difference decreased from 21 percentage points to 11 percentage points in 2011/2012.

Table 7.4 *Determinants of bad health status (binary analysis 0: 'good health', 1: 'bad health')*

	M1a	M1b	M2a	M2b	M3a	M3b
	2006/2007	2006/2007	2009/2010	2009/2010	2011/2012	2011/2012
Female (/ male)	0.023**	0.023**	0.030**	0.030**	0.025**	0.025**
	(5.91)	(5.91)	(7.26)	(7.17)	(6.74)	(6.69)
Migrant (/ national)	0.020+	0.020+	0.036*	0.036*	0.025+	0.024
	(1.68)	(1.70)	(2.55)	(2.56)	(1.67)	(1.64)
Age	0.011**	0.011**	0.011**	0.011**	0.011**	0.011**
	(27.59)	(27.98)	(40.12)	(41.18)	(30.74)	(30.82)
Unemployed	0.038**	0.038**	0.044**	0.044**	0.035**	0.034**
	(2.64)	(2.76)	(4.55)	(4.86)	(3.42)	(3.40)
Low education	0.099**	0.099**	0.118**	0.118**	0.112**	0.111**
	(10.33)	(10.34)	(11.46)	(11.60)	(8.55)	(8.62)
Medium education	0.046**	0.046**	0.067**	0.067**	0.064**	0.064**
	(9.10)	(9.08)	(11.24)	(11.72)	(12.80)	(12.86)
EU poor	0.031*	0.030*	0.023	0.022	0.034*	0.033*
	(2.30)	(2.34)	(1.52)	(1.50)	(2.27)	(2.23)
Healthcare access	0.178**	0.178**	0.181**	0.157**	0.189**	0.174**
	(22.41)	(21.51)	(8.32)	(6.43)	(11.33)	(8.19)
Arrears	0.026**	0.038**	0.014	0.034*	0.013	0.035**
	(2.63)	(3.79)	(1.17)	(2.38)	(1.17)	(2.76)
Capacity to afford life	0.070**	0.066**	0.057**	0.053**	0.065**	0.063**
	(8.59)	(6.85)	(5.66)	(4.04)	(7.21)	(5.07)
Macro-level (/EAP)						
BoP countries	0.209**	0.241**	0.212**	0.077	0.111*	0.078
	(5.01)	(5.69)	(5.08)	(1.06)	(2.00)	(1.08)
Central countries	0.025	0.040	0.029	0.008	0.026	0.016
	(0.57)	(0.85)	(0.66)	(0.24)	(1.07)	(0.46)
Peripheral no crisis	0.153**	0.171**	0.156**	0.093*	0.112**	0.094*
	(3.42)	(3.68)	(3.50)	(2.00)	(3.42)	(2.05)
BoP*access health		0.006		0.113**		0.078*
		(0.84)		(2.66)		(2.20)
BoP*arrears		−0.016		−0.037*		−0.040+
		(−0.98)		(−1.96)		(−1.87)
N	721431	721431	657322	657322	792009	792009
Chi2	158553	158576	148898	148586	169927	169806
R2	0,26	0,26	0,27	0,27	0,25	0,26
AIC	710964	710626	632076	631370	770805	770222
BIC	711136	710833	632247	631575	770978	770442
Log-likelihood	−355467	−355295	−316023	−315667	−385387	−385092

Note: Displayed are average marginal effects on being in subjective bad health. Confidence intervals in brackets. Significance levels: +p/z < 0.1; *p/z > 0.05; ** > 0.0.1 In M1b, M2b and M3b all cross-level interactions between healthcare access, arrears and afford life with BoP and EAP countries are controlled for, only significant ones are displayed.

At the same time, the difference between the eurozone centre and periphery does not seem to come to the fore with respect to health. While our analysis showed that the situation of households in the EAP countries is clearly worsening, the short-term effects of the crisis do not impact the overall health of their population. M2b and M3b also show that the interaction effects between EAP countries and social determinants are not significant. In contrast, the BoP countries are significantly different from the European average concerning access to healthcare during the crisis. In 2009/2010, unmet medical needs were associated with an 11% higher risk of bad health in these countries, while prior to the crisis no effect was visible. H2 can therefore only be accepted in part. On the one hand, the difference between BoP and EAP is significant because their medical determinants of health are more pronounced. On the other hand, the gap is becoming smaller.

Common models for the population of a country as a whole can however hide worsenings for certain societal groups. The differential impact of the social determinants on the income quintiles can be assessed by means of separate regression analysis (see Figure 7.3). It shows that there is a trend of rising problems in healthcare access and deprivation, which is most

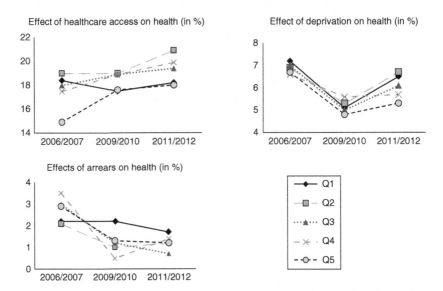

Note: Displayed are marginal effects of being in bad health retrieved from regression analysis, while controlling for the same variables as mentioned in Table 7.3. The dotted lines display not significant coefficients.

Figure 7.3   Impact of social determinants differentiated by income quintile

pronounced for the second income quintile. The first income quintile has some of the lowest risks of unmet medical needs and is only second when it comes to deprivation. Its exposure to arrears seems to be among the highest in 2011/2012, however this effect is not significant. This confirms the trend already visible in the descriptive statistics.

H3 has to be rejected entirely, as the poorest show neither the worst development for health nor the most pronounced impact of social determinants. The grey zone between the poor and the non-poor seems to have taken their place as the most precarious income quintile.

7.6 CONCLUSION

In this chapter we set out to answer the question of to what extent the global financial crisis and the subsequent European debt crisis with its austerity policies influenced the opportunity structure of Europeans in the periphery and thus their health. Clearly, the eurozone crisis brought about differential living conditions as well as health responses throughout the income groups. It appears that individuals from the lowest quintile in the European periphery are suffering less than expected in terms of health as a result of the financial crisis and the reduced economic opportunities and social welfare. It is rather those just above the borderline between the poor and the non-poor who are experiencing a setback and showing worse health outcomes. This can be explained as follows: when governmental support systems are reduced to covering the poorest part of the population only, due to reasons of cost reduction, other groups lose their support structure and may thus lose out on medical insurance and other essential services. The section of the population just above the poverty line will then be hit to the highest extent by austerity measures, as they are not protected to the same degree by governmental exemption rules as the most vulnerable (Eurofound 2014; Kiernan 2014). In the wealthier EAP countries this trend is shown by the development of the second and third quintile, while in the BoP countries, in particular Romania, the fifth quintile reported increasingly bad health. In most crisis countries, the risk levels of the first, second and third income quintile are therefore converging and overlapping. The income gradient to health shown first by the Black Report in the 1980s and afterwards prominently identified in almost all analyses of population health seems to have been altered with the current crisis. For the European peripheral countries it is no longer possible to say that higher social status – at least with respect to income – is linked gradually to better health. A slightly higher income does not seem to prevent the negative consequences of the crisis.

While governmental protection of the poorest section of the population in the form of exemptions from medical co-payments and other service costs can explain why the lowest quintile's health is not worsening, the actual improvement of health needs a further explanation. This fact could be attributed to their relative improvement in living conditions. When arrears and deprivation become more widespread among the middle of the population, they are deemed more acceptable. This buffers their effect on emotional distress, which renders them less detrimental to health. Moreover, the perception of the poorest of being less strongly affected by the crisis than others could be an explanation for the counter-intuitive results (Ragnarsdóttir et al. 2012). The aim of this chapter was solely to analyse the effects of absolute income on health during the crisis. A further exploration of the effect of relative deprivation by income quintile is needed to bring new insights as to why exactly the first income quintile is improving.

In terms of social determinants, the analysis was able to reveal its expected effect of worsening trends. In particular the EAP countries, Spain, Greece, Cyprus, Ireland and Portugal show increased difficulties in affording basic goods as well as higher arrears. Access problems to the healthcare system due to financial hardship could only be observed in Greece, while in Portugal the situation has improved and Spain has been able to maintain its universal healthcare system. Even though the EAP countries are showing a more dramatic change in social determinants of health, for Latvia and Romania the increased barriers to healthcare are worrying, as they are structural factors which can create significant lagged effects on health. All in all, the Eastern European countries seem to be mastering the crisis, because their recent improvements are still outweighing the effects of the crisis on health and its determinants. In the Mediterranean countries, however, late effects of the current policies might be appearing soon if the development of the social determinants of health continues in the same direction.

NOTES

1. The European Semester, an EU policy framework implemented in 2011, introduced for all EU countries Stability or Convergence Programmes (SCPs) and National Reform Programmes (NRPs), which constitute a 'new surveillance system for budgetary and economic policies' (European Commission 2014).
2. Accessed 30 April 2015 at http://www.nytimes.com/2011/12/27/world/europe/greeks-reeling-from-health-care-cutbacks.html.
3. Accessed 30 April 2015 at http://www.theguardian.com/world/2013/sep/05/spanish-helpline-rise-callers-considering-suicide.
4. Next to socio-economic factors 'new' factors, describing horizontal inequalities,

e.g. gender, sexual orientation, ethnicity etc., are important and will be as far as possible controlled for in the analysis.

5. The life-course theory will not be detailed out as a separate theory. It is seen as a cross-cutting theory, reinforcing the importance of material, psycho-social and medical factors in certain periods of life and cumulative over the life-course.

6. In an initial factor analysis the following variables were included: arrears on mortgage or rent payments (hs011), arrears on utility bills (hs021), arrears on hire purchase instalments (hs031), ability to keep home adequately warm (hs050), capacity to face unexpected financial expenses (hs060), do you have a telephone (hs070), do you have a colour television (hs080), do you have a washing machine (hs0100), ability to make ends meet (hs120), leaking roof, damp walls/floors (hs040), noise from neighbours or from the street (hs170), pollution (hs180), financial burden of the repayment of debts from hire purchases (hs150), financial burden of the total housing cost (hs140), ability to make ends meet (hs120), problems with the dwelling: too dark (hs160).

REFERENCES

Azzopardi-Muscat, N., T. Clemens, D. Stoner and H. Brand (2015), 'EU country specific recommendations for health systems in the European Semester process: trends, discourse and predictors', *Health Policy*, **119**, 375–383.

Bartoll, X., L. Palència, D. Malmusi, M. Suhrcke and C. Borrell (2013), 'The evolution of mental health in Spain during the economic crisis', *European Journal of Public Health*, **24** (3), 415–418.

Becker, J. and J. Jäger (2011), 'European integration in crisis: the centre-periphery divide', paper presented at the 17th Euromemo Workshop on Alternative Economic Policy, Vienna, 16–18 September 2011.

Beckfield, J. and S. Olafsdottir (2009), 'Empowering health: a comparative political sociology of health disparities', *Perspectives on Europe*, **39**, 9–12.

Blásquez, M., E. Cottini and A. Herrarte (2014), 'The socioeconomic gradient in health: how important is material deprivation?', *Journal of Economic Inequality*, **12**, 239–264.

Blyth, M. (2013), *The History of a Dangerous Idea*, Oxford: Oxford University Press.

Bolte, G. and M. Kohlhuber (2009), 'Soziale Ungleichheit bei umweltbezogener Gesundheit: Erklärungsansätze aus umweltepidemiologischer Perspektive', in M. Richter and K. Hurrelmann (eds), *Gesundheitliche Ungleichheit*, Second Edition, Wiesbaden: VS Verlag, pp. 99–116.

Bolte, G., C. Bunge and C. Hornberg (eds) (2012), *Umweltgerechtigkeit: Chancengleichheit bei Umwelt und Gesundheit: Konzepte, Datenlage und Handlungsperspektiven*, Bern: Verlag Hans Huber.

Bonaccio, M., A.E. Bonanni and A. Di Castelnuovo (2012), 'Low income is associated with poor adherence to a Mediterranean diet and a higher prevalence of obesity: cross-sectional results from the Moli-Sani study', *BMJ Open*, **2** (6), 1–9.

Bosma, H., R. Peter, J. Siegrist and M.G. Marmot (1997), 'Low job control and risk of coronary heart disease in the Whitehall II (prospective cohort) study', *British Medical Journal*, **314**, 558–565.

Branas, C.C., A.E. Kastaanaki, M. Michalodimitrakis, J. Tzougas, E.F. Kranioti, P.N. Theodorakis, B.G. Carr and D.J. Wiebe (2015), 'The impact of economic austerity and prosperity events on suicide in Greece: a 30-year interrupted time-series analysis', *BMJ Open*, **5**(1), e005619.

Braubach, M. and J. Fairburn (2010), 'Social inequities in environmental risks associated with housing and residential location – a review of evidence', *European Journal of Public Health*, **20** (1), 36–42.

Bryan, M.L. and S.P. Jenkins (2013), 'Regression analysis of country effects using multilevel data: a cautionary tale', Research Paper No. 2013-14. Essex: Institute for Social and Economic Research.

Burgard, S.A. and Kalousova, L. (2015), 'Effects of the Great Recession: health and well-being', *Annual Review of Sociology*, **41** (13), 1–21.

Burgard, S., K. Seefeldt and S. Zelner (2012), 'Housing instability and health: findings from the Michigan Recession and Recovery Study', *Population Studies Center Research Report* 12–749, Ann Arbor: University of Michigan.

Chen, L.C., T.G. Evans and R.A. Cash (1999), 'Health as a global public good', in I. Kaul, I. Grunberg and M.A. Stern (eds), *Global Public Goods: International Cooperation in the 21st Century*, Oxford: Oxford University Press, pp. 284–305.

Chzhen, Y. (2014), 'Child poverty and material deprivation in the European Union during the Great Recession', Innocenti Working Paper, No. 2014–06, Florence: UNICEF Office of Research.

Davies, J.C. (1962), 'Toward a theory of revolution', *American Sociological Review*, **27**, 5–19.

Doorslaer, E., C. Masseria and X. Koolman (2006), 'Inequalities in access to medical care by income in developed countries', *Canadian Medical Association Journal*, **174** (2), 177–183.

Eurofound (2014), 'Access to healthcare in times of crisis', Luxembourg: Publications Office of the European Union.

European Commission (2013), 'Europe 2020 – country specific recommendations', accessed 16 November 2014 at http://ec.europa.eu/europe2020/making-it-happen/country-specific-recommendations/.

European Commission (2014), 'The EU's economic governance explained', memo from 28 May 2014, accessed 16 November 2014 at http://europa.eu/rapid/press-release_MEMO-13-979_en.htm.

Evans, J., S. Hyndman, S. Steward-Brown, D. Smith and S. Petersen (2000), 'An epidemiological study of the relative importance of damp housing in relation to adult health', *Journal of Epidemiology and Community Health*, **54**, 677–686.

Fairbrother, M. (2011), 'Explaining social change: the application of multilevel models of repeated cross-sectional survey data', paper presented at ECPR, Reykjavik, August 2011, accessed 10 November 2014 at http://ecpr.eu/filestore/. . ./217a482c-55f1-4179-8808-1f44bed1fc6f.pdf.

Fayers, P. and M.A. Sprangers (2002), 'Understanding self-rated health', *The Lancet*, **359**, 187–188.

Gee, G.C. and D.C. Payne-Sturges (2004), 'Environmental health disparities: a framework integrating psychosocial and environmental concepts', *Environmental Health Perspectives*, **112**, 645–653.

Gili, M., M. Roca, S. Basu, M. McKee and D. Stuckler (2012), 'The mental health risks of economic crisis in Spain: evidence from primary care centres, 2006 and 2010', *European Journal of Public Health*, **23** (1), 103–108.

Graham, H. (2004), 'Social determinants and their unequal distribution: clarifying policy understandings', *The Milbank Quarterly*, **82** (1), 101–124.

Greer, S.L. and P. Kurzer (2013), *European Union Public Health Policy. Regional and Global Trends*, London: Routledge.

Hassel, A. (2006), *Wage Setting, Social Pacts and the Euro*, Amsterdam: Amsterdam University Press.

Jürges, H. (2007), 'True health vs response styles: exploring cross-country differences in self-reported health', *Health Economics*, **16**, 163–178.

Kaiser, H.F. (1974), 'An index of factorial simplicity', *Psychometrika*, **39** (1), 31–36.

Karanikolos, M., P. Mladovsky, J. Cylus, S. Thomson, S. Basu, D. Stuckler, J.P. Mackenbach and M. McKee (2013), 'Financial crisis, austerity, and health in Europe', *Lancet*, **381**, 1323–1331.

Kentikelenis, A., M. Karanikolos, A. Reeves, M. McKee and D. Stuckler (2014), 'Greece's health crisis: from austerity to denialism', *Lancet*, **383**, 748–753.

Kiernan, F. (2014), 'What price austerity – a nation's health? The effect of austerity on access to health care in Ireland', *The European Journal of Public Health*, **24** (supplement 2). http://dx.doi.org/10.1093/eurpub/cku165.110.

Krieger, J. and D.L Higgins (2002), 'Housing and health: time again for public health action', *American Journal of Public Health*, **92** (5), 758–768.

Kyriopoulos, I.I., D. Zavras, A. Skroumpelos, K. Mylona, K. Athanasakis and J. Kyriopoulos (2014), 'Barriers in access to healthcare services for chronic patients in times of austerity: an empirical approach in Greece', *Journal for Equity in Health*, **13** (1), 54–61.

Lapavitsas, C., A. Kaltenbrunner, D. Lindo, J. Michell, J.P. Painceira, E. Pires, J. Powell, A. Stenfors and N. Teles (2010), 'Eurozone crisis: beggar thyself and thy neighbour', *Journal of Balkan and Near Eastern Studies*, **12** (4), 321–373.

Macy, J.T., L. Chassin and C. Presson (2013), 'Predictors of health behaviours after the economic downturn: a longitudinal study', *Social Science & Medicine*, **89**, 8–15.

Marmot, M.G., M.J. Shipley and G. Rose (1984), 'Inequalities in death – specific explanations of a general pattern', *The Lancet*, **323**, 1003–1006.

Marmot, M.G., G. Davey Smith, S.A. Stansfeld, C. Patel, F. North, J. Head, I. White, E.J. Brunner and A. Feeney (1991), 'Health inequalities among British civil servants: the Whitehall II study', *The Lancet*, **337**, 1387–1393.

Mielck, A., R. Kiess, O. Kneseback and A. Kunst (2007), 'Association between access to health care and household income among the elderly in 10 western European countries', in J.P. Mackenbach et al. (eds), *Tackling Health Inequalities in Europe: An Integrated Approach*, Final Report, Rotterdam: University Medical Centre Rotterdam.

Newman, K. (1999), *Falling from Grace: Downward Mobility in the Age of Affluence*, Berkeley: University California Press.

Novoa, A.M., J. Bosch, F. Díaz, D. Malmusi, M. Darnell and C. Trilla (2014), 'El impacto de la crisis en la relacíon entre vivienda y salud. Políticas de buenas práctivas para reducer las desigualidades en salud asociadas con las condiciones de vivienda', *Gacetta Sanitaria*, **28** (1), 44–50.

OECD (2013a), 'Health at a glance 2013: OECD indicators', OECD Publishing, accessed at http://dx.doi.org/10.1787/health_glance-2013-en.

OECD (2013b), 'Crisis squeezes income and puts pressure on inequality and poverty. Results from the OECD income distribution database', Paris: OECD. Accessed 30 April 2015 at http://www.oecd.org/social/soc/OECD2013-Inequality-and-Poverty-8p.pdf.

Osoba, D. (1999), 'What has been learned from measuring health-related quality of life in clinical oncology', *European Journal of Cancer*, **35**, 1565–1570.

Penchansky, R. and J.W. Thomas (1981), 'The concept of access: definition and relationship to consumer satisfaction', *Medical Care*, **19**, 127–140.

Ragnarsdóttir, B.H., J.G. Bernburg and S. Ólafsdóttir (2012), 'The global financial crisis and individual distress: the role of subjective comparisons after the collapse of the Icelandic economy', *Sociology*, **47** (4), 755–775.

Schulz, A. and M. Northridge (2004), 'Social determinants of health: implications for environmental health promotion', *Health Education and Behaviour*, **31**, 455–471.

Siegrist, J. and M. Marmot (2006), 'Introduction', in J. Siegrist and M. Marmot (eds), *Social Inequalities in Health: New Evidence and Policy Implications*, Oxford: Oxford University Press, pp. 15–44.

Singh-Manoux, A.M, P. Martikainen, J. Ferrie, M. Zins, M. Marmot and M. Goldberg (2006), 'What does self-rated health measure? Results from the Whitehall II and French Gazel cohort studies', *Journal of Epidemiology and Community Health*, **60**, 364–372.

Smith, H.J., T.F. Pettigrew, G.M. Pippin and S. Bialosiewicz (2011), 'Relative deprivation: a theoretical and meta-analytic review', *Personality and Social Psychology Review*, **16** (3), 203–232.

Stafford, M. and M. McCarthy (2006), 'Neighbourhoods, housing and health', in M. Marmot and R. Wilkinson (eds), *The Social Determinants of Health*, Oxford: Oxford University Press, pp. 197–317.

Stuckler, D. and S. Basu (2013), *The Body Economic. Why Austerity Kills*, London: Allen Lane.

Veenstra, G. and S. Kelly (2007), 'Comparing objective and subjective status: gender and space (and environmental justice?)', *Health & Place*, **13**, 57–71.

Wendt, C. (2009), 'Mapping European healthcare systems: a comparative analysis of financing, service provision and access to healthcare', *Journal of European Social Policy*, **19**, 432–445.

WHO (1948), 'WHO definition of health', in Preamble to the Constitution of the World Health Organization as adopted by the International Health Conference, New York, 19–22 June, 1946 and entered into force on 7 April 1948.

WHO Europe (2012), *Health Policy Responses to the Financial Crisis in Europe*, Copenhagen: WHO Regional Office for Europe.

Wilkinson, R.G. and K. Pickett (2009), *The Spirit Level: Why More Equal Societies Almost Always Do Better*, London: Allen Lane.

APPENDIX

Table 7A.1   Latent factors from low income to poor health

(Latent) factors of income poverty	Link to bad health	Variables	Factor loadings	Reliability: Kaiser-Meyer-Olkin measure[1]
Difficulties of financing living	● Physical effect through incapacity to live a healthy living	● Ability to pay for usual expenses	−0,567	0,894
		● Keep house warm	0,727	0,778
		● Ability to afford a proper meal	0,708	0,794
Arrears	● Psychological stress of not being able to pay	● Arrears on mortgage or rent	0,763	0,837
		● Arrears on utility bills	0,783	0,811
		● Arrears on hire purchase instalments	0,745	0,839
Access to medical services	● Lagged physical effects of not addressing concerns immediately	● Unmet medical need for financial reasons		

Notes:
A low but acceptable Chronbach's alpha[2] of 0.64 shows that overall the variables have enough in common to warrant a factor analysis. A model divided by years shows the best goodness of fit, here the RMSEA[3] has a value of 0.044 – with 0.1, 0.05 and 0.01 indicating a good fit, very good fit and outstanding fit respectively. The Comparative Fit Index (CFI)[4] takes up 0.957 confirming the excellent fit of the model for our purpose.
1. Kaiser-Meyer-Olkin (KMO) measure of sampling adequacy takes values between 0 and 1. Historically, the following labels are given to values of KMO (Kaiser 1974): 0.00 to 0.49 unacceptable, 0.50 to 0.59 miserable, 0.60 to 0.69 mediocre, 0.70 to 0.79 middling, 0.80 to 0.89 meritorious, 0.90 to 1.00 marvellous.
2. Chronbach's alpha = $[Np / [1 + p(N - 1)]$ with 'N' being the number of variables and 'p' the mean inter-item correlation.
3. The RMSEA is based on analysis of residuals.
4. The CFI is based on the non-central X2 and is given by (X2 model – df model)/(X2 independence – df independence).

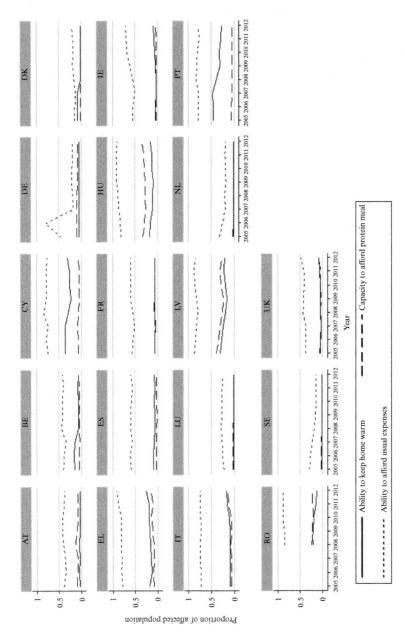

Note: Displayed is the headcount of individuals with different kinds of deprivation.

Source: EU-SILC data.

Figure 7A.1 Development of basic deprivation items (2005–2012)

192

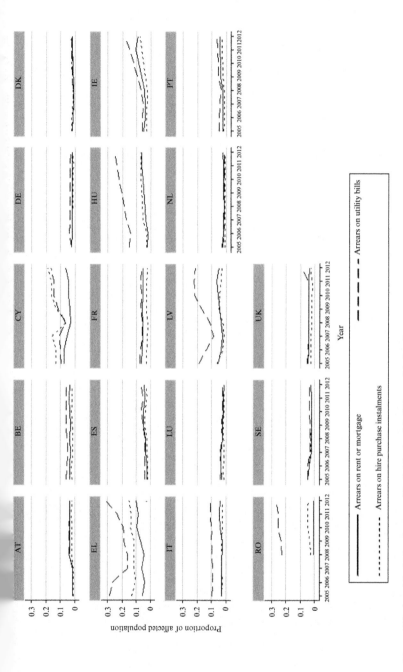

Note: Displayed is the headcount of individuals with different kinds of arrears.

Source: EU-SILC data.

Figure 7A.2 Development of arrears (2005–2012)

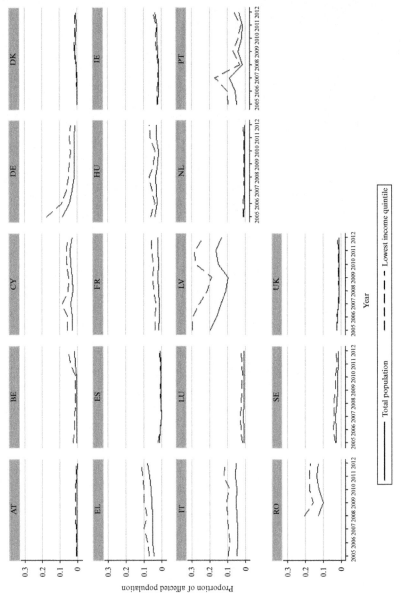

194

Note: Displayed is the headcount of individuals with income-related unmet medical needs (due to costs, transport cost, waiting lists).

Source: EU-SILC data.

8. Does the Europeanization of daily life increase the life satisfaction of Europeans?

Franziska Buttler

8.1 INTRODUCTION

With the onset of the severe economic crisis in 2008, life satisfaction worsened in many EU countries. Although on average the number of people stating they were happy with their lives remained broadly stable in the EU-28 between 2008 and 2012, it decreased sharply in the five countries under the auspices of the European bailout funds (ESM/EFSM/EFSF), i.e. in Greece, Spain, Portugal, Cyprus and Ireland, which all had to implement strict deficit-reducing policies. In the case of Greece, the country hit worst by the crisis, the share of the population stating they were satisfied with their lives fell by half from 65 per cent (2008) to 32 per cent (2012). Especially in these cases EU policies seem to have a negative impact on the subjective perception of living conditions (see Figure 8.1).

Despite such negative effects of the eurozone crisis and austerity policies (cf. Blyth 2013) on the life satisfaction in certain European countries, other aspects of the European integration project might have more positive effects. In particular, transnational social relationships may constitute an additional source of social support and a professional resource in a common European labour market, helping European citizens from crisis countries to overcome difficult economic and social conditions by moving, studying or working abroad. Such 'cross-border interactions between European countries in terms of communication, the exchange of ideas and meanings, collective mobilisation across borders as well as cross-border mobility and networks' have been termed 'horizontal Europeanisation' (Mau and Mewes 2012: 10). Previous studies of this phenomenon have shown the EU citizens' appreciation of cross-border relations and social practices (Díez Medrano et al. 2013; Favell 2008; Guiraudon 2011; Recchi et al. 2014), communication and mobility (Mau and Mewes 2012), as well as attitudes (Delhey et al. 2014; Gerhards and Lengfeld 2015). Some

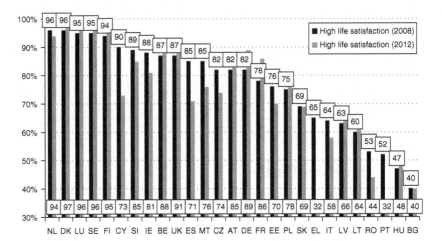

Note: Percentage of the national population which is very satisfied or fairly satisfied with life.

Source: Standard Eurobarometer 69 and 78.

Figure 8.1   Life satisfaction in the EU (2008 and 2012)

studies have quantified these processes of horizontal Europeanization and compared them across nation states and social classes (Delhey et al. 2014). A major result is that horizontal Europeanization has a clear class and territorial bias: transnational attitudes and social practices can be found mostly in higher social classes in wealthier Member States (Fligstein 2008; Kuhn 2011, 2015).

This chapter goes beyond the description and measurement of processes of horizontal Europeanization by investigating its potential impact on the lives of Europeans. The research question is whether cross-border networks, social relations and transnational patterns of communication in Europe improve the life satisfaction of European citizens due to an enlarged set of opportunities to work, travel and study beyond the national borders.

In order to capture the effect of social European integration, we will use the horizontal Europeanization index (HEI) (Buttler et al. 2013) to test whether cross-border interrelations such as the share of European *tourism, people working abroad, immigrants* and *European students* impacts on individual life satisfaction.

The next section reviews previous research on life satisfaction (section 8.2). It provides a working definition and summarizes previous studies on the individual and the contextual determinants of life satisfaction. Next, the potential impact of transnational interrelations on individual well-being and my own theoretical approach based on mobility theories is presented (section 8.3). After a short explanation of the data and methods used (section 8.4), the impact of growing cross-border relations in Europe is analysed on the basis of Eurobarometer data and the HEI (section 8.5). Finally, the results and conclusions are discussed (section 8.6).

8.2 LIFE SATISFACTION IN A MULTI-LEVEL PERSPECTIVE

Life satisfaction refers to the degree to which individuals evaluate their overall quality of life (emotionally) and perceive their aspirations as met (cognitively) (Veenhoven 2012: 67). This is firstly a multidimensional concept, since it depends on satisfaction in different life domains, such as work, family, health or leisure. Secondly, it is dynamic and may change with the conditions of these life domains over time (Frey and Stutzer 2002: 405). Thirdly, it is culture specific, as desired concepts of life and both expected as well as aspired living conditions vary among cultures (Joshanloo 2014: 489; Jürgens 2007: 176). In the following sections, essential results of individual and national characteristics that impact on life satisfaction will be summarized before discussing the relevance of the transnational level for subjective well-being.

8.2.1 Socio-demographic Determinants of Life Satisfaction

In general, after controlling for other socio-demographic variables such as age, education and income, women are happier than men (Jürgens 2007: 165; Lalive and Stutzer 2010: 936; Tesch-Römer et al. 2008: 330). The impact of age on life satisfaction is usually U-shaped (Kassenboehmer and Haisken-DeNew 2012: 238). While young people experience higher levels of joy, the mid-life decline in life satisfaction is attributable to high work intensity and family demands, whereas the elderly are on average more satisfied again (Blanchflower and Oswald 2007: 17; Diener 2009: 28). With regard to household composition, it has been shown that couples are on average happier than singles (Stavrova et al. 2012: 1064). Children contribute positively to life satisfaction when income is controlled for (Mencarini and Sironi 2012: 212). People with a higher income have a higher social status in society and have more opportunities to buy what they desire and need (Frey and Stutzer 2002: 409). Therefore, life satisfaction is higher – at least until a certain threshold is reached (about \$75 000 per year in the US;

cf. Kahneman and Deaton 2010). Unemployment reduces life satisfaction persistently, as the unemployed not only suffer a loss in income, but also experience non-monetary disadvantages such as a lack of social contacts or reduced self-esteem (Clark and Oswald 1994; Clark et al. 2010: 52; Gallie et al. 2003; Winkelmann and Winkelmann 1998). The positive effect of educational attainment on life satisfaction does not appear to be particularly strong and is highly intertwined with income (Diener 2009: 29). For most individuals, however, health is the most important aspect in their quality of life (Adena and Myck 2013: 1; Böhnke and Kohler 2010: 637; Powdthavee 2008: 1467). By virtue of good health, people are able to develop their full potential. People not only feel better in the absence of illness, they also benefit from the instrumental value of health, which increases productivity and possibilities to engage with the social environment (Husain et al. 2014: 123).

The relationship between transnational interconnectedness and life satisfaction has not been investigated deeply yet. However, after controlling for other socio-demographic variables such as income, education and household composition, Polgreen and Simpson (2010: 820) have shown that emigrated individuals report higher life satisfaction. Based on economic theory, emigration depends on comparing the utility of living in the country of origin with the utility of living abroad. If life perspectives seem more attractive in a foreign country and if migration costs remain low (e.g. family and friends left home, language barriers, etc.), individuals are more likely to emigrate.

Social contacts are an indispensable human need because they provide emotional bonds, interpersonal trust and opportunities to discuss important matters (Portela et al. 2013: 503; Powdthavee 2008: 1473). They are also a source of support and advice in the case of unpleasant life events and make people happier, healthier and reduce criminal behaviour (Böhnke 2007: 317; Böhnke 2008: 191; Rodríguez-Pose and von Berlepsch 2014: 359; Sander and Putnam 2010: 9). Therefore, one can assume that not only social contacts within a nation state but also transnational social contacts contribute positively to life satisfaction, as those experiences are especially worth having in times of dense cross-border exchange of goods, information and people (Kaufmann et al. 2004: 746; Kostakopoulou 2013: 44; Portela et al. 2013: 497).

8.2.2 National Determinants

In addition to individual, socio-demographic aspects, subjective well-being is also influenced by national institutions and the broader social and economic environment influence. *Economic prosperity* is associated with higher levels of life satisfaction, as income per capita can be seen as a proxy for a high coverage of material needs (Delhey and Kohler 2007: 397; Diener et al. 2009: 63). The fact that increasing income per capita in Western industrialized countries is not accompanied by a further increase in life satisfaction is known as the 'Easterlin Paradox' (Blanchflower and Oswald 2004: 1362; Diener and Seligman 2004: 3; Easterlin 1974: 106). This has also been observed in Europe (Alesina et al. 2001: 18). Easterlin explains this observation by the fact that not only do absolute income levels determine life satisfaction, but also relative ones, i.e. the gap between poor and prosperous countries. Once a certain living standard has been reached, life satisfaction seems to depend on other characteristics such as income inequality, human rights, quality of government or comparison processes with past prosperity or expected prosperity (Delhey and Dragolov 2013: 152; Delhey and Kohler 2007: 390; Frey and Stutzer 2002: 417).

The role of *government indebtedness* in life satisfaction is ambiguous. However, there are channels through which excessive government indebtedness may affect peoples' life satisfaction negatively. This negative effect of debt is mostly pronounced during crisis times when government debt increases due to a fall in tax income and increased spending for social securities. If a certain threshold of government debt is reached it may be the case that private actors start doubting that fiscal policy will be able to meet their debt obligations without increasing taxes in the (near) future or cut public spending. Rational households or firms will react to this by decreasing their individual spending, which reduces aggregate spending and hence GDP. Furthermore, as observed during the European debt crisis, financial markets recognize such unstable situations and lenders will demand an additional risk-premium for lending to a state in excessive debt. This in turn will lead to an increase in interest rates and hence real debt servicing costs – not only for governments but also for private companies and households. These channels will have an adverse effect on the economy and lead to an increase in unemployment as well as a reduction in social spending, thus reducing life satisfaction.

Next to current and future prosperity levels, the *employment rate* is important for subjective well-being. It is an indicator of the proportion of the population that can benefit directly from economic prosperity. Moreover, with a higher employment rate, the bargaining power of individuals increases, which enables them to shape their working conditions and buffer labour market risks – two factors that are crucial for life satisfaction (Clark et al. 2010: 53). Individuals outside the labour market will need to rely on welfare state mechanisms, which buffer life risks. In particular *social expenditures* will be positively associated with life satisfaction, since they guarantee not only an existential minimum of life but stabilize income in the case of temporary unemployment or sickness (Böhnke 2011: 165; Mau et al. 2012: 659).[1]

With the eurozone crisis, GDP and income per capita and employment rates have especially fallen in Southern Europe. The countries under the auspices of the European bailout funds (ESM/EFSM/ESM), such as Greece, Spain, Portugal, Cyprus and Ireland, were forced by the EU bailout agreements to reduce their debts and to reform their social security systems (see Chapter 9). This lowered the living standards and the life satisfaction of many Europeans. Given these negative consequences of the eurozone crisis, it remains to be seen to what extent the ongoing social integration (with the assumed positive consequences for life satisfaction) could countervail this process. In the following section it will be discussed how European social integration offers opportunities to the EU population which could help people to deal with unpleasant life events. Cross-border connections and exchange may be a resource that can be used to achieve individual aims, despite the current eurozone crisis.

8.3 DETERMINANTS OF LIFE SATISFACTION AT A TRANSNATIONAL LEVEL

Cross-border relations in Europe have an economic and a social dimension. The basis for economic and social integration in Europe is the *community acquis* of the EU, which guarantees the free movement of goods, services, capital and people across EU Member States. Due to these legal regulations, the EU has become an economically integrated space characterized by intense cross-border trade and mobility (Dreher et al. 2008). The possibility to study, work and live in other EU countries has improved the labour market opportunities of transnationally oriented Europeans. Europe has also become a social space characterized by dense cross-border transactions and social networks (Mau and Mewes 2012). Europeans can spend their holidays in other European countries, pay with the same currency in currently 19 countries, communicate or fall in love with other Europeans or marry them in the framework of common legal and administrative regulations.

These increased opportunities also affect individual life chances. Transnational social ties provide chances for people to satisfy their curiosity about other cultures. Cross-border interactions and transnational social ties are the basis of intercultural and linguistic competences (Gerhards 2014). These new interrelations of individuals within Europe broaden the opportunities for transnational employment, leisure and social relations (Gerhards and Hans 2013: 100). They may improve the social and professional status of Europeans and thus may also increase the life chances and life satisfaction of Europeans.

Different indices for measuring the transnationalization of economic exchange and cross-border relations have been proposed. König and Ohr (2013) developed an EU index which is composed of four sub-indices measuring the integration of the single market, EU homogeneity/convergence, the symmetry of business cycles and the conformity with EU rules. Particularly important for economic integration is the first sub-index, which sheds light on the cross-border transactions of goods, services, capital and labour. While this index mainly focuses on the economic and institutional integration of the EU, the Europeanization of Everyday Life Index proposed by Delhey et al. (2014) captures the respective relevance of the national, European and global space for individual interactions such as travelling and shopping. Additionally, cognitive dimensions of Europeanization such as solidarity and transnational cultural interests are included in this index. This index assumes that two geographic horizons, the national and the global one, are relevant when investigating horizontal Europeanization empirically. Therefore, it distinguishes between *European closure* towards the world and the *national openness* towards the EU.

In order to measure the impact of cross-border interactions in Europe on individual life satisfaction, I will use the HEI proposed by my colleagues and me (Buttler et al. 2013). This index captures both the social *and* economic dimension of horizontal Europeanization, but I will limit my analysis to the social dimension because it is not likely that economic cross-border interconnections have a direct influence on life satisfaction. An impact of cognitive Europeanization is also not expected in the literature. Similar to Delhey et al. (2014), the index distinguishes between European closure (EC) and national openness (NO), which captures the share of European interaction relative to national and global interactions.

The *social dimension* of the HEI is related to the free movement of people, which is an essential element of the EU. The construction of the composite indicator was based on an exploratory factor analysis, a tool for identifying a latent theoretical construct behind single indicators, in this case 'horizontal Europeanization'. This dimension comprises the following four cross-border interrelations: *tourism, working abroad, immigrants* and *European students*,[2] as those variables appeared to be closest related to cross-European social activities.[3] Some of these interactions occur on a more regular basis (e.g. tourism) while others are one-time decisions (e.g. immigration, or study abroad). Furthermore, these four European interactions capture *outbound* (working abroad, tourism) and *inbound* (student exchange and immigration) mobility. The way the index is constructed assumes that all groups of a nation state are somewhat affected by closer cross-border interactions – even people who do not benefit directly from travel abroad, because the probability of ordinary citizens coming into contact with European immigrants or foreign students is higher in countries with a high share of European inbound mobility.

In the following, the four components of the *social dimension* of the HEI and their expected impact on subjective well-being will be discussed in detail.

Outbound tourism: People enjoy travelling when they are curious about other countries and cultures or when they are keen to deviate from their daily routines and strive to escape at least temporarily from daily obligations and/or tensions at home or work (Ory and Mokhtarian 2004: 99). Outbound tourism affects only a short period of life. Kostakopoulou states that 'connections beyond and across boundaries can generate experiences worth having and enriched life options' (2013: 44). A high share of people travelling abroad for holiday, trips or recreation means that a large part of the population is influenced by the positive impact of tourism. Furthermore, due to low-cost airlines and a well-developed public transport network in Europe, a cross-border holiday is no longer restricted to particular social groups. On the contrary, the majority of people are financially able to afford a holiday in another European country. The hurdles to experiencing this type of Europeanization are thus low, as they require few financial and linguistic resources. It can be expected that *people with touristic experiences are on average more satisfied with their lives than other people, because experiences abroad satisfy curiosity, interrupt daily routines and relieve people from everyday obligations (H1a). This effect also remains stable on the aggregate level, since the majority of people are able to afford low-cost travel by using public transport networks in Europe (H1b).*

Working abroad: The free movement of employees is a fundamental principle of the EU. In general, labour market migration is assumed to increase subjective well-being because migration is likely to improve income. However, this economic advantage may be accompanied by shortcomings in other domains. For example, working abroad may result in disruptions to family and community relations. Furthermore, an insufficient match of an individual's professional knowledge and abilities with their assigned tasks may lead to deskilling (Bartram 2010: 346–347). Thus, a Europeanized labour market can have ambivalent effects on subjective well-being. *On the one hand, it can be expected that a high share of people who work abroad corresponds with a better income, resulting in a higher life satisfaction (H2a). On the other hand, income gains from working abroad may be balanced out by disruptions to social and family relations. This could have a negative effect on life satisfaction (H2b).*

Immigration: European labour markets not only influence the life perspectives of people who actively search for and find a job abroad – countries receiving immigrants are also affected by the right to free movement within Europe. Therefore, the effects of migration can be expected not only at the micro-level as previously discussed, but also at the macro-level. Although people from averagely unhappier and poorer countries generally migrate to happier and wealthier countries, the effects of a high share of immigrants on the subjective well-being of the whole population remain two-sided. On the one hand, the effect could be positive when nation states with a high share of immigrants perceive them as beneficial, since employed migrants increase taxes, social contributions and the aggregated demand of the population (Dustmann et al 2010: 29). Unemployment could decrease and GDP could increase, which could contribute to the rising well-being of the overall population (Akay et al 2014: 82). On the other hand, a high share of immigrants could also be perceived as costly or even threatening, as they might be expected to lower the wages and employment opportunities of the native population (cf. Ottaviano and Peri 2012). Nonetheless, in this chapter we follow the scientific evidence stating that the overall impact of European immigrants is positive on a country (Akay et al. 2014: 82). *Thus, it can be expected that a higher share of immigrants is positively correlated with the life satisfaction of the population because a growth in the labour force might improve public finances and the aggregated demand (H3).*

Studying abroad: The EU has launched various mobility initiatives for lower and higher education programmes, such as Comenius, Leonardo da Vinci, the Youth in Action Programme and Erasmus. Exchange programmes not only foster social and intercultural skills as well as openness towards diversity, adaptability and problem-solving abilities, they also strengthen participants' human capital (Murphy-Lejeune 2002). Participation in exchange programmes in higher education and interaction with other Europeans can lead to an approximation of each other's perspectives and norms – an essential competence for transnational professionals which can be translated in better job perspectives (Kuhn 2012: 997–998). However, those students who do not participate in an exchange programme but study at a university with a high amount of international students also have the chance to develop similar skills. Formulated as a hypothesis: students in *countries with a high share of international students benefit from a high quality of education as well as from the related evolution of professional knowledge and soft-skills. This could contribute positively to subjective well-being (H4).*

In sum, Europe has become a geographical entity with dense cross-border transactions and networks (Dreher et al. 2008; Mau and Mewes

2012). This has enlarged the opportunity structure of individuals. These new cross-border relations help people to deal with and overcome unpleasant life events (Kaufmann et al. 2004: 754; Ohnmacht et al. 2009: 2). Connectedness with other European countries serves as a resource that helps to maintain or improve social status. Hence, *it can be assumed that higher degrees of horizontal Europeanization are associated with higher subjective well-being among the EU citizens (H5)*.

8.4 DATA AND METHODS

In order to test these hypotheses, I will use the Eurobarometer survey (EB 78.2), which was fielded in 2012 in 23 countries with 20 287 observations. The dependent variable, which captures the overall life satisfaction in the nation state and the EU, was calculated by adding up the answers to the following questions: 'Please tell me to what extent you agree or disagree with each of the following statements:' A) 'You are happy living in (OUR COUNTRY)?' and B) 'You are happy in living in the EU?'. The answers to these questions vary between 1 ('totally disagree') and 4 ('totally agree'). These two variables are highly correlated ($r = 0.83$); therefore, I have added up the results in order to construct an additive index for life satisfaction that takes into account the opportunities offered by nation states and the EU for overall life satisfaction (Frey and Stutzer 2000: 925, 2002: 422; Tov and Diener 2009: 165). Following Kassenboehmer and Haisken-DeNew (2012), these outcomes were treated as interval-scaled rather than ordinal, as it is assumed that the differences between the answer categories are considered as equal by the respondents.[4]

Gender, age, years of education, health conditions and employment status were included as socio-demographic control variables in the analyses. Furthermore, we controlled for household composition and distinguished between single-person households, single parents and households with and without children. Due to the fact that income data are not available in the Eurobarometer, the item d60 'Difficulties in paying bills last year' was included as an indicator of material constraints. As our hypotheses assume that European interconnectedness conveys benefits on both the individual and aggregated level, the survey respondents' migration background and European travel experiences have also been included as approximations to individual European interconnectedness. Context variables capture country-specific effects on the outcome variable. We included the GDP per capita (as an indicator of the economic prosperity of the country), social expenditures as percentage of GDP (as an indicator of the national level of social protection), government debts in percentage of GDP (as an indicator of the risk of potential expenditures cuts due to austerity policies) and the employment rate (as an indicator of the inclusiveness of the national labour market). In order to evaluate the effect of horizontal Europeanization on life satisfaction, the social dimensions of the HEI were included. Table 8.1 summarizes the variables, their operationalization as well as the expected sign of the coefficient. In order to deal with the hierarchical structure of the data, a linear two-level random intercepts model with random intercept parameters was constructed with the Stata command *mixed*.

Life satisfaction 'y_{ic}' for an individual i in country c is a function of a range of individual-level characteristics such as income and other factors 'X_{ic}' as well as country-level features such as GDP per capita 'Z_c' and the intermediating factor 'horizontal Europeanization' (measured by vector 'H_c'). Measurement errors and bias on the individual level are subsumed under the error terms ε_{ic} at the individual and u_c at the country-level:

$$y_{ic} = X_{ic}\beta + Z_c\gamma + H_c\theta + u_c + \varepsilon_{ic} \qquad (1)$$

with $i = 1, \ldots, N_c$; $c = 1, \ldots, C$.

Robustness checks in terms of a log-log model which captures possible non-linear relationships as well as models that include welfare state specific dummy variables and interaction terms between welfare states and horizontal Europeanization show similar results as the linear OLS two-level regression.

8.5   RESULTS

8.5.1   Descriptive Statistics

Average life satisfaction in the EU varies relatively strongly among European countries. Figure 8.2 shows that most Southern as well as Central and Eastern European (CEE) countries report a relatively low life satisfaction. Continental, Scandinavian and liberal countries as well as Spain and some CEE countries report an above average life satisfaction. The distribution of horizontal Europeanization reveals a similar picture. Whereas most Eastern and Southern European countries are characterized by a relatively low level of horizontal Europeanization, people in Continental, Scandinavian and liberal countries are well interconnected within Europe. Horizontal Europeanization is strongly correlated with life satisfaction ($r^2 = 0.27$).

Table 8.1 Expected effects of the selected variables for the multivariate multi-level regression

Variable	Operationalization and data source	Expected sign
Dependent		
Life satisfaction	Scale of 2 to 8, where 2 means very dissatisfied/ unhappy and 8 means very satisfied/happy. Composite indicator variable. Question one (qa1_1): 'You are happy living in (OUR COUNTRY)?' Question two (qa1_2) 'You are happy in living in the EU?' Both answer categories range from totally disagree (1) and totally agree (4).	
Independent	*Individual level*	
Gender	(0 = male; 1 = female) [d_10]	+
Age and age square	Age at time of interview [vd11]	Concave
Age when full-time education stopped	'How old were you when you stopped full-time education?' [d8] 1 = up to 15 years (Ref.); 2 = 16–19 years; 3 = +20 years	+
Unemployed	Unemployed at the time of the interview. (0 = no; 1 = yes) [c14]	−
Economic difficulties	Difficulties in paying bills [d60]	−
Household composition	[d7r3] 1 = Single parents (Ref.); 2 = Couples without children; 3 = Couples with children; 4 = Single	+
Migrant background	Citizen of another EU or non-EU country [q1_1 – q1_29] (0 = no; 1 = yes)	+
EU trips	In the last 12 months, have you purchased goods or services, whilst on holiday or in a business trip in another EU Member State? [qb2_2] (0 = no; 1 = yes)	+
Independent	*Country level*	
Social protection expenditures	Percentage of GDP which is expended for the social security functions sickness/health care, disability, old age, survivors, family/children, unemployment, housing, social exclusion [Eurostat: spr_exp_fto]	+
Government debts	General government gross debts (in % of GDP) [Eurostat: gov_10dd_edpt1]	−
Employment rate	Employment rate in % of all persons aged 15–64 [Eurostat: lfsi_empa]	+

Table 8.1   (continued)

Variable	Operationalization and data source	Expected sign
Independent	*Country level*	
GDP per capita	Gross domestic product (at market prices) per capita [Eurostat: nama_gdp_c]] (logarithmized)	+
	Europeanization factors	
Outbound tourism	Share of EU outbound tourism relative to the population of sending country (Eurostat)	+
Working abroad	Share of people working abroad in the EU relative to the population of sending country (Eurostat)	+/−
Immigrants	Share of EU immigrants relative to the population of receiving country (Eurostat)	+/−
European students	Share of EU students relative to the number of native students in respective receiving country (Eurostat)	+
Horizontal Europeani- zation (social dimension)	Weighted (by factor loadings of CFA) overall summary of all four components in the social dimension. (Data source from Buttler et al. 2013.)	+

Furthermore, all components of the social horizontal Europeanization are positively related with life satisfaction, with outbound tourism playing the most important role ($r^2 = 0.31$), followed by the share of European students ($r^2 = 0.06$), the share of people working abroad ($r^2 = 0.04$) and the share of European immigrants ($r^2 = 0.04$). Overall, it seems that the population in prosperous countries, which have high GDP per capita, low government debts, high social expenditures and high employment rates, are characterized by higher rates of cross-border contacts and exchanges. These first descriptive statistics provide some positive evidence that supports the hypotheses 1b, 2a, 3, 4 and 5. A multivariate investigation of the individual, national and transnational driving factors of life satisfaction will be accomplished in the next section.

8.5.2   Multi-level Analyses

Multi-level analyses (see the results in Table 8.2.) account for the hierarchical structure of the data and thus allow the total variance to be broken down into the variance at the individual level (1) and the national level (2). Statistically, the importance of context factors is indicated by the reduction

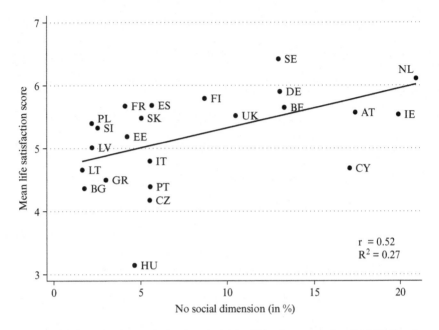

Note: This figure has been calculated on the basis of Eurobarometer data 2012 (78.2) and the Horizontal Europeanization Index proposed by Buttler et al. (2013).

Figure 8.2   Life satisfaction and the social dimension of horizontal Europeanization

of between-nation variance. As we are focusing on the European interconnectedness of individuals and countries, socio-demographic variables – which have the expected sign – are not shown in Table 8.2 (see however Table 8A.1 in the appendix).

The random intercept only (RIO) model – a model without explanatory variables – shows the total and between-country variance which will be reduced by variables at the individual and national level respectively. Here, between-country variance is 0.54, which means that 30 per cent of the total variance (1.82) in life satisfaction in Europe can be explained by national characteristics. Model 1 and the following models include individual socio-demographic variables, which however are not shown in Table 8.2 (see however Table 8A.1). As expected, individual migration and travelling experiences are positively correlated with life satisfaction. Thus, H1a can be confirmed on the individual level. The individual socio-demographic background and the two transnational variables at the individual level included in model 1 explain 33 per cent of the variance.

Table 8.2 Determinants of life satisfaction of the European population

	Model 0	Model 1	Model 2	Model 3	Model 4	Model 5	Model 6	Model 7	Model 8
Individual determinants									
Migration background	0.163+	0.162+	0.162+	0.162+	0.162+	0.163+	0.163+	0.162+	0.162+
	(1.67)	(1.67)	(1.67)	(1.66)	(1.66)	(1.67)	(1.67)	(1.66)	(1.66)
EU trips	0.073***	0.073***	0.073***	0.073***	0.073***	0.073***	0.073***	0.073***	0.073***
	(3.16)	(3.15)	(3.15)	(3.15)	(3.15)	(3.15)	(3.15)	(3.15)	(3.15)
Horizontal Europeanization									
Outbound tourism			0.011***						
			(3.62)						
Working abroad			0.772						
			(0.99)						
Immigration			−0.109						
			(−1.40)						
EU students			−0.015						
			(−0.40)						
Comprehensive HE Index				0.049***	0.042***	0.045***	0.038**	−0.030	
				(3.29)	(3.23)	(3.83)	(2.13)	(−0.63)	
National context									
Social expenditures					0.056**	0.081***	0.073**	−0.013	
					(2.40)	(3.62)	(2.21)	(−0.19)	
Government debts						−0.006***	−0.005**	−0.007***	
						(−3.12)	(−1.98)	(−3.21)	
Employment rate							0.013	−0.000	
							(0.34)	(−0.00)	
GDP per capita (log)								2.265+	1.362***
								(1.88)	(4.04)

209

Table 8.2 (continued)

	Model 0	Model 1	Model 2	Model 3	Model 4	Model 5	Model 6	Model 7	Model 8
No.	20287	20287	20287	20287	20287	20287	20287	20287	20287
Chi^2	·	715990	1695916	839954	921512	982637	1512505	988598	744061
Between-country variance	0.54	0.40	0.29	0.32	0.28	0.25	0.24	0.19	0.24
Variance (total)	1.817	1.728	1.728	1.728	1.728	1.728	1.728	1.728	1.728
Intra-class correlation	0.30	0.23	0.17	0.19	0.16	0.15	0.14	0.11	0.14
R^2	·	0.33	0.37	0.38	0.39	0.41	0.41	0.44	0.41
AIC	69825	68816	68816	68812	68812	68811	68813	68809	68806
BIC	69848	68927	68959	68931	68938	68945	68955	68959	68925
Log-likelihood	−34909	−34394	−34390	−34391	−34390	−34388	−34388	−34385	−34388

Note: Linear multi-level models. Levels of significance: $+ \, p < .1$; $*p < .05$; $**p < .01$. t-values are given in parentheses. Socio-demographic characteristics are controlled for but not shown here (see appendix Table 8A.1). The test statistics of testing for the joint significance of all variables in the fixed effects model are given by Chi^2. The AIC (Akaike information criterion) and the BIC (Bayes information criterion) are measures of the relative quality of the model specification.

Source: Own calculations on the basis of Eurobarometer data 2012 (78.2).

In model 2, the previously explained indicators of horizontal Europeanization at the national level are included. Whereas a higher share of outbound tourism increases life satisfaction significantly, this cannot be observed for the share of people who are working abroad, immigrants and European students. This indicates that outbound tourism is a dominant transnational predictor of life satisfaction. Model 3 adds the overall index for horizontal Europeanization, which is also positively associated with life satisfaction. As expected by H1b, the aggregated impact of tourism is positive, while the effects of working abroad, immigration and European students vanish when the other dimensions of horizontal Europeanization are included. Hence, H2a/b, H3 and H4 cannot be confirmed empirically on the aggregated level, even though individual migration experiences are linked to a higher life satisfaction.

Models 4, 5 and 6 test whether the effects of horizontal Europeanization on life satisfaction are stable when other national context factors are included. Therefore, we included social expenditures, government debts and employment rates. Whereas increasing social expenditures contribute positively to life satisfaction by functioning as a collective protection net against all sorts of biographical risks, increasing employment rates do not play a significant role. Increasing government debts are negatively associated with life satisfaction, as they erode the protective function of the welfare state and lead to insecurities in the time of the economic crisis. Even when these context factors are controlled for, the effect of horizontal Europeanization remains stable and positive. This changes in model 7 when GDP is added and has a highly significant impact on life satisfaction. However, this does not necessarily imply that GDP per capita is a more accurate causal explanation for life satisfaction. This construct of national income is rather a 'black box' (Ng and Muntaner 2014), which is highly correlated with the level of social expenditures, the employment rate and horizontal Europeanization, but does not identify any mechanism on its own by which life satisfaction can be directly increased. For horizontal Europeanization (in addition to social expenditures and public debts), however, a strong causal effect on life satisfaction can be founded theoretically. This assumption is supported by the higher reduction of the between-country variance in model 6 in comparison to model 8.

In sum, European interconnectedness (on the individual as well as on the aggregated level) offers an enlarged set of opportunities to cope with unpleasant life events, even when we control for other nation state characteristics such as social expenditure, government debt and employment rate (a result which confirms H5). Transnationally mobile and interconnected Europeans are better off in terms of life satisfaction than Europeans living in countries with lower levels of cross-border connections. Thus, countries where people make use of the new possibilities of transnational experiences (e.g. via the European job market, education system or holidays) have more chances to satisfy their needs and desires. However, the transnational population is mostly located in wealthier countries, which indicates growing cleavages in Europe, especially in times of crisis.

8.6   CONCLUSION

This chapter discussed the relationship between life satisfaction and horizontal Europeanization. Horizontal Europeanization refers to social and economic interactions which extend beyond the nation state border, such as mobility, consumption and communication (Mau et al. 2008) or the exchange of goods, capital and knowledge (Sandholtz and Stone Sweet 1998). In this chapter we focused on the social dimension of these interactions and argued that horizontal Europeanization can be seen as a resource that broadens opportunities in the areas of employment, leisure and social relations. European integration thus enlarges the opportunity set of transnationally-oriented individuals (Kostakopoulou 2013: 44).

Three insights can be derived. Firstly, life satisfaction corresponds positively to horizontal Europeanization. Especially the share of *outbound tourism* at the aggregate level is strongly associated with life satisfaction. The share of persons working abroad, immigrants and Erasmus students, on the other hand, is not particularly strong related to life satisfaction. Secondly, the effect of horizontal Europeanization remains stable when we control for other national characteristics such as social expenditures, government debts and employment rates. Breaking down the national context helps to clarify the pathways by which national income leads to higher life satisfaction. It is thus not the amount of money but the way in which it is used by individuals and nation states which determines life satisfaction. European social relations (travelling, working, living in other EU countries) enhance opportunities for dealing with problematic situations in life and facing new challenges. Such interrelations have positive effects on the satisfaction of living in the respective nation state and the EU. They contribute to experiences 'worth having'. Improving an individual's labour market position, intercultural knowledge and transnational social ties can become an important resource, and can help in mastering adverse social and economic times.

NOTES

1. Furthermore, a high degree of *income inequality* brings about poor health, insecurity and anxiety which weakens solidarity and cohesion and thus reduces life satisfaction not only for the objectively disadvantaged but for the whole society (Böhnke 2011: 163; Wilkinson and Pickett 2010: 18). It had been shown that Europeans are especially inequality adverse (Alesina et al. 2001: 4) With respect to basic constitutional rules it can be seen that *democratic institutions*, in particular the right to participate in elections or referenda, contribute positively to life satisfaction as politicians are more motivated to rule according to the interest of the voters. A reliable government and low corruption increases the chances of high life satisfaction (Frey and Stutzer 2000: 925, 2002: 422). Next to the objective individual and country-specific factors that contribute to the explanation of life satisfaction, the subjective perception of the social and institutional environment is also a matter of recent research. There it had been shown that, in particular in times of crises, the substantial decrease in *social and institutional trust* may be additionally responsible for the decline in well-being in Europe (Delle Fave 2014: 119). Distrust in fellow natives and *status anxiety* are the main mediators for reduced life satisfaction in unequal societies (Delhey and Dragolov 2013: 152).
2. The required weighting factors are the factor loadings observed in the construction of the HEI.
3. Further variables were included in the factor analysis, namely knowledge of foreign languages, frequency of discussions about EU topics, trust in the EU, broadband connection, passenger transport, overnight stays, participation in EU elections, as well as import and export of books and other printed media.
4. Ordered logistic regressions (OLR) have been conducted and are available upon request. The robustness test of the results of our ordinary least square (OLS) estimates (in comparison to OLR) show no meaningful differences in the results.

REFERENCES

Adena, M. and M. Myck (2013), 'Poverty and Transitions in Health', *WZB Discussion Paper SP II 2013-307*, 1–29, accessed 28 April 2016 at: http://bibliothek.wzb.eu/pdf/2013/ii13-307.pdf.

Akay, A., A. Constant and C. Giulietti (2014), 'The Impact of Immigration on the Well-being of Natives', *Journal of Economic Behavior & Organization*, **103**(7–8), 72–92.

Alesina, A., R. Di Tella and R. MacCulloch (2001), 'Inequality and Happiness. Are Europeans and Americans Different?', *National Bureau of Economic Research Working Paper Series*, 8198, 1–37.

Bartram, D. (2010), 'International Migration, Open Borders Debates, and Happiness', *International Studies Review*, **12**(3), 339–361.

Blanchflower, D.G. and A.J. Oswald (2004), 'Well-Being Over Time in Britain and the USA', *Journal of Public Economics*, **88**(7), 1359–1386.

Blanchflower, D.G. and A. Oswald (2007), 'Is Well-being U-shaped Over the Life Cycle?', in *National Bureau of Economic Research Working Paper Series* 12935, 1–27, accessed 12 September 2014 at: http://www.nber.org/papers/w12935.pdf.

Blyth, M. (2013), *Austerity: The History of a Dangerous Idea*, Oxford: Oxford University Press.

Böhnke, P. (2007), 'Feeling Left Out. Patterns of Social Integration and Exclusion', in J. Alber, T. Fahey and C. Saraceno (eds), *Handbook of Quality of Life in the Enlarged European Union*, New York: Routledge, pp. 304–327.

Böhnke, P. (2008), 'Does Society Matter? Life Satisfaction in the Enlarged Europe?', *Social Indicators Research*, **87**(2), 189–210.

Böhnke, P. (2011), 'Gleichheit und Sicherheit als Voraussetzung für Lebensqualität?', *WSI Mitteilungen*, **4**, 163–170, accessed 12 September 2014 at: http://www.boeckler.de/wsimit_2011_04_Boehnke.pdf.

Böhnke, P. and U. Kohler (2010), 'Well-Being and Inequality', in S. Immerfall and G. Therborn (eds), *Handbook of European Societies. Social Transformations in the 21st Century*, New York: Springer, pp. 629–666.

Buttler, F., C. Ingensiep, S. Israel and C. Reimann (2013), 'Connected Europe(ans)? The Quantitative Measurement of Horizontal Europeanization', *Pre-Prints of the DFG Research Unit Horizontal Europeanization*, **2014**(2), accessed 12 April 2015 at: http://www.horizontal-europeanization.eu/downloads/pre-prints/PP_HoEu_2014-02_buttler_etal.pdf.

Clark, A.E. and A.T. Oswald (1994), 'Unhappiness and Unemployment', *The Economic Journal*, **104**(424), 648–659.

Clark, A.E., A. Knabe and S. Rätzel (2010), 'Boon or Bane? Others' Unemployment, Well-being and Job Insecurity', *Labour Economics*, **17**, 52–61.

Delhey, J. and G. Dragolov (2013), 'Why Inequality Makes Europeans Less Happy: The Role of Distrust, Status Anxiety, and Perceived Conflict', *European Sociological Review*, **30**(2), 151–165.

Delhey, J. and U. Kohler (2007), 'Where we Stand in Europe. Citizens' Perceptions of European Country Rankings and their Influence on Subjective Well-being', in J. Alber, T. Fahey and C. Saraceno (eds), *Handbook of Quality of Life in the Enlarged European Union*, New York: Routledge, pp. 385–403.

Delhey, J., E. Deutschmann, T. Graf and K. Richter (2014), 'Measuring the Europeanization of Everyday-Life: Three New Indices and an Empirical Application', *European Societies*, **16**(3), 355–377.

Delle Fave, A. (2014), 'Well-being in Times of Crisis: Interdisciplinary Evidence and Policy Implications', *Journal of Happiness Studies*, **15**(1), 119–123.

Diener, E. (2009), 'Subjective Well-Being', in E. Diener (ed.), *The Science of Well-being. The Collected Works of Ed Diener*, Social Indicators Series, **37**, Dordrecht: Springer, pp. 11–58.

Diener, E. and M.E.P. Seligman (2004), 'Beyond Money. Toward an Economy of Well-Being', *Psychological Science in the Public Interest*, **5**(1), 1–31.

Diener, E., M. Diener and C. Diener (2009), 'Factors Predicting the Subjective Well-Being of Nations', in E. Diener (ed.), *Culture and Well-Being: The Collected Works of Ed Diener*, Social Indicators Series, **38**, Dordrecht: Springer, pp. 43–91.

Díez Medrano, J., C. Cortina, A. Safranoff and T. Castro-Martín (2013), 'Euromarriages in Spain: Recent Trends and Patterns in the Context of European Integration', *Population, Space and Place*, **20**(2), 157–176.

Dreher, A., N. Gaston and P. Martens (2008), *Measuring Globalisation. Gauging its Consequences*, New York: Springer.

Dustmann, C., T. Frattini and C. Halls (2010), 'Assessing the Fiscal Costs and Benefits of A8 Migration to the UK', *Fiscal Studies*, **31**(1), 1–41.

Easterlin, R.A. (1974), 'Does Economic Growth Improve the Human Lot? Some Empirical Evidence', in P.A. David and M.W. Reder (eds), *Nations and Households in Economic Growth: Essays in Honor of Moses Abramovitz*, New York: Academic Press, pp. 89–125.

Favell, A. (2008), *Eurostars and Eurocities: Free Movement and Mobility in an Integrating Europe*, Malden, MA: Blackwell.

Fligstein, N. (2008), *Euroclash*, Oxford: Oxford University Press.

Frey, B.S. and A. Stutzer (2000), 'Happiness, Economy and Institutions', *Economic Journal*, **110**(446), 918–938.

Frey, B.S. and A. Stutzer (2002), 'What Can Economists Learn from Happiness Research?', *Journal of Economic Literature*, **40**(2), 402–435.

Gallie, D., S. Paugam and S. Jacobs (2003), 'Unemployment, Poverty and Social Isolation: Is There a Vicious Circle of Social Exclusion?', *European Societies*, **5**(1), 1–32.

Gerhards, J. (2014), 'Transnational Linguistic Capital: Explaining English Proficiency in 27 European Countries', *International Sociology*, **29**(1), 56–74.

Gerhards, J. and S. Hans (2013), 'Transnational Human Capital, Education and Social Inequality. Analyses of International Student Exchange', *Zeitschrift für Soziologie*, **42**(2), 99–117.

Gerhards, J. and H. Lengfeld (2015), *European Citizenship and Social Integration in the European Union*, Abingdon: Routledge.

Guiraudon, V. (2011), 'Mobilization, Social Movements and the Media', in A. Favell and V. Guiraudon (eds), *Sociology of the European Union*, New York: Palgrave Macmillan, pp. 125–149.

Husain, Z., M. Dutta and N. Chowdhary (2014), 'Is Health Wealth? Results of Panel Data Analysis', *Social Indicators Research*, **117**, 121–143.

Joshanloo, M. (2014), 'Eastern Conceptualizations of Happiness: Fundamental Differences with Western Views', *Journal of Happiness Studies*, **15**, 475–493.

Jürgens, H. (2007), 'True Health vs Response Styles: Exploring Cross-Country Differences in Self-reported Health', *Health Economics*, **16**, 163–178.

Kahneman, D. and A. Deaton (2010), 'High Income Improves Evaluation of Life But Not Emotional Well-Being', *Proceedings of the National Academy of Sciences*, **107**(38), 16489–16493.

Kassenboehmer, S.C. and J.P. Haisken-DeNew (2012), 'Heresy or Enlightenment? The Well-being Age U-shape Effect is Flat', *Economics Letters*, **117**(1), 235–238.

Kaufmann, V., M.M. Bergmann and D. Joye (2004), 'Motility: Mobility as Capital', *International Journal of Urban and Regional Research*, **28**(4), 745–756.

König, J. and R. Ohr (2013), 'Different Efforts in European Economic Integration: Implications of the EU Index', *Journal of Common Market Studies*, **51**(6), 1074–1090.

Kostakopoulou, D. (2013), *Co-creating European Union Citizenship. A Policy Review*, Luxembourg: Publications Office of the European Union.

Kuhn, T. (2011), 'Individual Transnationalism, Globalisation and Euroscepticism: An Empirical Test of Deutsch's Transactionalist Theory', *European Journal of Political Research*, **50**(6), 811–837.

Kuhn, T. (2012), 'Why Educational Exchange Programmes Miss Their Mark: Cross-Border Mobility, Education and European Identity', *Journal of Common Market Studies*, **50**(6), 994–1010.

Kuhn, T. (2015), *Experiencing European Integration: Transnational Lives and European Identity*, Oxford: Oxford University Press.

Lalive, R. and A. Stutzer (2010), 'Approval on Equal Rights and Gender Differences in Well-being', *Journal of Population Economics*, **23**(3), 933–962.

Mau, S. and J. Mewes (2012), 'Horizontal Europeanization in Contextual

Perspective: What Drives Cross-border Activities Within the European Union?', *European Societies*, **14**(1), 7–34.

Mau, S., J. Mewes and A. Zimmermann (2008), 'Cosmopolitan Attitudes Through Transnational Social Practices?', *Global Networks*, **8**(1), 1–24.

Mau, S., J. Mewes and N.M. Schöneck (2012), 'What Determines Subjective Socio-economic Insecurity? Context and Class in Comparative Perspective', *Socio-Economic Review*, **10**(4), 655–682.

Mencarini, L. and M. Sironi (2012), 'Happiness, Housework and Gender Inequality in Europe', *European Sociological Review*, **28**(2), 203–219.

Murphy-Lejeune, E. (2002), *Student Mobility and Narrative in Europe: The New Strangers*, London: Routledge.

Ng, E. and C. Muntaner (2014), 'A Critical Approach to Macrosocial Determinants of Population Health: Engaging Scientific Realism and Incorporating Social Conflict', *Current Epidemiological Reports*, **1**(1), 27–37.

Ohnmacht, T., H. Maksim and M.M. Bergmann (eds) (2009), *Mobilities and Inequality – An Introduction*, Farnham: Ashgate.

Ory, D.T. and P.L. Mokhtarian (2004), 'When is Getting There Half the Fun? Modelling the Liking for Travel', *Transportation Research*, **39**(A), 97–124.

Ottaviano, G.I.P. and G. Peri (2012), 'Rethinking the Effect of Immigration on Wages', *Journal of the European Economic Association*, **10**(1), 152–197.

Polgreen, L.A. and N.B. Simpson (2010), 'Happiness and International Migration', *Happiness Studies*, **12**, 819–840.

Portela, M., I. Neira and M. del Mar Salinas-Jiménez (2013), 'Social Capital and Subjective Wellbeing in Europe: A New Approach on Social Capital', *Social Indicators Research*, **114**, 493–511.

Powdthavee, N. (2008), 'Putting a Price Tag on Friends, Relatives, and Neighbours: Using Surveys of Life Satisfaction to Value Social Relationships', *The Journal of Socio-Economics*, **37**(4), 1459–1480.

Recchi, E., J. Salamońska, T. Rossi and I.G. Baglioni (2014), 'Cross-border Mobilities in the European Union: An Evidence-based Typology', in E. Recchi (ed.), *The Europeanisation of Everyday Life*, Final Report, accessed 30 April 2016 at: http://nbn-resolving.de/urn:nbn:de:0168-ssoar-395269.

Rodríguez-Pose, A. and V. von Berlepsch (2014), 'Social Capital and Individual Happiness in Europe', *Journal of Happiness Studies*, **15**(2), 357–386.

Sander, T.H. and R.D. Putnam (2010), 'Still Bowling Alone? The Post-9/11 Split', *Journal of Democracy*, **21**(1), 9–16.

Sandholtz, W. and A. Stone Sweet (1998), *European Integration and Supranational Governance*, Oxford: Oxford University Press.

Stavrova, O., D. Fetchenhauer and T. Schlösser (2012), 'Cohabitation, Gender and Happiness: A Cross-Cultural Study in Thirty Countries', *Journal of Cross-Cultural Psychology*, **43**(7), 1063–1081.

Tesch-Römer, C., A. Motel-Klingebiel and M.J. Tomasik (2008), 'Gender Differences in Subjective Well-Being: Comparing Societies with Respect to Gender Equality', *Social Indicators Research*, **85**(2), 329–349.

Tov, W. and Diener, E. (2009), 'The Well-Being of Nations: Linking Together Trust, Cooperation, and Democracy', in E. Diener (ed.), *The Science of Well-being. The Collected Works of Ed Diener*, Dordrecht et al.: Springer, pp. 155–174.

Veenhoven, R. (2012), 'HAPPINESS: Also Known as Life Satisfaction and Subjective Well-being', in K.C. Land, A.C. Michalos and M.J. Sirgy (eds),

Handbook of Social Indicators and Quality of Life Research, Dordrecht: Springer, pp. 63–77. doi: 10.1007/978-94-007-2421-1_3.

Wilkinson, R. and K. Pickett (2010), *The Spirit Level. Why Equality is Better for Everyone*, London: Penguin Books.

Winkelmann, L. and R. Winkelmann (1998), 'Why are the Unemployed so Unhappy? Evidence from Panel Data', *Economica*, **65**(257), 1–15.

APPENDIX

Table 8A.1 *Individual determinants of life-satisfaction of the European population (linear multi-level model)*

Individual determinants	Model 0	Model 1	Model 2	Model 3	Model 4	Model 5	Model 6	Model 7	Model 8
	Empty model								
Women		0.108***	0.108***	0.108***	0.108***	0.108***	0.108***	0.108***	0.108***
		(6.18)	(6.18)	(6.19)	(6.19)	(6.19)	(6.19)	(6.18)	(6.18)
Age		−0.179***	−0.179***	−0.179***	−0.179***	−0.179***	−0.179***	−0.179***	−0.179***
		(−3.12)	(−3.12)	(−3.12)	(−3.12)	(−3.12)	(−3.12)	(−3.12)	(−3.12)
Age^2		0.024***	0.024***	0.024***	0.024***	0.024***	0.024***	0.024***	0.024***
		(4.40)	(4.40)	(4.40)	(4.40)	(4.40)	(4.40)	(4.40)	(4.40)
Years of education		0.149***	0.149***	0.149***	0.149***	0.149***	0.149***	0.149***	0.150***
		(6.80)	(6.79)	(6.80)	(6.80)	(6.79)	(6.78)	(6.81)	(6.81)
Unemployed		−0.178***	−0.177***	−0.177***	−0.177***	−0.177***	−0.177***	−0.178***	−0.177***
		(−4.83)	(−4.82)	(−4.83)	(−4.83)	(−4.82)	(−4.83)	(−4.82)	(−4.83)
Difficulties paying bills		−0.325***	−0.325***	−0.325***	−0.325***	−0.325***	−0.325***	−0.324***	−0.325***
		(−11.56)	(−11.58)	(−11.57)	(−11.59)	(−11.56)	(−11.56)	(−11.55)	(−11.60)
Ref.: Single parent									
Single person		−0.006	−0.006	−0.006	−0.007	−0.007	−0.007	−0.007	−0.007
		(−0.15)	(−0.15)	(−0.15)	(−0.15)	(−0.15)	(−0.15)	(−0.15)	(−0.15)
HH without child(ren)		0.088**	0.088**	0.088**	0.088**	0.088**	0.088**	0.088**	0.088**
		(2.11)	(2.10)	(2.10)	(2.10)	(2.10)	(2.10)	(2.11)	(2.10)
HH with child(ren)		0.126***	0.126***	0.126***	0.126***	0.126***	0.126***	0.126***	0.126***
		(2.65)	(2.66)	(2.65)	(2.65)	(2.66)	(2.66)	(2.66)	(2.65)

	(1)	(2)	(3)	(4)	(5)	(6)	(7)	(8)	(9)
Migrant background		0.163+	0.162+	0.162+	0.162+	0.163+	0.163+	0.162+	0.162+
		(1.67)	(1.67)	(1.66)	(1.66)	(1.67)	(1.67)	(1.66)	(1.66)
EU trips		0.073***	0.073***	0.073***	0.073***	0.073***	0.073***	0.073***	0.073***
		(3.16)	(3.15)	(3.15)	(3.15)	(3.15)	(3.15)	(3.15)	(3.15)
HEI components: social dimension, European and national context factors	*(See Table 8.2)*								
No.	20287	20287	20287	20287	20287	20287	20287	20287	20287
Chi²	.	715990	1695916	839954	921512	982637	1512505	988598	744061
Between-country variance	0.54	0.40	0.29	0.32	0.28	0.25	0.24	0.19	0.24
Variance (total)	1817	1728	1728	1728	1728	1728	1728	1728	1728
Intra-class correlation	0.23	0.19	0.14	0.16	0.14	0.13	0.12	0.10	0.12
R²		0.33	0.37	0.38	0.39	0.41	0.41	0.44	0.41
AIC	69824.60	68815.98	68816.04	68812.48	68811.61	68810.75	68812.57	68808.58	68806.01
BIC	69848.35	68926.83	68958.56	68931.25	68938.29	68945.35	68955.09	68959.02	68924.78
Log-likelihood	−34909.30	−34393.99	−34390.02	−34391.24	−34389.81	−34388.37	−34388.28	−34385.29	−34388.01

Note: Significance intervals: +p/z < 0.1; *p/z > 0.05; ** > 0.01. t-values are given in parentheses. The test statistics of testing for the joint significance of all variables in the fixed effects model are given by Chi². The AIC (Akaike information criterion) and the BIC (Bayes information criterion) are measures of the relative quality of the model specification.

Source: Own calculations on the basis of Eurobarometer data 2012 (78.2).

9. The European integration process and the social consequences of the eurozone crisis

Jenny Preunkert

9.1 INTRODUCTION

Since 2010, comprehensive European crisis management has been gradually introduced to avoid a potential shortfall in payments by any member of the eurozone. The bailout funds enable vulnerable EU Member States to apply for support in the form of credits and securities (Blyth 2014; Hall 2014; Hodson 2015).[1] However, the common currency area has been challenged not only by the fiscal and economic problems of some of its member countries, but also by the dangers of social disruption. A growing social divergence has been observed between the core members of the European common currency area and its periphery. The Southern members and Ireland have been confronted with an increasing number of social problems in terms of increasing (long-term) unemployment rates and a deterioration in living conditions (see the previous chapters in this volume). Thus, the crisis has serious social consequences – in particular high (youth) unemployment rates, widespread poverty, social exclusion and health problems. Consequently, it is an empirically and politically relevant question to ask how these social problems have been dealt with, and perhaps even caused by, European crisis management. In particular, the three European bailout funds – the EFSM, EFSF and ESM – may thus play an important role in dealing with these social problems through their obligations (generally known as the Economic Adjustment Programme (EAP)), which suggest the reorganization of national welfare systems.

The aim of this chapter is to understand whether the bailout funds have not only an economic dimension but also a social dimension. The main questions of this chapter therefore are: have the previously described social problems – the increasing gap between different social groups and between Northern and Southern European countries – been defined as politically relevant issues in European crisis management? And how have these challenges been treated within the framework of bailout funds?

Two scenarios will be discussed in the following sections. The first scenario proposes that the bailout funds have focused on the fiscal and economic side of the crisis while so far ignoring the social problems. In this scenario, social policy has been defined as a cost factor which must be reduced in order to overcome the fiscal problems. The second scenario assumes that European crisis management has defined the social problems as political challenges and therefore supports national social policy measures in order to tackle the negative social developments.

The bailout funds are analysed in five steps. In the next section the two scenarios are developed on the basis of the state of the art, followed by a description of the research design. In the third and the fourth step the empirical findings are presented. The findings show that the social problems have been recognized within the European crisis policy, but so far social security systems have been treated mainly as a cost factor that has to be reduced. National assistance has been demanded only in terms of programmes for particular groups. The final step provides a summary of the results.

9.2 PATHS OF THE EUROPEAN INTEGRATION PROCESS IN TIMES OF CRISIS: TWO SCENARIOS

The EU has few redistributive resources and limited direct competence to act in the field of social policy (Leibfried and Pierson 1995; Leibfried 2015). Legal competences only exist in the fields of health protection for employees, gender equality and anti-discrimination (Lindberg and Vollaard 2014; Leibfried 2015). 'The welfare state remains one of the few key realms where national governments have usually resisted losses of policy authority not least because of the electoral significance of most social programmes' (Leibfried 2015: 267). Nonetheless, the European integration process has influenced governments' scope of action with regard to social policy in different ways. Governments are no longer able to define the mechanism of social security alone and without paying regard to European regulations and law, a development that is highly disputed. While on one side this process of Europeanization is seen as a danger to social standards, others define it as a chance to develop common high standards on the European level.

Building on different strands of arguments (regarding the debate see Lindberg and Vollaard 2014; Leibfried 2015), two diametrically different answers can be found to the question of how the current European policy deals with social problems. One strand argues that European policy contributes to a retrenchment of welfare states and therefore to a reduction in social protection within the European Union. Another strand contrarily claims that the EU is breaking new ground in social policy, enabling welfare states to converge towards a high standard of provision and therefore strengthening Europeans' social security. These two considerations of a 'Social Europe' basically reflect the divergence between Streeck (2014) and Habermas (2012) on a more general level and thus the ongoing debate on the future of the European Union. In the following, the two streams of thought in conceiving a 'Social Europe' are reconstructed in detail and two scenarios are developed accordingly. This will help to analyse the question of what role the social problems and social policies play in setting the agenda of European crisis management.

One research stream that analyses the EU's influence on national welfare states stresses that the European integration process has an economic bias and consequently promotes a retraction of national welfare states and a cutback in social security. The starting point of this argumentation is that the creation of a common market is not the only target of European integration, but that '[m]arket-making no longer implies [only] enforcement of non-discrimination but the abolition of potential institutional impediments to free markets' (Höpner and Schäfer 2010: 344). In other words, integration is aimed at an economic liberalization process, driven by a powerful coalition of the European Commission (the European Court of Justice) and national governments with a liberal market orientation (Streeck 2014). Consequently, non-economic issues are ignored and other policy fields are subordinated to the goal of market creation on the European level. The creation of the common single market strengthens tendencies towards the marketization and privatization of social benefits, contributing to a cut in social benefits and a tightening of access requirements (Scharpf 2002; Menz 2003; Lindstrom 2010; Streeck 2014; Leibfried 2015).

If the European integration process is interpreted in this way, welfare states are under pressure to conform with the requirements of the European internal market (Ferrera 2012a, 2012b). Moreover, national economic systems within the common single market come into competition with one another. As a result, social protection becomes a cost factor which is taken into consideration in the location decision of businesses (Leibfried and Pierson 1995; Leibfried 2015). Thus, European integration is considered to be a conversion process of the welfare states to the lowest common denominator. All social security systems have to be subordinated to market logics and social standards have to be reduced under the pressure of the internal market (Streeck 2014).

When we adopt this view of EU social policy *in the first scenario*, it has to be expected that the European crisis policy has focused on market-stabilizing and market-protecting mechanisms (Hall 2014), while social problems have been considered as non-crucial to the European common market and therefore play a subordinate role within current European strategies for dealing with the crisis (for an overview of the first scenario see Table 9.1). Consequently, the European crisis policy is aimed at tackling the fiscal problems of states that are having problems with refinancing themselves on the financial markets. *The first thesis is therefore that the European crisis management policy focuses on sovereign defaults and debt restructurings and ignores the social dimension and consequences of the crisis.*

On the basis of this economic-centred understanding of the crisis, it has to be assumed that within the framework of the European crisis policy, social policy is primarily regarded as a cost factor. Social expenditure is considered a burden on the national budget (Blyth 2014). In order to consolidate the domestic public budget and to combat the public fiscal problems within the common currency area in the short and long term, European crisis management is pushing towards a reduction in social policy spending, i.e. a reduction in national social services (Armstrong 2012). 'Social policy objectives and instruments have been marginalized within the new governance architecture' (Crespy and Menz 2015: 765). *The second thesis is that within the European crisis policy, socio-political measures are generally treated as a cost factor. Cuts in the social safety nets are requested as a one-fit-all solution in order to overcome the fiscal problems.*

Within the first scenario it has to be assumed that social problems are not seen as European challenges within European crisis management politics and that therefore no support is given to national efforts to help those citizens affected by the crisis. Following the second strand of arguments, it can be said that since the 1990s social policy has become an independent policy aim at the European level (Habermas 2012). In this approach, the European integration process not only concentrates on the creation of a common single market, but also serves and supports the development of high social standards. The European agenda is understood as the object of bargaining processes between the economic-oriented and the social-oriented politicians in both the European Commission and the governments (Kriesi et al. 2006; Hartlapp et al. 2014). Therefore, the issue of how much the European policy cares about social problems is an open empirical question.

In general, firstly the European Employment Policy and the Lisbon Strategy and now the Europe 2020 strategy are seen as processes that 'created new ideas and instruments to modernize social and labour market systems in order to achieve a new balance between competitiveness and social cohesion' (Bieling 2012: 256; see also Zeitlin 2005; Zeitlin and Vanhercke 2014). It is also supposed that activation of unemployed people and social safeguarding of particularly vulnerable groups are fostered and supported by the EU (Marlier et al. 2007; Zeitlin 2010). Concerning the current crisis, Zeitlin and Vanhercke (2014) stress that while at the beginning of the crisis the European political agenda was dominated by economic-orientated actors, the social policy actors were able to later regain influence on the European policy agenda. The EU is understood in this strand of arguments as a political project that at least has the potential to help its Member States to improve their standards of welfare provision. However, it is also assumed that because of the differences between national institutions, European integration will not result in a convergence process but in a process of domestic adaption. The European agenda gives incentives to improve social standards by means of common goals, indicators, benchmarking and peer reviews. As the initiatives are only soft law instruments, their implementation varies depending on the domestic institutional framework and may differ from state to state. Thus, in this version one has to conclude that the European integration process is based not only on economic agreements but also on social agreements, representing a domestic adaption of the European agenda.

The basic assumption of *the second scenario* is that the European integration process has a social dimension (for an overview of the second scenario see Table 9.1). If the main assumption is that minimizing social problems is part of the European agenda, it can be expected that crisis-related social problems are considered a challenge at the European level. The third thesis *is therefore that within the European crisis management policy not only the fiscal issues but also the social problems are defined as politically-relevant challenges which the bailout funds need to respond to.* On the basis of this problem definition, it can be expected that within the framework of European crisis management an approach is developed that supports national policy in tackling social problems.

The fourth thesis is *that although the main aim of the European crisis policy is to overcome the fiscal problems, it also advises the affected states to combat social problems and endorses the strengthening or at least the reorganization of the domestic social safety net.* In the second scenario, it can therefore be predicted that social problems are of relevance to the current European policy projects. Thus, European measures are introduced to support national strategies for dealing with the social consequences of the current crisis.

To summarize, the eurozone is facing its deepest crisis since its creation. Some of its member countries face or have faced the danger of losing access to financial markets and have been exposed to an economic

Table 9.1   Developing two scenarios

	Scenario 1: EU has no social dimension	Scenario 2: EU has social dimension
Defining the most important current problems	Having a one-dimensional problem perception. Focus on economic problems, ignoring the social ones.	Having a multi-dimensional problem perception. Defining the growing social problems as political challenges.
Role of social policy	Social policy is defined as a cost factor that has to be reduced. Cuts of social expenditures are supported and requested as a one-fit-all solution.	Social policy is necessary to counteract social problems. National social policy measures are supported and requested.

recession and growing social problems. This chapter poses the question of how the European crisis policy deals with social problems and what kind of social-political measures and reforms are required within the bailout funds. On the basis of the state of the art of a 'Social Europe', two scenarios have been developed that give two diametrically opposed answers to the question of how the growing social problems in parts of the eurozone have been tackled. They also diverge in their assumption as to which kind of social policy is perceived as appropriate by the European crisis policy. Following the understanding that the EU is an economic project, it has to be expected that the European crisis policy only focuses on the economic and fiscal side of the crisis. If the assumption is that there is a social Europe, it can be expected that the European crisis management policy also has a social dimension. In the next step, the empirical material and methods used as the basis of the analysis are presented.

9.3   RESEARCH DESIGN

Two different scenarios were developed in the previous section. In the following, the implementation process of the European crisis policy and its functionality are reconstructed and explained. The four EAPs that are at the centre of the empirical analysis are then introduced and described. Finally, the research design of the article is discussed.

Since 2010, the institutional framework of the EU has been radically changed. To guarantee the financial liquidity of the eurozone countries, the no-bailout clause of the Maastricht Treaty (currently Art. 125 TFEU) was de facto eroded and a comprehensive European crisis management policy has been incrementally developed. Firstly, Greece was granted unique bilateral aids by other governments of the eurozone in April 2010. After it became clear that other countries also needed help, a general but temporary assistance programme was introduced in the form of the European Financial Stability Facility (EFSF) and subsequently the European Financial Stabilization Mechanism (EFSM) in spring 2010. Despite an increase in the volume of aid, the crisis management policy failed to resolve the situation (Advisory Council 2011). Therefore, the European Stability Mechanism (ESM), a permanent bailout fund of around 700 billion euros, was subsequently established by the governments of the eurozone, the European Commission and the International Monetary Fund (IMF) in September 2012 (Eichengreen 2012; De Grauwe 2014). The ESM supports governments and banks at risk of financial problems with loans and guarantees. Since 2012 the European Central Bank (ECB) has had the option to buy government bonds on the secondary markets as part of the programme called Outright Monetary Transactions (OMT), which has not been used to date (March 2016).

According to the guidelines of the programme and similar to the standard operating procedure of the IMF, it was decided that transnational help should only be offered if the affected state had previously applied for help to the ESM and accepted its conditions. In the case that a state is confronted with the problem of refinancing its own debt, support from the EFSM, EFSF, ESM and the ECB is available, but only if the concerned state is ready to accept several conditions (Matthijs 2014). Most of these conditions are targeted at reducing public debt by cutting government spending and/or increasing state income, and require the implementation of structural reforms intended to strengthen the competitive position of the affected state (Becker and Jäger 2012: 180; Schimmelfennig 2014: 322).

Asking for support from the bailout funds therefore implies the willingness to accept a close monitoring and controlling report system, the aforementioned EAP. Each EAP starts by defining the conditions for aid in the memorandum of economic and financial policies (MEFP)[2] and the memorandum of understanding (MoU). Both documents are an agreement between the government that asked for support from the bailout fund and the lenders. Without this agreement and the implementation of the MEFP and MoU there is no financial support. The MEFP lays down the kind of policy reforms that will be implemented in the state that is asking for support, while the MoU defines the timetable for the reform process.

However, the MEFP and MoU in combination with the Loan Agreement are just general agreements between the money-lender and money-receiver. They set out the conditions of support and the total amount of loans that the asking government can receive incrementally over a certain period as well as the preconditions for the first disbursement.

Within the EAP the economic situation of the state and the political developments are evaluated by the European Commission, the ECB and the IMF twice a year. On the basis of their assessment of past developments, the affected state and its international partners agree on updates of the MEFP and the MoU. These updates specify the next steps and form the basis for further disbursements. In order to understand the role of social problems and social policy in the bailout funds, it is necessary to analyse both the MEFP and the MoU together with their updates. They thus form the central empirical basis for the following analysis.

Following payment difficulties, four eurozone countries have so far claimed support from the bailout programmes of the common currency area in order to serve their public debts.[3] Greece had three EAPs: the first was from 2010 to 2013, and a second one for the years 2012 to 2014 was later extended to the end of June 2015. Since August 2015, there has been a third programme. However, because of the political situation in Greece, the regular EAP stopped in summer 2014, which is why my analysis of the second Greek EAP also ends with the fourth updates of the MoU and the MEFP in April 2014. The EAP for Ireland started in December 2010 and covered the period from 2010 to 2013. The Portuguese EAP began in 2011 and ended in mid-2014. The EAP with Cyprus started in April 2013 and covers the period from 2013 to 2016.

To summarize, the centre of the following analysis is the five EAPs of four states, the main empirical data are the MEFP and the MoU and their updates during the period of time between 2010 and 2014 (for an overview see Table 9.2).

The empirical data was studied in a documentary analysis in two steps: firstly by asking how often the keywords can be found in the documents

Table 9.2   Economic Adjustment Programs (EAPs)

	Timelines	Amount of loans
Cyprus	2013–2016	10 billion euros
Greece: 1st Programme	2010–2012	80 billion euros
Greece: 2nd Programme	2012–2015	130 billion euros
Ireland	2010–2013	85 billion euros
Portugal	2011–2014	78 billion euros

and secondly by interpreting their political meaning and the political consequences. The first part of the analysis concerns the phrasing of the social
problems. I argue that some social problems such as unemployment (youth
unemployment), poverty or problems in paying bills are mentioned within
the MEFP, the MoU and their updates. I then analysed in detail whether
the social problems are only named or whether a political need for action
is derived from them. In this second part of the analysis, I examined the
treatment of social policy within the documents. Again, I began by analysing how many and what kinds of social policy fields are named in the
documents. I then evaluated whether in the document the lenders require
the social safety net to be cut or whether it has to be strengthened or at
least maintained.

To summarize, the empirical analysis concentrates on the bailout funds
and their five EAPs for the time between 2010 and 2014. It is an evaluation
of a specific European mechanism. The analysis excludes the domestic
level and by so doing it ignores questions concerning the implementation of the European requirements and their results on the national level.
Further European mechanisms that may influence the other EU Member
States are also not accounted for in the analysis. This chapter is therefore
unable to provide answers regarding the development of the European
integration process as a whole.

9.4   SOCIAL PROBLEMS AS CHALLENGES FOR THE EUROPEAN BAILOUT PROGRAMMES?

A common factor in all EAPs is that three broad policy fields are defined as
the central issues in order to overcome the problems of the crisis-affected
states: stabilization of the banking and financial sector, public fiscal con-
solidations and structural reforms. Thus, in line with the first thesis, it
could be concluded that the growing social problems are ignored by the
bailout funds. However, in the following analysis it will be shown that the
reforms requested in the EAP also consider the growing social problems.
The aim of the following empirical analysis is to reconstruct which social
problems are defined as political challenges in the programmes and therefore can be considered as the recognized European problems. As the programmes regarding the banking sectors and the financial markets have no
social dimension, they are excluded in the following.

Public fiscal consolidation means two things: increasing the income
of the state and reducing its expenditure. As social security systems are
one important part of public spending, a reduction in public expenditure
is demanded in all of the analysed documents. However, in all EAPs it

is also stressed that the most vulnerable people in society need protection and that their social support by the state should be excluded from the austerity package. For instance, in the Irish MoU it was pointed out that 'For the duration of the EU/IMF financial assistance programme the Irish authorities will take all the necessary measures to ensure a successful implementation of the programme and minimise the costs to the taxpayers, while protecting the most vulnerable' (European Commission 2013a: 45, similar statements can be found in the other Irish MoUs and in other EAPs). In particular since 2012, high poverty and deprivation rates have gained attention. However, it is still an open question which policy approach was recommended in the EAP to protect the most vulnerable of the crisis-affected states.

The analysis of the programme sections focusing on structural reforms shows that at the beginning of the crisis in 2010, unemployment was not defined as a European challenge in the EAPs. It was not even mentioned in the Irish documents and it was only noticed as a problem in the EAPs of Greece and Portugal (Cyprus did not participate in the programme at that time). The situation changed in 2012 and 2013 when not only did the level of unemployment hit its peak in Greece, Ireland and Portugal (in Cyprus the highest rate was in 2014), but these high numbers of jobless people were also considered to be an urgent political challenge that needed a political reaction in all four EAPs (for an overview see Table 9A.1 in the appendix). For instance, it was stated in the Cypriot MEFP that 'the situation remains difficult, with unemployment, especially for youth, rising toward very high levels, while disposable incomes are falling.' (European Commission 2014: 101).

In summary, my analysis shows that in line with the second scenario, the growing social problems of affected states have been increasingly considered as political challenges over the course of the crisis.[4] In particular the problems of neediness and unemployment were considered more and more over the course of the crisis as political issues in the analysed EAPs. On the basis of these results, in the next step it will be discussed which kind of social policy reforms were demanded in the EAPs. Has the growing attention to the social problems observed over the course of the crisis resulted in demands for better social protection?

9.5 THE REQUESTED SOCIAL POLICY REFORMS IN THE ECONOMIC ADJUSTMENT PROGRAMMES

The following analysis of the treatment of social policy in the EAPs will show that cuts in public spending have been demanded in all fields of social policy. The level and the scope of the social security system in general have had to be reduced in all four programme countries. In the individual cases in which an increase in social protection was demanded, it was requested in order to introduce (temporary) programmes for certain groups.

As previously mentioned, one central aim of all EAPs is the consolidation of public debts.

> Greece was forced into one of the most draconian austerity programmes in history, designed to reduce its budget deficit by 11 percentage points of GDP within three years. Alongside difficult structural reforms, Ireland was asked to reduce its budget deficit by 9 percentage points of GDP in five years, and Portugal by 6 per cent within three years. For comparative purposes, note that the oil price shock of 1974 that ushered in a traumatic recession took roughly 4 per cent out of European GDP. (Hall 2014: 1231)

A reduction in costs was demanded for the pension, health and unemployment systems as well as for further welfare programs in all EAPs at all times during the crisis (see appendix Table 9A.2). Thus, EAPs face a dilemma because the claim of protecting the most vulnerable people conflicts with the goal of cutbacks in public expenditure, i.e. also in the field of social policy. Empirically, the claim of providing social protection is subordinate to the goal of cutbacks. For instance, in the first MoU for Cyprus it is determined that '[t]he plan, which will include proposals to consolidate welfare programs, improve targeting, and streamline administration, will aim to attain the budget savings required to reach our program fiscal targets, while ensuring that the poor and vulnerable groups are adequately protected' (European Commission 2013b).

Most of the EAPs lack a clear definition of which social standards have to be fulfilled, despite the cutbacks to the social security systems. In cases where the EAP defines a minimum collateral (for instance in the field of pensions in the second EAP of Greece), it is always stressed that this kind of social protection is only possible as long as it does not contradict the aim of budget consolidation. Thus, an analysis of the MEFP, the MoU and their updates shows that European support for avoiding public illiquidity is accompanied by the requirement of making savings in the social safety nets.

The question of how much unemployment insurance should be paid to jobless people is not only discussed in the programme dedicated to fiscal consolidation, it is also an issue in the field of structural reforms. In all EAPs it is stressed that employment policy reforms are necessary to increase the pressure on jobless people to find and secure a job. In the first Portuguese MEFP, for example, it is pointed out that in order to

[r]evise the unemployment insurance system to change incentives, increase employment ... and strengthen social safety nets. We [the Portuguese government, JP] will reduce the maximum duration of unemployment insurance benefits to no more than 18 months, and cap unemployment benefits at 2.5 times the social support index and introduce a declining profile of benefits after six months of unemployment (a reduction of at least 10 per cent in benefits), without reducing accrued-to-date entitlements. (European Commission 2011: 52, similar statements can be found in other EAPs)

Thus, cuts in the duration and the amount of unemployment insurance are not only following the aim of budget consolidation, they are also seen as an appropriate instrument for tackling the high number of unemployed people.

Recognition of the growing social problems thus has not changed the policy approach within the EAPs. Instead, as a solution to the precarious situation of a growing number of people, first the Greek then also the Cypriot MEFP and MoU proposed the introduction of programmes of public welfare for particular groups.

To help cushion the impact of our fiscal adjustment on the most vulnerable, we have strengthened social spending programs. Support for the unemployed will be increased by €55 million by 2014, through two new programs (now being piloted): (i) an income-tested benefit scheme that targets long-term unemployed and provides income payable for a year; and (ii) a minimum income guarantee scheme targeting families in areas with difficult socioeconomic profiles. We will also expand our job-training and job matching programs, to be financed where possible by better leveraging available EU structural funds. (European Commission 2012: 160)

While the social security of broad parts of society has been reduced, (temporary) programmes for particular groups were introduced to mitigate their social problems.

To sum up, in line with the first scenario and here in particular the second thesis, the empirical results indicate that social problems are subordinate to the goal of fiscal solidity. Growing recognition of social problems has not resulted in a rethinking of the demanded social policy reforms. In all EAPs, the one-fit-all solution of public fiscal consolidation is the reduction of public spending and therefore a reduction in the costs of the social security systems. In the field of employment policy, a reduction in unemployment insurance is even seen as an appropriate instrument for increasing the pressure on jobless people to find a job and therefore to reduce the high level of unemployment. In order to combat the problems of the vulnerable people in particular, temporary and group-related programmes have been proposed and requested.

9.6   CONCLUSION

The starting point of this analysis was the observation that the Southern eurozone Member States especially are facing serious social problems and increasing social inequality as a consequence of the financial and sovereign debt crises from 2008 onwards. In this chapter it has been discussed how these developments have been taken into account and what kind of social reforms were requested in the five EAPs under examination. Two possible scenarios have been identified.

Following the first scenario, in the continuity of the market-dominated European integration process, it can be expected that the European crisis policy is concentrating on the stability of the markets and subordinate social problems under this goal. Contrary to this view, the second scenario expects that the European integration process includes a social dimension and therefore that the European crisis policy recognizes the social problems and supports the national political level in overcoming them. In line with the second scenario, the results show that the growing social problems have been viewed and recognized at the European level. However, in keeping with the first scenario, the results also indicate that fiscal consolidation is a top priority of the European agenda. Huge European efforts have been made to achieve the aims of lowering interest rates for the crisis-affected states and ensuring balanced budgets for all members of the eurozone. The growing social problems have clearly been receiving attention at the European level, but they are still not considered as systemically important. The perception that the nation-states are responsible for social problems remains unchanged. A social bailout similar to the fiscal ESM has not been undertaken so far.

The European rescue measures are showing results – especially the announcement by the President of the ECB in 2012 that the ECB will 'do whatever it takes to preserve the euro'. However, social problems and in particular high unemployment rates do not disappear at the same speed as high interest rates (cf. Chapter 1). A social gap remains between the core of the eurozone and its periphery in terms of social exclusion poverty, unemployment and health condition. Social inequality is still increasing between the crisis-affected states and the rest of the eurozone. These persistent social problems are not only a challenge for the affected people; the protests and political crises in Italy, Greece and Spain indicate that they are also a challenge for the affected states.

A report by the International Labour Organization (2013) emphasizes that the observed social problems in combination with political instability are endangering the social peace in the affected societies. Thus, the EU is facing the challenge of reducing the social tensions within and between its

Member States. Summarizing my analysis, it is doubtful that the European response to the crises so far will lead to a stable fiscal, social and political currency area and therefore to a stable EU in the future. 'In so far as the European crisis management hitherto has succeeded in avoiding the worst – a catastrophic breakdown which quite well could have been the result of the repercussions of the global financial crisis – it can be called a "success". However, this is already the end of good news' (Deutschmann 2014: 344).

NOTES

1. A similar provision is made for EU Member States that are not part of the single currency. They, too, can apply to the European Commission for financial support.
2. All monitoring reports and further statements can be found at http://ec.europa.eu/ economy_finance/assistance_eu_ms/index_en.htmhttp://ec.europa.eu/economy_finance/ assistance_eu_ms/portugal/index_en.htm.
3. Spain also asked for support (in the period 2012–2013), however the support was for the banking system and not the government, which is why the Spanish EAP focuses on the reforms of the banking system. The Spanish fiscal, economic and social policy has been controlled by the European Semester. Spain is therefore excluded from the analysis.
4. This understanding of problems is in line with the public statements of the members of the common currency; who have started to expound the problems of people in the crisis affected states since 2012 for instance (European Council 2012c, 2012b, 2012a, 2013b, 2013a). 'Combating youth unemployment is a particular and immediate objective, considering the unacceptably high number of young Europeans who are unemployed' (European Council 2013b: 1). In particular, the growing number of jobless (young) people has been identified as a social problem that must be addressed in the European political debate.

REFERENCES

Advisory Council (2011), *Verantwortung für Europa wahrnehmen, 2011/12*, Wiesbaden: Statistisches Bundesamt.

Armstrong, K.A. (2012), 'EU social policy and the governance architecture of Europe 2020', *Transfer: European Review of Labour and Research*, **18** (3), 285–300.

Becker, J. and J. Jäger (2012), 'Integration in crisis: a regulationist perspective on the interaction of European varieties of capitalism', *Competition and Change*, **16**, 169–187.

Bieling, H.-J. (2012), 'EU facing the crisis: social and employment policies in times of tight budgets', *Transfer: European Review of Labour and Research*, **18** (3), 255–271.

Blyth, M. (2014), 'The sovereign debt crisis that isn't: or, how to turn a lending crisis into a spending crisis and pocket the spread', ACES Cases 2014.1, American Consortium on European Union Studies.

Crespy, A. and G. Menz (2015), 'Commission entrepreneurship and the debasing of social Europe before and after the Euro crisis', *Journal of Common Market Studies*, **53** (4), 753–768.

De Grauwe, P. (2014), *Economics of Monetary Union*, 10th edition, Oxford: Oxford University Press.

Deutschmann, C. (2014), 'The future of the European Union: a "Hayekian" regime?', *European Journal of Social Theory*, **17** (3), 343–358.

Eichengreen, B. (2012), 'European monetary integration with benefit of hindsight', *JCMS: Journal of Common Market Studies*, **50**, 123–136.

European Commission (2011), The Economic Adjustment Programme for Portugal, June 2011.

European Commission (2012), The Second Economic Adjustment Programme for Greece, First Review December 2012, Brussels, December 2012.

European Commission (2013a), The Economic Adjustment Programme for Ireland, Winter 2012 Review, Brussels, April 2013.

European Commission (2013b), The Economic Adjustment Programme for Cyprus, 2013.

European Commission (2014), The Economic Adjustment Programme for Cyprus, Third Review Winter 2014, Brussels, March 2014.

European Council (2012a), *Conclusions*, 13–14 December 2012, CO EUR 19, CONCL 5. Brussels.

European Council (2012b), *Conclusions*, 18–19 October 2012, CO EUR 15, CONCL 3. Brussels.

European Council (2012c), *Conclusions*, 28–29 June 2012, CO EUR 4, CONCL 2. Brussels.

European Council (2013a), *Conclusions*, 24–25 October 2013, CO EUR 13, CONCL 7. Brussels.

European Council (2013b), *Conclusions*, 27–28 June 2013, CO EUR 9, CONCL 6. Brussels.

Ferrera, M. (2012a), 'Modest beginnings, timid progresses: what's next for social Europe?', in B. Cantillon, H. Verschueren and P. Ploscar (eds), *Social Inclusion and Social Protection in the EU: Interactions between Law and Policy*, Cambridge: Intersentia Publishing Ltd, pp. 17–41.

Ferrera, M. (2012b), 'The new spatial politics of welfare in the EU', in G. Bonoli and D. Natali (eds), *The Politics of the New Welfare State*, Oxford: Oxford University Press, pp. 256–287.

Habermas, J. (2012), *The Crisis of the European Union: A Response*, Cambridge: Polity Press.

Hall, P.A. (2014), 'Varieties of capitalism and the euro crisis', *West European Politics*, **37**, 1223–1243.

Hartlapp, M., J. Metz and C. Rauh (2014), *Which Policy for Europe? Power and Conflict Inside the European Commission*, Oxford: Oxford University Press.

Hodson, D. (2015), 'Policy-making under economic and monetary union. Crisis, change, and continuity', in H. Wallace, M.A. Pollack and A.R. Young (eds), *Policy-Making in the European Union*, 7th edition, Oxford: Oxford University Press, pp. 263–292.

Höpner, M. and A. Schäfer (2010), 'A new phase of European integration: organised capitalisms in post-Ricardian Europe', *West European Politics*, **33** (2), 344–368.

International Labour Organization (2013), *World of Work Report 2013: Repairing the Economic and Social Fabric*, Geneva: International Institute for Labour Studies.

Kriesi, H., E. Grande, E. Lachat, M. Dolezal, S. Bornschier and T. Frey (2006), 'Globalization and the transformation of the national political space: six European countries compared', *European Journal of Political Research*, **45**, 921–956.

Leibfried, S. (2015), 'Social policy. Left to courts and markets?', in H. Wallace, M.A. Pollack and A.R. Young (eds), *Policy-Making in the European Union*, Oxford: Oxford University Press, pp. 263–292.

Leibfried, S. and P. Pierson (1995), 'Semi-sovereign welfare states: social policy in a multi-tiered Europe', in S. Leibfried and P. Pierson (eds), *European Social Policy – Between Fragmentation and Integration*, Washington, DC: The Brookings Institution, pp. 43–77.

Lindberg, D. and H. Vollaard (2014), 'Implementing social Europe in times of crises: re-established boundaries of welfare?', *West European Politics*, **37** (4), 677–692.

Lindstrom, N. (2010), 'Service liberalization in the enlarged EU: a race to the bottom or the emergence of transnational political conflict?', *Journal of Common Market Studies*, **5** (48), 1307–1327.

Marlier, E., A.B. Atkinson, B. Cantillon and B. Nolan (2007), *The EU and Social Inclusion*, Bristol: The Policy Press.

Matthijs, M. (2014), 'Mediterranean blues: the crisis in Southern Europe', *Journal of Democracy*, **25**, 101–115.

Menz, G. (2003), 'Re-regulating the Single Market: national varieties of capitalism and their responses to Europeanization', *Journal of European Public Policy*, **10** (4), 532–555.

Scharpf, F.W. (2002), 'The European social model: coping with the challenges of diversity', *Journal of Common Market Studies*, **40** (4), 645–70.

Schimmelfennig, F. (2014), 'European integration in the euro crisis: the limits of postfunctionalism', *Journal of European Integration*, **36** (3), 321–337.

Streeck, W. (2014), *Buying Time: The Delayed Crisis of Democratic Capitalism*, New York: Verso Books.

Zeitlin, J. (2005), *Social Europe and Experimentalist Governance: Towards a New Constitutional Compromise?*, European Governance Papers (EUROGOV) No. C-05-04.

Zeitlin, J. (2010), 'Towards a stronger OMC in a more social Europe 2020: a new governance architecture for EU policy coordination', in E. Marlier and D. Natali with R. van Dam (eds), *Europe 2020: Towards a More Social EU?*, Brussels: PIE Lang, pp. 253–273.

Zeitlin, J. and B. Vanhercke (2014), *Socializing the European Semester? Economic Governance and Social Policy Coordination in Europe 2020*, Report No. 7. Published by the Swedish Institute for European Policy Studies.

APPENDIX

Table 9A.1   *Mentioning unemployment as a political issue*

		Unemployment	Long-term unemployment	Youth unemployment
Cyprus	MEFP and MoU 2013	++	+	+
	Updates summer 2013	++	+	+
	Updates autumn 2013	+	+	+
	Updates winter 2013/2014	++	+	+
	Updates spring 2014	++	+	+
	Updates summer 2014	++		+
	Updates summer 2015	+	+	+
Greece 1st	MEFP and MoU 2010	+	−	−
	Updates summer 2010	−	−	−
	Updates autumn 2010	+	−	−
	Updates winter 2010/2011	−	−	−
	Updates spring 2011	+	−	−
	Updates autumn 2011	+	−	+
Greece 2nd	MEFP and MoU 2012	+	−	−
	Updates winter 2012/2013	++	+	+
	Updates spring 2013	++	+	++
	Updates summer 2013	++	+	++
	Updates spring 2014	++	+	+
Ireland	MEFP und MoU 2010	−	−	−
	Updates summer 2011	−	−	−
	Updates autumn 2011	+	+	−

Table 9A.1   (continued)

		Unemployment	Long-term unemployment	Youth unemployment
	Updates winter 2011/2012	+	+	−
	Updates spring 2012	+	+	−
	Updates summer 2012	++	+	−
	Updates autumn 2012	+	−	−
	Updates winter 2012/2013	+	+	−
	Updates spring 2013	++	+	+
	Updates summer 2013	++	+	+
	Updates autumn 2013	+	−	+
Portugal	MEFP and MoU 2010	+	+	+
	Updates summer 2011	+	+	−
	Updates autumn 2011	+	+	−
	Updates winter 2011/2012	++	+	+
	Updates spring 2012	++	+	+
	Updates summer 2012	++	+	−
	Updates autumn 2012	++	+	−
	Updates winter 2012/2013	++	+	−
	Updates summer 2013	+	+	−
	Updates winter 2013/2014	+	+	−
	Updates spring 2014	−	+	−

Note: + named as problem, ++ named as an urgent problem or as a political priority, − not named in the documents.

Table 9A.2 Treatment of social policy in the Economic Adjustment Programmes

		Demand of cuts in the field of social policy					Demand of protection for vulnerable people	
		General	Pension	Health	Unemployment	Social care	Income support	Social security
Cyprus	MEFP and MoU 2013	+	+	+	+	+	+	–
	Updates summer 2013	+	+	+	+	+	+	–
	Updates autumn 2013	+	+	+	+	+	+	–
	Updates winter 2013/2014	+	+	+	+	+	+	–
	Updates spring 2014	+	+	+	+	+	+	–
	Updates summer 2014	+	+	+	+	+	+	–
	Updates summer 2015	+	+	+	+	+	+	–
Greece 1st	MEFP and MoU 2010	+	+	+	+	+	–	–
	Updates summer 2010	+	+	+	+	+	–	–
	Updates autumn 2010	+	+	+	+	+	–	–

	C1	C2	C3	C4	C5	C6	C7
Greece 2nd							
Updates winter 2010/2011	−	−	+	+	+	+	+
Updates spring 2011	−	−	+	+	+	+	+
Updates autumn 2011	−	−	+	+	+	+	+
MEFP and MoU 2012	+	+	+	−	+	+	+
Updates winter 2012/2013	+	+	+	−	+	+	+
Updates spring 2013	+	+	+	−	+	+	+
Updates summer 2013	+	+	+	−	+	+	+
Updates spring 2014	+	+	+	−	+	+	+
Ireland							
MEFP und MoU 2010	−	−	+	+	+	+	+
Updates summer 2011	−	−	−	+	+	+	+
Updates autumn 2011	−	−	−	+	+	+	+
Updates winter 2011/2012	−	−	−	+	−	+	+
Updates spring 2012	−	−	−	+	−	+	+

Table 9A.2 (continued)

		Demand of cuts in the field of social policy					Demand of protection for vulnerable people	
		General	Pension	Health	Unemployment	Social care	Income support	Social security
	Updates summer 2012	+	+	+	+	−	−	−
	Updates autumn 2012	+	+	+	+	−	−	−
	Updates winter 2012/2013	+	+	+	+	−	−	−
	Updates spring 2013	+	+	+	+	−	+	−
	Updates summer 2013	+	+	+	+	−	+	−
	Updates autumn 2013	+	−	+	+	−	+	−
Portugal	MEFP and MoU 2010	+	+	+	+	+	−	−
	Updates summer 2011	+	+	+	+	+	−	−
	Updates autumn 2011	+	+	+	+	+	−	−
	Updates winter 2011/2012	+	+	+	+	+	−	−

Updates spring 2012	–	–	+	+	+	+	+
Updates summer 2012	–	–	+	+	+	+	+
Updates autumn 2012	–	–	+	+	+	+	+
Updates winter 2012/2013	–	–	+	+	+	+	+
Updates summer 2013	–	–	+	+	+	+	+
Updates winter 2013/2014	–	–	–	+	+	+	+
Updates spring 2014	–	–	–	+	+	+	+

Note: + demanded as reform, – not mentioned in the documents.

Index

active labour market policies (ALMP)
  potential negative effects on
    employment 144–5
austerity policies 18, 23, 34, 53, 108,
    110–11, 117, 120, 165, 185, 205,
    229
  concept of 8
  criticisms of 25
  fiscal 34–5
  impact on public services 110
  inequality-enhancing potential of
    25
  influence on employment rates of
    women 17, 109, 125, 131, 135
  lack of consistent effect on economic
    stress 41
  negative employment effects of 125,
    195
Austria 53
  public health in 182
average marginal effects (AME) 82, 120
  concept of 36

Balance of Payment Programmes
    (BoPs) 18, 170, 173
  arrears indicators 177–8
  countries subject to 18, 165
    bad health issues in 178, 182–3
    issues of arrears in 177
    rise of indebtedness in 170
  development of bad health 178–9,
    185
  regression analysis of 182, 184
Beck, U.
  definitions of poverty 50
Behrendt, C.
  observations of causes of poverty
    52
Belgium
  income inequality in
    Gini coefficient of 25–6

permanent poverty in 56
public health in 182
temporary employment levels in
    139
Bettio, F.
  focus on added worker effect 111
Black Report
  impact of 167
  income gradient to health 167, 185
Blanchard, O.J.
  concept of 'hysterical effect of LTU'
    70
Blásquez, M.
  observations of bad health incidents
    among income quintiles in
    peripheral countries 179
Bryan, M.L. 120, 124
  application of logit models by 82
Bulgaria 13, 42, 54, 110
  LTU in 71
  permanent poverty in 57
  public health in 182
  rates of transition from
    unemployment to employment
    in 76

Caminada, K.
  poverty analyses efforts of 51–2
capital 146
  European integration in 31
  exchange of 200–201, 212
  flows 15, 25–6
  globalization of 8
  human 203
  inflows 42
capitalism
  egalitarian 7
Croatia
  income inequality in
    Gini coefficient of 25
  LTU in 71

243